"An impeccably researched and intimate narrative of the events leading up to America's participation in World War II, especially the highly consequential rivalry between nativism and democracy that still echoes in today's harrowing political climate. *Awakening the Spirit of America* adds new and important information in the highly traveled road of FDR biography."

—Dr. Steven Lomazow, author *FDR's Deadly Secret*
and *FDR Unmasked*

"Powerfully portrays the political genius of FDR as he confronted global authoritarian forces, which had taken root in America, threatening the essence of democratic ideals and democratic aspirations. Sparrow, breathing life into one of the most critical periods in American history, clearly makes the case that FDR's wisdom and international leadership in his day offers guidance in today's struggle with anti-democratic forces both domestic and foreign."

—Michael Zuckerman, former *USA Today* Washington editor,
investigative reporter, and author of *Vengeance is Mine*

"A truly suspenseful history. Sure, we know President Franklin Roosevelt prevailed against the isolationists, antisemites, and Nazi sympathizers of the America First Committee and rallied Americans to defend democratic life against the ambitions and forces of Hitler, Mussolini, and the Japanese imperialists. But Sparrow makes us critically aware of how FDR had to first pursue battles against the Committee's popular champion Charles Lindbergh—and how things might have gone otherwise had FDR faltered. Sparrow makes clear to us the power of FDR's words, the words that reminded Americans of who they were and what they had to do."

—Harvey J. Kaye, professor emeritus of Democracy and Justice
at the University of Wisconsin-Green Bay and author of
The Fight for the Four Freedoms and *FDR on Democracy*

AWAKENING *the*
SPIRIT *of* AMERICA

AWAKENING *the* SPIRIT *of* AMERICA

FDR'S WAR OF WORDS WITH CHARLES LINDBERGH— AND THE BATTLE TO SAVE DEMOCRACY

PAUL M. SPARROW

PEGASUS BOOKS

NEW YORK LONDON

AWAKENING THE SPIRIT OF AMERICA

Pegasus Books, Ltd.
148 West 37th Street, 13th Floor
New York, NY 10018

First Pegasus Books cloth edition June 2024

Interior design by Maria Fernandez

Library of Congress Cataloging-in-Publication Data is available.

ISBN: 978-1-63936-667-5

10 9 8 7 6 5 4 3 2 1

Printed in the United States of America
Distributed by Simon & Schuster
www.pegasusbooks.com

With special thanks to the National Archives

and Records Administration

CONTENTS

PREFACE

No president in American history had a more significant impact on both American and world history than Franklin Roosevelt. He transformed the very concept of what a democratic government should do for its people, what rights its citizens have, and even what constitutes fundamental human rights for *all* people. In his battle to save democracy from fascism, to protect freedom and justice, he used every weapon at his disposal; his charisma and mellifluous voice; the power of the federal government; radio, newspapers, magazines; and boisterous rallies. All to shift public opinion in favor of supporting an ally in desperate need. Yet at the core of all of Roosevelt's weapons were his words. His words brought hope to a desperate world, comfort to those suffering hunger and deprivation, and a vision of a better world for those crushed by totalitarian oppression and hatred. This book seeks to put the reader in the room with FDR's team and his equally charismatic foil, the famed transatlantic pilot Charles Lindbergh, as they devise their linguistic strategy and craft the words that would decide the fate of all freedom loving people. I was fortunate to serve as the director of the Franklin D. Roosevelt Presidential Library and Museum for some years. After a long career in broadcasting and museum leadership, running a historically significant archive was a humbling experience. As I delved deeper and deeper into the collection (more than 17 million pages of documents, 10,000 pieces of art, 25,000 artifacts, 50,000 books), the power and impact of his words and deeds moved me. When I first entered the secure stacks of the FDR Presidential

Library, operating under the auspices of the National Archives, I was familiar with the well-known narrative of his life. Over time I came to understand a deeper truth—his remarkable success rested on a profound belief in the American spirit, the soul of America.

The one aspect of the Roosevelt narrative that intrigues me the most is how incredibly relevant it is today. Nearly every major issue he dealt with in the 1930s and 1940s is still a part of our daily lives: global conflicts, weapons of mass destruction, terrorism, income inequality, environmental degradation, propaganda and misinformation, authoritarianism, health care, social safety nets, racism, and antisemitism. In revisiting one of the most consequential periods of FDR's twelve years in the White House, I seek to provide some guidance for us today.

Over a two-year period, from September 1939 until January 1942, President Roosevelt persuaded the world that free people could overcome the terror of mechanized militaries controlled by brutal totalitarian governments. Understanding why and how FDR was able to confront and conquer the grave challenges America faced then is the driving force behind this book. Examining his words and deeds provide lessons for us today in an America struggling with dangerous factions bent on undermining democracy.

Today's political environment, where violent militias spout fascist ideology and antisemitism, is directly descended from the America First Committee that emerged during the lead up to World War II. Neo-Nazi protestors proudly wearing "Camp Auschwitz" T-shirts and shouting "We Will Not Be Replaced" threaten attacks on Jews and deface synagogues in tactics that mimic the brown-shirted Storm-troopers of Hitler's Germany. Now, as then, the spread of disinformation to undermine democracy and encourage racist, anti-immigrant, and antisemitic conspiracy theories poses an imminent threat. Hitler's invasion of Poland and the powerful political groups who opposed support for England and France are reflected today in political and media figures opposing aid to Ukraine in its existential battle with Russia.

During his campaign for president in 1940 Roosevelt said this about the information war he was fighting: "Certain techniques of propaganda, created and developed in dictator countries, have been imported into this campaign. It is the very simple technique of repeating and repeating and repeating falsehoods, with the idea that by constant repetition and reiteration, with no contradiction, the misstatements will finally come to be believed. They are used to create fear by instilling in the minds of our people doubt of each other, doubt of their government, and doubt of the purposes of their democracy."

This specific period of Franklin Roosevelt's presidency reveals how FDR confronted isolationists, fascists, and anti-immigrant politicians with a clear vision for a better world. His hope that Americans would rise to the challenge of defending democracy was built on the founding principle of the United States, the commitment to fight for freedom.

When Hitler plunged Europe into the chaos of World War II and the British Empire teetered on the brink of collapse, the future of democracy rested on one man's shoulders. Franklin Roosevelt battled fierce resistance as he sought to provide support for Great Britain in its time of desperate need. The handsome and world-famous aviator Charles Lindbergh emerged as Roosevelt's nemesis, and led the isolationist opposition to the president's efforts. Lindbergh spoke for many, and his allies included FDR's own Ambassador to Great Britain Joseph Kennedy, media titan William Randolph Hearst, and automobile tycoon Henry Ford.

President Roosevelt had his own allies, chief among them Prime Minister Winston Churchill. The two men forged a transatlantic partnership hailed as the most important alliance in American history. Roosevelt's team of advisors and writers included Harry Hopkins, a New Dealer who became the president's closest advisor; Judge Samuel Rosenman who started helping FDR with his speeches in the late 1920's and the Pulitzer Prize–winning playwright Robert Sherwood who added poetry and passion to Roosevelt's prose. And of course, his wife Eleanor Roosevelt, the most influential first lady in American history. All helped him in his fight for the soul of America and the battle between democracy and fascism.

During his 1936 campaign for reelection, Franklin Roosevelt told his supporters that "This generation has a rendezvous with destiny." That simple phrase set the tone of Roosevelt's leadership for the rest of his life. Alone among American leaders he foresaw early on the danger Hitler and fascism posed for democracy and freedom around the world. While many, including Charles Lindbergh, praised Hitler and his resurgent Germany as the world struggled through the Great Depression, Roosevelt saw a madman intent on global domination. Most Americans wanted nothing to do with war in Europe, and FDR faced an enormous challenge in convincing them the United States had a moral responsibility to rise to the occasion and embrace its destiny as a superpower.

Amid drama, conflict, and tension, Franklin and his team confronted entrenched antipathy and impossible deadlines as they labored to change public opinion. Night upon night, Winston Churchill and the British people struggled to survive bombing raids Hitler believed would break that nation's spirit. A German invasion seemed imminent. If the United States did not provide military supplies, food, and fuel the British Empire would fall. President Roosevelt strained against the strictures of the Neutrality Acts, which prevented him from providing arms to belligerent nations. The campaign to win the hearts and minds of Americans took place on the battlefield of public opinion, primarily delivered by way of radio and the print media.

His opponents also relied on mass media and political rallies, often with clandestine support from Nazi Germany. Soon after the invasion of Poland, Lindbergh utilized his boyish charm, good looks, and heroic status to rally millions to his cause. His passionate belief that America should remain neutral arose from his profound admiration for Germany, his disdain for Great Britain, and a deeply hidden antisemitism. His strong opposition to war echoes his father's pacifist stand during World War I, when he was one of only a handful of congressmen to vote against the Unites States entry into the war. He also harbored resentment toward the freedom enjoyed by the press, having suffered under the glare of tabloid flashbulbs after the tragic death of his infant son. One reporter went so far as to sneak into the morgue to photograph the murdered baby's corpse.

Franklin Roosevelt had faith in the American people, and fought back with words of his own. His devoted writers and advisors helped him construct a compelling and persuasive case against fascism that encouraged people to believe in democracy and its future.

The alliance between Franklin Roosevelt and Winston Churchill, forged in the fires of war, defeated the forces of hatred and oppression and created the world we live in today. It is a world that is far from perfect, but also far from the mass murder and destruction of the mid-twentieth century. My hope is that Franklin Roosevelt's belief that the American spirit will rise to any challenge when freedom is threatened will inspire others as it has inspired me.

—Paul M. Sparrow
Lewes, Delaware

PART ONE

THE WAR BEGINS

Proof sheet of portraits by Marcel Sternberger, taken at the White House, December 5, 1939.

Hitler watching German soldiers march into Poland, September 1939.

1

"GOD HELP US ALL"

WASHINGTON, D.C.—SEPTEMBER 1939

President Roosevelt's private secretary, Marguerite "Missy" LeHand, was sound asleep in her third-floor bedroom at the White House when her bedside telephone rang, startling her awake. It was shortly after 2:45 A.M. on September 1, 1939. She answered and heard the voice of William Bullitt, the American ambassador to France. Normally charming and flirtatious—he was a suitor of hers—Bullitt's manner was hard and brusque.[1]

"I need to speak to him right away. I just heard from Ambassador Biddle in Poland," Bullitt said. "The Germans have attacked. Can you tell the switchboard to put me through to his room?"

"Oh, my God!" she exclaimed. "Yes, hold on." Overnight operators had orders not to wake the President without an okay from Missy, who controlled access to Roosevelt night and day. She ran downstairs to the president's bedroom and woke him. The operator put the call through.[2]

Roosevelt picked up the handset. "Mr. President, I just got off the phone with Biddle," Bullitt said. "It's bad." The president and his assistant listened as Bullitt explained that German forces had crossed the Polish border in massive numbers and were bombing cities and slaughtering civilians. When Bullitt finished, the president sighed. "Well, Bill, it has come at last," he said. "God help us all."

Roosevelt hung up and sat in silent thought. Taking up the notepad and pencil he kept at bedside, he recorded a message for posterity. "The President received word at 2:50 A.M. by telephone from Ambassador Biddle through Ambassador Bullitt that Germany has invaded Poland and that four cities are being bombed. The Pres. Directed that all Navy ships and army commands be notified by radio at once. In bed 3:05 A.M. sept. 1 '39 FDR"[3]

The president immediately called the secretaries of state, army, and navy and gave them the news. Assistant press secretary William Hassett notified the media and went on the radio announcing the German invasion.

World War II began in Germany at 5:40 A.M., when Adolf Hitler, surrounded by his top military leaders, declared, "The Polish state has refused the peaceful settlement of relations which I desired, and appealed to arms . . . In order to put an end to this lunacy I have no other choice than to meet force with force from now on."[4]

As dawn was breaking over Poland, German artillery, tanks, and forty-two divisions of jackbooted troops unleashed a fusillade on unsuspecting Poles. Thousands of Luftwaffe bombers and fighters dropped death on peaceful cities while Wehrmacht armored battalions and infantry raced across the land, introducing the tactic of *blitzkrieg*, or "lightning war." In the face of overwhelming force, the Polish army displayed incredible bravery. Desperate to slow the attack, about 250 Polish cavalrymen charged an invading infantry unit, driving off the enemy foot soldiers—until German armored trucks mounting heavy machine guns laid waste to the men on horseback. Nearly a third were killed or wounded.

Hitler, wearing Wehrmacht field grey to address a hastily assembled Reichstag, pledged to remove his uniform only in victory or in death. Radio, his favored propaganda tool, broadcast his vile, lie-filled speech worldwide.[5]

Franklin Roosevelt was among the millions listening, and at 5:00 A.M. he called his wife Eleanor, who was at their home in Hyde Park, New York, and told her to tune in.[6]

In harsh tones that dripped scorn and anger, the Führer claimed the Poles had forced his hand by thwarting his numerous attempts to achieve a peaceful solution to the Polish problem. He bragged about having enlisted a new ally: the Soviet Union.

"I am happy particularly to be able to tell you of one event . . . I no longer see any reason why [Germany and The U.S.S.R.] should still oppose one another . . . We have, therefore, resolved to conclude a pact which rules out for ever any use of violence between us . . . Russia and Germany fought against one another in the World War. That shall and will not happen a second time." Hitler's announcement of a nonaggression pact with the Soviet Union was a stunning reversal—his hatred of Stalin and his belief that the Bolsheviks were controlled by Jews formed the foundation of his worldview.[7]

Raising his voice, the dictator rationalized his actions. "I am resolved to remove from the German frontiers the element of uncertainty, the everlasting atmosphere of conditions resembling civil war," he said. "I will not war against women and children. I have ordered my air force to restrict itself to attacks on military objectives." This was a blatant lie. Even as he spoke, German bombs were killing Polish civilians.

"I will continue this struggle, no matter against whom, until the safety of the Reich and its rights are secured. If our will is so strong that no hardship and suffering can subdue it, then our will and our German might shall prevail."[8]

England and France soon declared war with Germany to honor their treaties with Poland. Millions of Americans feared the U.S. would be drawn into the war. Hitler's new alliance with the Soviets tipped the balance of power in Europe in Germany's favor. The next day, in her weekly syndicated newspaper column, Eleanor Roosevelt dismissed Hitler's speech. "How can you say that you do not intend to make war on women and children and then send planes to bomb cities?" she asked.

By midmorning journalists were packing the White House lobby, demanding explanations from press secretary Stephen Early. Behind the closed door to the president's office, Roosevelt was with Hugh Wilson, accepting Wilson's previously tendered resignation as ambassador to Germany while seeking insights from him into Hitler's latest horror show. Secretary of State Cordell Hull joined them.[9] At 10:40 A.M. the president signaled Early to admit the press and he sounded the buzzer that alerted the reporters. Earl Godwin, who had been covering Roosevelt for years, was first into the room. A conservative former print reporter, Godwin was now an influential presence on the NBC Blue radio network.

Seated behind a large mahogany desk in a green velvet swivel chair, American and presidential flags flanking him, the president pulled the cigarette holder from his mouth and asked Godwin, "What time did you get up?"[10]

"About 3:00 or 3:15, right after you aroused the nation. Felt like I belonged to the village fire department."

"Yes, you were not the only one."[11]

As one last reporter was elbowing into the crowded room, Early called out, "All In!"

Roosevelt had an easy rapport with the journalists nearly encircling him. Unlike predecessors, he regularly appeared, often twice a week, at lively press conferences during which he made clear what was on the record and what was for "background" only. He was on a first-name basis with many reporters. Even newshounds who disagreed with him politically liked the man, and all honored an unspoken agreement never to write of his withered legs or photograph him in his wheelchair or being carried in and out of vehicles. Interactions between FDR and the press were usually playful and informal. Not so today.

"I think a good many of us had a somewhat sleepless night," Roosevelt said. "Bill Hassett has told you of what happened at the White House last night, beginning at 2:50 A.M. I do not believe at this particular time of this very critical period in the world's history that there is anything which I can say except to ask for full cooperation of the press throughout this country in sticking as closely as possible to facts. Of course, that will be the best thing for our own nation, and I think for civilization."

Rumors and falsehoods were swamping newsrooms nationwide, and the president stressed the need to prize accuracy over speed. The first question addressed exactly what everyone wanted to know.

"I think what is probably uppermost in the minds of all the American people today is—Can we stay out? Would you like to make any comment at this time?"

Without hesitation Roosevelt answered in strong, righteous tones. "Only this, that I not only sincerely hope so, but I believe we can and that every effort will be made by the administration so to do."

"May we make that a direct quote?"

"Yes" the president replied with finality. That simple question—"Can we stay out?"—came to dominate political discourse in the United States for the next two years, with powerful voices demanding America isolate itself from the carnage of another European ground war.

As the press conference ended, George Durno, the senior wire service reporter, ritually called out, "Thank you Mr. President!"[12] Instantly newsmen scrambled to be first to a bank of phones reserved for their use in the press room two doors over. Dashing past Secret Service agents stationed at the doorway, they crashed through Missy's office, around the huge round mahogany table in the lobby, and into the press room. In less than a minute reporters were dictating the president's statement to newsrooms. The headline of the early afternoon edition of the Washington *Evening Star* read, ROOSEVELT PLEDGES EVERY EFFORT TO KEEP U.S. OUT OF WAR.

LONDON

Prime Minister Neville Chamberlain summoned Winston Churchill to 10 Downing Street shortly after noon on September 1. For years Churchill had been in political exile as his militant views on Hitler and Mussolini put him at odds with "His Majesty's Government." His strident calls from the back benches of Parliament for an aggressive stance regarding Hitler earned him few friends. His disdain for, and public disparagement of, Chamberlain's policy of appeasement had made President Roosevelt see in Churchill a potential British partner. Chamberlain had little respect for American leadership, and Roosevelt thought the Prime Minister an appeaser and a fool.

Churchill entered Downing Street at his customary quick step, smoking a cigar, and feeling vindicated for his predictions regarding the Nazis. Chamberlain, clearly shaken and unsure of what to do, met him in the Cabinet Room.

"I see no hope of averting war," the prime minister said. "I shall have to form a small War Cabinet of Ministers without departments to conduct it.[13] It would exclude the war, admiralty and RAF ministers. I hope to form a national coalition, but Labor has declined. I would like you to be a part of this."

Churchill agreed. The two began discussing who should serve and who should not. Chamberlain assured Churchill that "unless Berlin ceases all aggressive action against Poland and withdraw their forces already there His Majesty's government would fulfill its obligations to the Poles without hesitation."[14] That promise languished for days. Before a session of Parliament that evening, with most members expecting a declaration of war, the prime minister again procrastinated, saying Whitehall was awaiting word from Berlin regarding the situation.

Response to Chamberlain's meekness was overwhelmingly negative, even outraging members of his own Cabinet. On September 3, Chamberlain finally went on the BBC to announce England was at war with Germany. Churchill addressed the next session of Parliament, delivering the first of many memorable wartime speeches. "Outside the storms of war may blow and the lands may be lashed with the fury of its gales, but in our own hearts this Sunday morning there is peace," he declared. "Our consciences are at rest . . . We are fighting to save the whole world from the pestilence of Nazi tyranny and in defense of all that is most sacred to man." Chamberlain met with Churchill afterward and offered him the post he most intensely desired—first lord of the admiralty, the position he had held during the First World War.[15]

The concept of fighting Hitler to save the world would become the cornerstone to the complex relationship between Winston Churchill and Franklin Roosevelt. This notion of a global crusade also came to stand at the core of the argument that Roosevelt made to the American public as he struggled in coming years to lead their country away from an isolationist worldview and toward acceptance of America's rendezvous with destiny in defeating fascism. This "defense of all that is most sacred to man" was the essence of FDR's efforts to save the soul of America and inspire its citizens to rise to the challenge facing them. But before he could come to Churchill's aid, he had to walk the razor thin line between truth and lies—agreeing America should remain neutral, while secretly preparing for war.

THE WHITE HOUSE

On the day that Churchill became first lord, Roosevelt hosted key advisors at the White House to hone the text of the fireside chat he was to give that evening. One of his closest aides, Assistant Secretary of State Adolf Berle, had submitted a draft, but FDR insisted on writing his own remarks.

President Roosevelt sat at a table near the white marble fireplace in the Lincoln study. He wore a short-sleeved shirt; outside the temperature was 85°, and the swampy Potomac humidity made conditions feel even warmer. At 3:52 P.M. Berle, Secretary of State Cordell Hull, Undersecretary of State Sumner Welles, and Assistant Secretary of War Louis Johnson entered the room in silence. All were feeling the weight of history. Roosevelt distributed copies of his reworking of the speech.

"Mr. President this is a tremendous improvement over anything I have done," Berle said.[16]

There was much discussion of the need to declare America's neutrality, with Secretary Hull insistent on language affirming that status as official U.S. policy. The meeting broke up at 5:00 P.M. Roosevelt had a quiet dinner with Missy LeHand and her assistant Grace Tully after the women had finished typing a final reading copy of his speech.

At 8:55 P.M. a Secret Service agent wheeled Roosevelt into the Diplomatic Reception Room. That space, in the White House basement, had been transformed into a broadcast studio from which the president had delivered many radio addresses. The thirteen-foot vaulted stone ceilings gave the room a feeling of depth and sanctuary, like a cathedral crypt. On this night, though, the makeshift studio was bustling with dozens of radio and newsreel technicians arranging and rearranging microphones, cables, and lights. At exactly 9:00 P.M. the president leaned in close to an array of microphones and began speaking to fellow Americans in a relaxed, clear voice, as one neighbor might talk with another over the dining room table. This was his fourteenth fireside chat, and one of his most important.

"My countrymen and my friends: Tonight, my single duty is to speak to the whole of America," Roosevelt said. "Until four-thirty this morning I had hoped against hope that some miracle would prevent a devastating war in Europe and bring to an end the invasion of Poland by Germany.

"For four long years a succession of actual wars and constant crises have shaken the entire world and have threatened in each case to bring on the gigantic conflict which is today unhappily a fact."[17]

Wherever the moment found them, millions of Americans were leaning toward radios, hanging on his every word. Fear of war was rampant, and the public craved reassurance from their leader that the United States was safe. Roosevelt denounced the invasion of Poland, and despite his own feelings to the contrary the president delivered the words the State Department requested—a statement that America would remain neutral. But he offered an important caveat, inserting his personal perspective over his diplomats' objections.[18]

"But I cannot ask that every American remain neutral in thought as well," Roosevelt said. "Even a neutral has a right to take accounts of facts. Even a neutral cannot be asked to close his mind or his conscience." Just three days after the start of the war, Franklin Roosevelt addressed the issue that was to drive him for the next two years. The Neutrality Acts might prevent the country from taking sides in this conflict, but individual Americans had to decide for themselves what direction their moral compasses pointed. He later called this his quest to save the soul of America. Roosevelt knew in his heart that someday, perhaps soon, the United States would have to confront Hitler and fascism. But he repeated his oft-voiced declaration that "I have said not once but many times that I have seen war and I hate war. I say it again and again. I hope the United States will keep out of this war. I believe that it will. And I give you assurance and reassurance that every effort of your government will be directed toward that end."

And so, President Roosevelt walked the razor's edge between truth and deception. He used words that would inform the public without

alarming them while doing everything he could to prepare for the very
action that he denied he was going to take.

New York City

Charles Lindbergh arrived in New York City by train at 7:40 A.M. after an
overnight journey from Washington D.C.[19] The tall, lanky aviator strode
across the marble floor of Grand Central Station. The huge headlines on
the morning papers fronting the cluttered newsstands—GERMAN TROOPS
ENTER POLAND—shouted out to him. War had come. The famed pilot
of the *Spirit of St. Louis* and international hero had recently returned to
the United States after spending four years in Europe. After his infant
son's kidnapping and death in 1932, and years of ensuing media mayhem,
in 1935 Charles and wife Anne had fled flashbulbs and prying eyes to
seek peace in Great Britain. The tall handsome pilot and his beautiful,
fashionable wife were recognized everywhere they went and treated as
celebrities. The German government invited Lindbergh to visit that
reviving nation's aircraft factories and landing fields. He met several times
with Luftwaffe Commander in Chief Hermann Göring, who presented
Lindbergh with the Service Cross of the German Eagle at an American
Embassy event. German warplanes profoundly impressed Lindbergh.
In detailed reports to the American Embassy, he observed that German
aviation technology and design were far outpacing that of the U.S. He
praised Germans' vitality and energy.[20]

In September 1939, facing the reality of Hitler's aggression, Lindbergh wrote in his diary, "What stand should America take in this war?
This is now our most pressing issue. We have enough internal problems
without confusing them with war. I see trouble ahead even in times of
peace. War would leave affairs chaotic—and always the best men lost."[21]

After listening to President Roosevelt's fireside chat, Lindbergh wrote,
"I wish I trusted him more. Much as I dislike taking part in politics and

public life, I intend to do so if necessary to stop the trend which is now going on in this country."[22]

Many Americans shared Lindbergh's view that the country should not involve itself in European wars. War's inevitable byproduct—refugees— had been hotly debated for years. Just a week before Germany invaded Poland, Lindbergh had met in Washington, D.C., with William R. Castle, former ambassador to Japan and state department official under Herbert Hoover, and archconservative radio commentator Fulton Lewis Jr. Over dinner at Castle's house the three found common ground in their opposition to American involvement in the war. They also shared a dislike for Jews.[23]

Painfully seasoned by his experiences with the media, Lindbergh spoke bluntly. "We are disturbed about the effect of the Jewish influence in our press, radio, and motion pictures," the aviator told the former diplomat and the newsman. "It may become very serious."

Lewis told of an experience he had had while working in radio. "There was one instance when a Jewish advertising firm threatened to remove all their advertising from the Mutual system if a certain feature were permitted to go on the air," he said. "The threat was powerful enough to have the feature removed!"

Lindbergh responded, "I do not blame the Jews so much for their attitude, although I think it unwise from their own standpoint."[24]

"If an antisemitic movement starts in the United States, it may go far," he wrote in his journal that night. "It will eventually affect the good Jews along with the others."

WASHINGTON

At 11:00 P.M. on Sunday, September 10, having spent the weekend inspecting progress on the Presidential Library being built at the Roosevelt family estate known as Springwood, the president left Hyde Park for Highland, New York, across the Hudson River. At the train station he boarded his private Pullman car and departed for an overnight ride to Washington, D.C. He arrived at the White House at 8:45 A.M. and at the desk in his private study composed a personal note to Winston Churchill, the pugnacious aristocrat recently appointed Britain's first lord of the admiralty for a second time. The first had been during World War I, while Roosevelt was assistant secretary of the navy. Bypassing the State Department and centuries of diplomatic protocol, the president wrote in an informal and friendly tone: "My dear Churchill, it is because you and I occupied similar positions in the World War that I want you to know how glad I am that you are back again in the Admiralty."[25]

For a president to directly contact a foreign military officer is a serious breach of political etiquette. Roosevelt did not care. He had little respect for British Prime Minister Neville Chamberlain, who had indulged in a disastrous course of appeasement with Adolf Hitler. Roosevelt was eager to connect with someone who shared his deep concerns regarding the Nazi threat to the world.

"What I want you and the Prime Minister to know is that I shall at all times welcome it if you will keep me in touch personally with anything you want me to know about," FDR wrote. "You can always send sealed letters through your pouch or my pouch."

This remarkable communique began a friendship that has been called the most significant of the twentieth century. Over the next six years, Roosevelt and Churchill exchanged thousands of messages and letters and spent 113 days together at private and official military conferences. Understanding the sensitive nature of this letter, Churchill shared it with the War Cabinet and with their input replied to Roosevelt that he looked forward to further communication.

In keeping with his position, Churchill headed his response "The Following From Naval Person." He used this unique salutation throughout thousands of exchanges, substituting "Former Naval Person" when he became prime minister. This wartime correspondence between the leaders of two countries has no parallel in modern history. Most of the dispatches were labeled top secret and not declassified until 1972. They reveal the depth of the pair's intense involvement in nearly every aspect of World War II, the planning for the post-war world, their disagreements, and their friendship and senses of humor.

In his six-volume history of World War II, Churchill writes, "I was delighted to receive a personal letter from President Roosevelt. I responded with alacrity, using the signature of "Naval Person" and thus began that long and memorable correspondence."

A few weeks later, on October 5, Churchill was having dinner in his London apartment with the director of naval construction, Sir Stanley Goodall, and Rear Admiral Bruce Fraser. They were discussing the latest developments with the Royal Navy when the phone in the front hall rang. The valet answered. After a moment he entered the dining room and Churchill barked "Who is it?"

"I don't know, sir."

"Well, say I can't attend to it now."

"I think you ought to come, sir."[26]

A nettled Churchill pushed his chair back from the table and stomped to the phone. Goodall and Fraser both wondered who would dare telephone the notoriously testy Churchill at this hour. After a silence, they heard Churchill say, "Yes, sir."

"Who on earth could that be?" Fraser later recalled thinking. "There are few people he would address as sir."

Churchill strode back into the room. "Do you know who that was?" he said. "The president of the United States! It is remarkable to think of being rung up in this little flat in Victoria Street by the president himself in the midst of a great war. This is very important. I must go see the prime pinister at once."

The dinnertime interruption had arisen from a false flag operation. The Germans had warned the president that the British were about to sink an American liner, the *Iroquois*, and blame it on the Germans. The whole thing was a ruse, but Roosevelt had thought it serious enough to contact Churchill directly. This set the stage for a deepening of their relationship, as FDR pushed against boundaries imposed by the Neutrality Acts on assisting belligerent nations (and wanted to make sure any ploys to disturb this were disproved) and Churchill did everything in his considerable power to entice the president to join the war on the side of Britain.

*Charles Lindbergh delivering a radio address over the Mutual Broadcasting System,
October 13, 1939.*

2

A Shot Across the Bow

Charles Lindbergh had been out of the public eye for years; he had last done a radio broadcast in August 1931. His new friend, conservative radio host Fulton Lewis Jr., saw Lindbergh as a potential spokesman for the isolationist movement. Lewis, a vocal supporter of Hitler's regime before Germany's invasion of Poland, had strong connections with Nazis in America. Years later, after World War II had ended, Allied analysts reviewing sheaves of dispatches seized from the German Embassy in Washington found one in which Lewis suggested in detail how Hitler could cultivate a friendly relationship with Roosevelt as a means of ensuring continued American neutrality. Lewis went so far as to draft specific language for the dictator to use.[1]

Lewis arranged for Lindbergh to make the case for neutrality by radio from the nation's capital on September 15. Lindbergh took the assignment seriously and spent days writing a script. Knowing his remarks would stir a furor, he arrived in Washington on Thursday, September 14, 1939, to meet with U.S. Army Air Corps Commander General Henry "Hap" Arnold. Arnold, who had been privy to the results of Lindbergh's reconnaissance of German airpower, had enormous respect for the "Lone Eagle." He read and approved Lindbergh's speech, suggesting that the aviator, a member of the Air Corps Reserve, resign that commission.

Arnold undoubtedly passed word up the army chain of command. On Friday, scheduled to speak that evening, Lindbergh got an urgent message from his friend Colonel Truman Smith. The men had met in Berlin, where Smith had been the American military attaché when Lindbergh was visiting German air force facilities, and had become close. Now Smith was an advisor to U.S. Army Chief of Staff George C. Marshall.

Smith arrived at Lindbergh's room in the Carlton Hotel, a magnificent eight-story Beaux Arts building two blocks from the White House, around 4:00 P.M.; Lindbergh was to speak at 9:45. "The administration is very much worried about your intentions to promote neutrality," Smith told Lindbergh. "They are willing to create a cabinet position of secretary of air for you, if you will support the president."

Lindbergh said he would be speaking his mind as planned.

"Well, you see they are worried," Smith replied, laughing.[2]

At 8:30, after dinner at Fulton Lewis's home, Lindbergh and his wife Anne joined Lewis and his wife, Alice, and headed back to the Carlton Hotel, site of the multinetwork broadcast. Charles wore a dark suit and tie, and a black fedora. Anne dressed fashionably in a black dress with a fur stole.[3] In the Carlton lobby a horde of reporters and photographers rushed the famously reclusive pair, who escaped the flurry of flashbulbs and shouted questions by ducking into an elevator.

The impromptu studio occupied an upper-floor room. Technicians were just finishing their handiwork. Cables crisscrossed the floor, and on a table stood six microphones. All three major radio networks—CBS, NBC, and Mutual—were to carry the broadcast. At the appointed time, Charles Lindbergh began.

"In times of great emergency men of the same belief must gather together for mutual counsel and action," he said. "I speak tonight to those people in the United States who feel that the destiny of this country does not call for our involvement in European wars."

He spoke in a slow, calm voice with a detached air and lacking any noticeable emotion. His flat Midwestern accent and plain language made his opinion easy to understand.

"We cannot count on victory merely by shipping abroad several thousand airplanes and cannon. We are likely to lose a million men, possibly several millions—the best of American youth. If we enter fighting for democracy abroad, we may end by losing it at home."[4]

Lindbergh unquestionably understood what he was doing. The words he was speaking were his own, and they accurately expressed views that he held strongly. He was particularly concerned with the rise in what he considered to be a stream of misinformation and outright lies being put forth by a press he had come to loathe for its brutality to his family. But he also gave veiled vent to antisemitic feelings deep within his psyche.

"We will be deluged with propaganda, both foreign and domestic," he continued. "Much of our news is already colored and we must ask who owns and who influences the newspaper, the news picture, and the radio station. Let us look to our own defense and to our own character. If we attend to them, we have no need to fear what happens elsewhere. If we do not attend to them, nothing can save us."

And so, Charles Lindbergh fired his first shots across Franklin Roosevelt's bow. The two men had met only once. On April 20, 1939, fresh from his and Anne's European sojourn, the thirty-seven-year-old Lindbergh called on the president. Having met that morning with Secretary of War Harry H. Woodring to discuss military aviation in Europe and the United States, Lindbergh arrived at the White House at noon. In the president's office, he admired FDR's remarkable collection of historic naval prints and ship models. Roosevelt remained seated behind his desk and leaned forward to offer the aviator his hand in greeting. Only later did Lindbergh realize Roosevelt was "crippled."

"Thank you for coming. How is your lovely wife, Anne?" the president said. "You know she went to Miss Chapin's School with my daughter Anna."

The men undoubtedly discussed the situation in Europe and the state of American air power, which was dismal compared to that of Germany. When Lindbergh tried to leave the executive mansion, he faced a raucous and unavoidable gantlet of photographers and reporters who had every exit covered. Escorting him off the grounds, two uniformed police officers kept the press from swarming him.

In his diary Lindbergh recorded his impression of the president. "He is an accomplished, suave, interesting conversationalist," he wrote. "I liked him and feel that I could get along with him well. Acquaintanceship would be pleasant and interesting. But there is something about him I did not trust, something a little too suave, too pleasant, too easy. Still, he is our President, and there is no reason for any antagonism between us in the work I am now doing. It is better to work together as long as we can, yet somehow, I have a feeling that it may not be for long." Lindbergh was right.[5]

The lead headline of the September 16 *New York Times* blared, LINDBERGH URGES WE SHUN THE WAR. By the time the Lindberghs returned to Lloyd Manor, their beautiful new Long Island home outside Huntington, New York, the press was dissecting the speech for its political implications. Congratulatory telegrams and letters arrived by the hundreds. Even Secretary of War Woodring thought Lindbergh's speech "was very well worded and very well delivered." Former president Herbert Hoover, who detested FDR and fought against all his policies, sought out Lindbergh for a private meeting and told him, "Roosevelt definitely wants to get us into this conflict."[6]

But not everyone found Lindbergh's remarks inspiring. Popular *New York Herald Tribune* columnist Dorothy Thompson, famed for her "On the Record" byline, noted that Lindbergh's "inclination toward fascism" was well known among his friends. Thompson also took exception to his oblique but obvious comment about Jewish ownership of newspapers and radio stations. She listed his many interactions with the Nazis, including accepting the Service Cross of the German Eagle. She ended with a typically sharp comment of her own.[7]

"But since he himself has warned that all who speak in the present situation should have their personal interests inquired into, he cannot object to an inquiry into his own biases," Thompson concluded. "And his are not the predilections of the majority of Americans or of democracies anywhere."

Two days after Lindbergh's radio address and without warning, the Soviet Union attacked Poland from the east—the first violent fruit of the Molotov-Ribbentrop Pact, a mutual nonaggression deal made by Germany and the U.S.S.R a week before Hitler invaded Poland. There followed the subjugation of Poland under its totalitarian masters, whose unexpected reconciliation after years of bitter opposition stunned both Churchill and Roosevelt, threatening a military juggernaut that could crush Western democracies under the tracks of their tanks.

The government of Poland, overwhelmed by two massive foreign armies on that beleaguered nation's soil, withdrew to Romania and ordered Polish units to reassemble in France. Within weeks the invaders had demolished Polish resistance and divided the country in two.

THE WHITE HOUSE

The situation in Europe was chaotic. Most Americans did not want their country to entangle itself in another senseless bloodbath. Franklin Roosevelt saw the situation very differently. He wanted to provide support for England and France in their efforts to thwart Hitler's quest for world domination. But the Neutrality Acts prevented him from doing much of anything. One article of the act specifically forbade selling weapons to any belligerents in a military conflict, in effect imposing a total arms embargo. Roosevelt wanted to amend that constraint to allow sale of weapons and matériel on a "cash and carry" basis. While this language appeared to describe a neutral policy, the reality greatly favored England and France, whose navies controlled the Atlantic Ocean. Cargo vessels sailing under those nations' flags could easily transport armaments, although the German submarine fleet posed a deadly challenge. Lindbergh had not singled out the proposed "cash and carry" amendment for attack, pleasing the president as he prepared for a major address to Congress.

Roosevelt had scheduled that speech for September 21. Time was short, and the stakes remarkably high. Missy LeHand called Judge Sam Rosenman, an old friend of FDR's who had worked with him for years, and asked him to come to the White House on September 20. Rosenman arrived at 5:30 P.M., and Missy gave him two drafts of the speech. One was the work of Adolf Berle. The other FDR had dictated. Speechwriting usually took place in the Cabinet Room, so Rosenman installed himself there and began editing the sharply contrasting versions into one coherent draft. By the time Secretary of State Cordell Hull and Berle arrived at 8:30 P.M. the long dark table in the center of the ornate room was covered with stacks of paper. Moments later President Roosevelt entered in his wheelchair.[8]

"Well, let's get this started" FDR said, jutting his chin and looking confident. For hours, the four worked at achieving the elusive perfect balance of logic, emotion, honesty, and politics. The always cautious Hull pushed for an overarching statement.

"It would be politically expedient if you were to make a commitment that we would never, under no circumstances and whatever happened, go to war," he told the president.[9] Roosevelt looked at Hull for several tense moments, his normally bright blue eyes now a cold steely grey.

"Can you guarantee that?" Roosevelt finally said. "Can I guarantee it?"

After another fraught silence, Berle tried to break the tension. "I do not see how anyone could guarantee the future in the next eight months," he said. "All we can do is to say that until the Atlantic line is seriously threatened or crossed, we will not go to war." Everyone agreed, and that language ended up in the final draft. Hull and Berle left around 11:00 P.M. The president went to bed. Rosenman continued working with Grace Tully to produce a coherent revised draft. They wound up at 2:30 A.M.

A few hours later Rosenman joined the president, awake and working but still in bed in his private suite. Sitting up and wearing an old sweater, Roosevelt scrutinized each page of the update, making notes and handing sheet upon sheet to Tully, who would run from the room with each mark-up and type that portion of what became the final reading copy. They finished at 12:30 P.M., and the president's valet came in to help him dress for the journey to the Capitol.

By convening Congress for an emergency joint session Roosevelt established the urgency of the situation and set the tone for the start of a contentious debate over the arms embargo. Senators and representatives had received thousands of letters and telegrams, mostly opposed to dropping the embargo from the 1937 Neutrality Act. Congress convened two hours before the president was to speak. The mood was tense. As House Speaker William Bankhead (D-Alabama) gaveled the meeting into session, Senator Charles Tobey (R-New Hampshire) moved to insert the text of the Lindbergh speech into the Congressional Record. Senate Foreign Relations Chairman Key Pittman (D-Nevada) stood and objected strongly, precluding insertion of the text. Murmurs of dissent amplified the tension in the room.[10]

The session's historic nature had filled the gallery with spectators. Crowds stood outside the Capitol, waiting for any news.

As in all such settings, it was necessary for the president to wear steel leg braces under his trousers. Tightly gripping the arm of his close aide,

General Edwin "Pa" Watson, he set about imitating a man who was able to walk. Starting in the mid-1920s, he had mastered the trick of using the muscles of his core to swing one paralyzed leg forward while balancing on the other. When he was within reach of the podium, he grabbed it with one hand, then released his grip on Watson's arm. There were some cheers, but not the usual exuberant greeting. He began with a somber declaration:

"I have asked the Congress to reassemble in extraordinary session in order that it may consider and act on the amendment of certain legislation, which, in my best judgment, so alters the historic foreign policy of the United States that it impairs the peaceful relations of the United States with foreign nations.[11]

"For many years, the primary purpose of our foreign policy has been that this nation and this Government should strive to the utmost to aid in avoiding war among nations. But if and when war unhappily comes, the Government and the nation must exert every possible effort to avoid being drawn into the war."

As he often did in speeches, the president took on the role of teacher. He laid out the historical record of American involvement in foreign wars, and the nation's policy in regard to trading with active belligerents. He admitted to having been reluctant to sign the Neutrality Act of 1937, the law he was now trying to change.

"I regret that the Congress passed that Act," he said. "I regret equally that I signed that Act. On July fourteenth of this year, I asked the Congress in the cause of peace and in the interest of real American neutrality and security, to take action to change that Act. I now ask again that such action be taken in respect to . . . the embargo provisions. I ask it because they are, in my opinion, most vitally dangerous to American neutrality, American security and, above all, American peace."

Standing for extended periods, even when he was able to steady himself by grasping a podium, was exhausting for FDR due to those ten-pound leg braces and the need to keep his balance while reading the speech. But on this night and in this moment his voice never wavered, his resolve never faltered. His message was clear.

"I seek a greater consistency through the repeal of the embargo provisions, and a return to international law," he said. "I seek reenactment of the historic and traditional American policy which, has served us well from the very beginning of our Constitutional existence. The result of these last two objectives will be to require all purchases to be made in cash, and all cargoes to be carried in the purchasers' own ships, at the purchasers' own risk. Repeal of the embargo and a return to international law are the crux of the issue that faces us."

Standing tall, looking out at the assembled legislators, Franklin Roosevelt ended his address with a heartfelt plea for unity of purpose, and an indirect reference to what he considered "the soul of America," that traces back to the founding of the country and the Golden Rule of Christianity—do unto others as you would have them do unto you.

"In a period when it is sometimes said that free discussion is no longer compatible with national safety, may you by your deeds show the world that we of the United States are one people of one mind, one spirit, one clear resolution, walking before God in the light of the living."

The president turned from the podium, took Watson's arm, and made his way out of the chamber. Hundreds of congressmen and senators stood and cheered as he exited the room. Many adamantly opposed ending the arms embargo but, understanding the burden they now carried, all respected the articulate passion of the president's remarks.[12]

The president met with multiple senators the next day, urging both Democrats and Republicans to repeal the arms embargo. For six weeks the debate raged, with isolationists blasting the effort at repeal and interventionists fighting to help Great Britain and France.

Public opinion shifted, and in a poll 60 percent of those asked supported eliminating the arms embargo, although a vast majority of Americans still opposed any involvement in the war itself. Truman Smith urged his friend Charles Lindbergh to meet with Representative

George Tinkham (R-Massachusetts), like Smith an isolationist. Smith
and likeminded people realized that Lindbergh would be a highly effective advocate for their cause and encouraged him to speak out again.
Lindbergh needed little encouragement.

At 9:30 on the evening of October 13, 1939, Lindbergh sat at a Mutual
Radio microphone and explained his position on neutrality and war, his
voice reaching millions of listeners. "Tonight, I speak again to the people
of this country who are opposed to the United States entering the war
which is now going on in Europe," he said. "We are faced with the need of
deciding on a policy of American neutrality. The future of our nation and
of our civilization rests upon the wisdom and foresight we use."[13]

In a near-monotone Lindbergh provided specifics. He recommended
continuing to embargo offensive weapons but allow the sale of "purely
defensive" weapons—a distinction most people found meaningless. He
proposed to prohibit American ships from the ports of warring nations
and adjacent "danger zones." Finally, in the strongest terms he opposed
providing credit to any belligerent nation or its agents.[14]

Lindbergh made his point in chillingly graphic terms. "I do not
want to see American bombers dropping bombs which kill and mutilate
European children, even if they are not flown by American pilots," he
told listeners.

In describing the combatants facing off in Europe, Lindbergh made
clear whom he favored. "From 1936 to 1939, as I traveled through European countries, I saw the phenomenal military strength of Germany
growing like a giant at the side of an aged, and complacent England. In
the past we have dealt with a Europe dominated by England and France,"
he said. "In the future we may have to deal with a Europe dominated by
Germany. But we are often told that if Germany wins this war, cooperation will be impossible, and treaties no more than scraps of paper. I
reply that cooperation is never impossible when there is sufficient gain
on both sides. Our accusations of aggression and barbarism on the part
of Germany, simply bring back echoes of hypocrisy and Versailles."

Without a formal declaration, Charles Lindbergh and Franklin Roosevelt had entered into a war of words that now took on a new intensity. The day after Lindbergh's appearance on Mutual, the president's allies in Congress spoke out against the aviator. "The most unfortunate part of Colonel Lindbergh's statement is that it encourages the ideology of the totalitarian governments and is subject to the construction that he approves of their brutal conquest of democratic countries through war!" Senator Pittman declared.[15]

A chorus of newspapers also faulted Lindbergh for his remarks, most stridently Dorothy Thompson, who denounced him as "a somber cretin" and a "pro-Nazi recipient of a German medal."[16]

In her October 19 "My Day" column, Eleanor Roosevelt described meeting friends for lunch amid constant talk of war. "We were all interested in . . . Dorothy Thompson's column today," Mrs. Roosevelt wrote. "She sensed in Col. Lindbergh's speech a sympathy with Nazi ideals which I thought existed but could not bring myself to believe was really there."

Interior view of the destroyed Fasanenstrasse Synagogue, Berlin, burned on Kristallnacht.

3

THE PERSECUTION OF THE JEWS

NUREMBERG, GERMANY—SEPTEMBER 1935

Thousands of flags ringed the rim of Nuremberg Stadium, fluttering above tens of thousands of Germans overflowing the arena. Each pennant's red field held a white circle, and within that circle was a black swastika. It was September 15, 1935, the day Chancellor Adolf Hitler declared a new official national flag of Germany. Hitler had replaced the traditional colors of the old imperial banner with a black, red, and white symbol of hatred, religious bigotry, and militarism.[1]

On the grounds at the foot of the stadium's stage troops staged mock battles. Hundreds of tanks, artillery, and armored personnel carriers criss-crossed at high speed beneath squadrons of bombers flying overhead. On their perch overlooking the spectacle, Hitler and his generals looked down and smiled, fully aware that their martial display unabashedly violated the Treaty of Versailles which had ended the Great War. They did not care. At 9:00 P.M. that evening, Hitler presided over the seventh Nazi Party Congress, delivering a short but shocking speech. He proudly proclaimed the resurrection of the German Army, and announced new laws institutionalizing what had been until then the brutal but informal persecution of his country's Jews.

"In order to reach an amicable relation between the German people and the Jews the government will try to bring about legal regulation," the dictator declared. "If Jewish agitation within and without Germany continues, we will then examine the situation again."[2]

Hitler turned the microphone over to Reichstag President Herman Göring to read the new laws. The legislation deprived Jews of citizenship, banned sexual activity and marriage between Jews and Germans, and invalidated existing mixed marriages. The "Nuremberg Laws" marked an intensification of state-sponsored terrorism that soon spawned a nationwide campaign of violence, imprisonment, and murder.

In the 1930s, the average American, along with most Europeans, held a negative view of Jews. Nearly every country strictly controlled the number of people allowed to immigrate. Antisemitism was rampant. Data from multiple polls in 1938 showed that 71 to 85 percent of Americans opposed enlarging refugee quotas to admit more Jews. A year later, 66 percent opposed implementation of a one-time exception that would have allowed 10,000 Jewish refugee children to enter the country. Other poll results illustrated the ugly face of American bigotry, as more than 50 percent of respondents labeled Jews greedy and dishonest. During the war, 15 to 24 percent of Americans polled said they considered Jews a "menace to America."[3]

As the Nazi campaign against Jewish Germans was taking form, Roosevelt made few public comments but did act behind the scenes. In a November 13, 1935, letter to New York Governor Herbert Lehman, the president explained that he had instructed the State Department to give "the most generous and favorable treatment possible under the laws of this country" to German Jews applying for visas to come to the United States. FDR acknowledged that the number of immigrants admitted from Germany in 1935 had been far below the official quota of 25,957.[4]

Historically, critics have scored the Roosevelt administration poorly for its interwar actions—and inactions—regarding refugees. One reason for this sorry record is that at the time staff ranks at the U.S. State Department and other agencies were rife with antisemites who made no bones about disdaining Jews. Many officials deliberately slow-walked applications through the visa process or made it difficult, even impossible, for German Jews to obtain visas for which they had applied. The American Embassy in Berlin initially denied Albert Einstein a visa and subjected the scientist and his wife to an in-person interrogation.[5] Consul General George Messersmith personally intervened to allow Einstein to emigrate to the United States. Charles Lindbergh's unspoken antisemitism was widely shared by many Americans.

On March 12, 1938, the German 8th Army, part of the newly expanded Wehrmacht, crossed the border into Austria. That afternoon Adolf Hitler drove to a warm welcome from cheering crowds. When he reached Vienna, 200,000 people publicly demonstrated their support for *Anschluss*, or annexation by Germany. Austrian officials offered no open resistance as Hitler declared Austria part of the German Reich in violation of the Treaty of Saint-Germain that had ended World War I. Hitler's actions galvanized a Europe seeing the form, if not the fact, of renewed German aggression. Annexation put Austria's Jews at risk and further complicated the refugee problem.[6]

WASHINGTON

On March 18, 1938, President Roosevelt called a Cabinet meeting, the first since the annexation. Seated around the dark mahogany table were the department secretaries assigned to implement the president's policies, including Treasury Secretary Henry Morgenthau, himself a Jew, and Secretary of State Cordell Hull. Roosevelt challenged his team to find novel solutions for the Jewish refugee crisis.

"Why can't we combine the immigration quotas of Germany and Austria to increase the number of refugees who can come here?" he asked. "After all, America had been a place of refuge for so many fine Germans in the time period of 1848 and why couldn't we offer them again a place of refuge at this time."[7]

"I do not think that would be legal," said Labor Secretary Frances Perkins, the mother of social security and the first woman in U.S. history to hold a Cabinet position.

"Could we increase the quota by getting Congress to act?"

Several people at the table expressed strong opinions that the level of hostility on Capitol Hill made this an impossibility.

"Perhaps the International Labor Bureau in Geneva could handle this?" Perkins suggested.

"That's a good idea," FDR said. "If we could appeal to different countries, depending on their size, perhaps they might take 100 to 1,000 families each, and this way we could find homes for 10,000 or even 15,000 families."

"I'll get the process started," Morgenthau volunteered. With Undersecretary of State Sumner Wells, Morgenthau began planning an international conference on the refugee crisis. They invited thirty-two countries to participate in this historic summit, from July 6th through the 15th, 1938, in Évian, France.

WARM SPRINGS, GEORGIA

Five days after the Cabinet meeting President Roosevelt traveled by train to Warm Springs, Georgia, where he had transformed a rundown rustic resort into the world's premier polio rehabilitation clinic. The "Little White House" there was a favorite place to recharge and escape the pressures of the presidency. Amid the balmy weather of Georgia's early spring and abundant local hospitality, he was able to relax as well as exercise in the naturally warm waters filling the therapy pools. On March 25, while sitting in his car outside his small white clapboard cottage near the facility, he met with the press. A wire service reporter posed a question.[8]

"With respect to the Secretary of State's invitation of yesterday to other powers on the plight of political refugees, from a practical point of view that means the Jews in Germany and Austria . . . "

" . . . it means a great many Christians too, a very large number," the president interjected.

"I wondered if any spokesmen of Catholic and Lutheran groups had also requested it?"

"I don't know, categorically," FDR said after a pause. "But I think so."

"To give practical application to it, would not legislation be required in order to relax our immigration laws?"

"No," Roosevelt answered curtly. "Why?"

"For example, there are 200,000 Jews . . ."

Roosevelt again cut him off. "The law says that if a country ceases to exist and is merged in another country, that the two quotas are merged into one quota."

"Then we have the total for both Germany and Austria together? It would run up to . . . ?"

"26,000," the president answered quickly and confidently.

Roosevelt's responses reflect his strategy of not focusing on Jewish refugees but instead including all categories of people the Nazis were persecuting.

The Évian Conference, for which Roosevelt had high hopes, convened as planned. The representatives of thirty-two countries gathered, along with officials from more than twenty international organizations and some two hundred journalists. The event's most visible accomplishment was the creation of the Intergovernmental Committee on Refugees (IGCR), a body that ultimately proved ineffective. Some countries did answer Roosevelt's call to help find homes for refugees, but few changed their policies.

In 1938 the U.S. issued 19,552 visas to Germans; 7,818 quota slots went unused with 139,163 on a waiting list. In 1939 those numbers increased to the full quota of 27,370 with 240,748 on the waiting list.[9] In 1940 15 visas went unused, with 301,935 Germans waiting. Most were Jews. Australia allowed 15,000 refugees to enter over those years. Many countries, including Canada and France, turned away refugees exceeding their quotas.

The Dominican Republic agreed to allow up to 100,000 refugees to enter the country and later designated land for arrivals to use, but only about 800 ever made it. In the end, FDR's opponents accurately derided the Évian Conference as a failure, and Nazi propaganda mocked the effort.

GERMANY

Emboldened by the lack of repercussions for his annexation of Austria, Hitler ratcheted up violence against Jews. Year by year since his seizure of power in 1933, German Jews alert to the implications had been leaving, first in a trickle, then in a stream. By 1938 about 150,000, almost 25 percent of Germany's Jewish population, had fled the country to escape increasingly harsh treatment by the Gestapo and the brown-shirted stormtroopers, *Sturmabteilung* (SA)—the National Socialist Party's street fighters. On November 9, 1938, Hitler unleashed the SA nationwide. Stormtroopers beat and humiliated thousands of Jews while smashing and burning seventy-six synagogues, 117 residences, and 815 businesses. Shards of broken windows littering the streets of German cities gave rise to the term *Kristallnacht*—"the night of the broken glass." Nazi authorities arrested more than 2,000 Jews, imprisoning hundreds in concentration camps.

WASHINGTON

The president invoked *Kristallnacht* during a November 15 press conference. "The news of the past few days from Germany has deeply shocked public opinion in the United States," he said. "Such news from any part of the world would inevitably produce a similar profound reaction among American people in every part of the nation. I myself could scarcely believe that such things could occur in a twentieth-century civilization. With a view to gaining a first-hand picture of the current situation in Germany I have asked the Secretary of State to order our Ambassador in Berlin to return at once for report and consultation."

A reporter asked about America's ambassador to England, Joseph P. Kennedy, a Roosevelt appointee and father of future president John F. Kennedy. "There are reports from London that Mr. Kennedy has made a suggestion to the British government concerning a place wherein the Jewish refugees would be taken care of," the newsman said.

"I cannot comment on the report, because I know nothing of what has been happening in London," Roosevelt replied. "We do know that the International Refugee Commission is at work trying to extend its help to take care of an increasingly difficult situation."

A serious but so far private rift had been widening between Roosevelt and Kennedy over dismissive remarks attributed to Kennedy regarding England's prospects in a war with Germany. The president did not want that quarrel going public right now.

"Mr. President, can you tell us whether you feel that there is any place in the world where you could take care of mass emigration of the Jews from Germany?" the reporter asked. "Have you given thought to that?"

"I have given a great deal of thought to it," Roosevelt said. Though he did not want to elaborate, he had spent much time dealing with exactly this issue. There were no easy solutions.

GERMANY

The day before *Kristallnacht*, Charles Lindbergh wrote to Ambassador Kennedy of his visits to German aviation facilities. "I am extremely anxious to learn more about Germany and I believe a few months spent in that country would be interesting from many standpoints," Lindbergh told Kennedy.[10] He explained that his wife was looking at houses in Wannsee, a suburb of Berlin. Lindbergh had also written to Army Air Corps chief Hap Arnold, urging the general to come to Germany and see for himself the Luftwaffe's accomplishments.

In October 1938, a month before *Kristallnacht*, Lindbergh visited a Junkers Aircraft and Motor Works factory whose production line was building engines for the new Junkers 88, a multipurpose warplane intended to be Germany's premier bomber. He flew a JU-52 and inspected several other military aircraft at the factory. That evening he attended a party at the American Embassy. In the course of that evening the second most powerful man in Germany, Hermann Göring, bestowed on Lucky Lindy "by order of the Führer" a golden cross with four small swastikas hanging from a red ribbon, the Service Cross of the German Eagle. Back at their Berlin accommodations, Charles showed the medal to Anne, who presciently dubbed the decoration "The Albatross." This was the medal Dorothy Thompson and others would refer to in the coming years.

In December, the Lindberghs rented an apartment in the 16th arrondissement in Paris, having decided against relocating to Berlin after the brutality of *Kristallnacht*.[11]

WASHINGTON

In the week following *Kristallnacht*, the president and his closest advisors frantically tried to reach beyond diplomatic posturing and accomplish something practical. At a press conference on November 18, 1938, FDR announced that he would allow any German or Austrian citizens currently in the United States on temporary visitor permits to have their visas extended indefinitely.

"Now, as a matter of practical fact, a great many of these people—who are not all Jews by any means, since other religions are included in very large numbers among them, if they were to get back to Germany . . . a great many of them believe that their treatment on reaching home might be a very serious problem," Roosevelt said. "In other words, it is a question of concentration camps, et cetera and so on. They are not here under a quota, so we have a very definite problem as to what to do. I don't know, from the point of view of humanity, that we have a right to put them on a ship and send them back to Germany under the present conditions."

The president could not allow refugees into the country in excess of congressionally mandated quotas, but he could unilaterally extend visitor permits—a small gesture in the face of atrocities but basically all that was feasible. Behind the scenes, he continued to press Sumner Welles about other countries' willingness to accept Jewish refugees. Welles provided a list of twenty-two countries, but few loosened their restrictive immigration policies.

In the months following *Kristallnacht*, an estimated 115,000 German Jews left the country. In 1939, the combined German-Austrian annual immigration quota of 27,370 for the United States was filled for the first time during the Nazi era. But Hitler had made emigration increasingly difficult for Jews, insisting they forfeit their savings, their businesses, and their homes. Hitler's invasion of Poland exacerbated a refugee problem that had no easy solution.

The White House State Dining Room has large floor-to-ceiling windows along two walls. On October 17, 1939, the curtains on those windows were pulled back to admit sunlight. Above the large fireplace hung a famed portrait of Abraham Lincoln painted by George Healy in 1869. The high-ceilinged, wood-paneled room was lit by a crystal chandelier over the table at its center. Shortly after noon that warm autumn day, the dining room began filling with delegates of the Intergovernmental Committee on Refugees. The IGCR, established at the Évian Conference in 1938 in response to the Jewish refugee crisis, was now facing a global crisis brought on by war. The president had invited the committee members to join him for a luncheon before their conference at the State Department. Representatives from all thirty-two countries were participating, along with a number of ambassadors, Secretary of State Hull, and Undersecretary of State Welles.[12]

A few minutes after 1:00 P.M. President Roosevelt entered the room and gave an opening statement. "In March 1938, it became clear to the world that a point had been reached where private agencies alone could no longer deal with the masses of unfortunate people who had been driven from their homes," FDR said. "These men, women, and children were beating at the gate of any nation which seemed to offer them a haven."[13]

The delegates listened intently. Their committee's future existence was uncertain. Support was waning, as hopes for rescuing refugees diminished, stymied now not only by bureaucratic indifference and antisemitism, but also Nazi enmity, barbed wire, and machine guns.

"Most of these fellow human beings belonged to the Jewish Race, though many thousands of them belonged to other races and other creeds," Roosevelt said. "The flight from their countries of origin meant chaos for them and great difficulties for other nations, which for other reasons—chiefly economic—had erected barriers against immigration. Many portions of the world which in earlier years provided areas for immigration had found it necessary to close their doors."

World War II's outbreak caused seismic shifts in the world's response to the refugee problem and made the October 17 meeting of the IGCR in Washington especially important. The president, perhaps more than any American politician, understood the long-term challenges. In the safe haven of the White House State Dining Room, delegates feared they could do little to alleviate European Jews' pain and suffering. The president reviewed the committee's accomplishments and pointed to the work remaining.

"A year and a half ago I took the initiative by asking thirty-two governments to cooperate with the Government of the United States in seeking a long-range solution of the refugee problem," Roosevelt said. "Since that time, this Intergovernmental Committee has greatly helped in the settling of many refugees, (and) in providing temporary refuge for thousands of others. Things were going well, although I must confess slowly, up to the outbreak of the war in Europe. Every war leaves behind it tens of thousands of families who for very many different reasons are compelled to start life anew in other lands." Roosevelt looked down at his notes. When he looked up, he made a prediction that shook the audience.

"When this ghastly war ends there may be not one million but ten million or twenty million men, women, and children belonging to many races and many religions, living in many countries and possibly on several continents, who will enter into the wide picture—the problem of the human refugee."[14]

The delegates shifted in their seats subtly but noticeably. This was a brutally honest statement that carried enormous political risk for the president. All present knew he was facing a Congress hostile to refugees and a public wanting nothing to do with the war in Europe. History shows that the post-war population of international refugees exceeded even FDR's grim estimate. The war displaced between 20 and 50 million people, and in the process of resettlement unknown hundreds of thousands died. Roosevelt wanted the IGCR to deal with both the immediate problem and the inevitable crisis to come.

"I ask, therefore, that as the second great task that lies before this committee, it starts at this time a serious and probably a fairly expansive effort to survey and study definitely and scientifically this geographical and economic problem of resettling several million people in new areas of the earth's surface," he continued. "This problem involves no one race group—no one religious faith. It is a problem of all groups and all faiths.

It is not enough to indulge in horrified humanitarianism, empty resolutions, golden rhetoric, and pious words. We must face it actively if the democratic principle based on respect and human dignity is to survive, and if world order, which rests on the security of the individual, is to be restored."

Once again Roosevelt was seeking to focus not solely on the Jewish refugee problem, but on global suffering. He wanted to appeal to what he believed to be Americans' basic goodness, a core belief that his and theirs was a country that welcomed those in need. He ended his remarks with a powerful image.

"Remembering the words written on the Statue of Liberty, let us lift a lamp beside new golden doors and build new refuges for the tired, for the poor, for the huddled masses yearning to be free."

Eighteen days later Congress repealed the arms embargo, and the president signed a revised Neutrality Act authorizing him to sell weapons to England and France on a cash and carry basis.

President Roosevelt with his wife Eleanor, his mother Sara, and Mrs. Endicott Peabody at St. James's Episcopal Church on March 4, 1940, the seventh anniversary of his first inauguration.

4

HOPPING MAD

WASHINGTON—MARCH 1940

The first yellow crocus blossoms of the year showed their pretty faces to the sun in the little protected garden on the south side of the White House.[1] A wisp of spring brightened life for winter weary Washingtonians on March 16, 1940. Two stories above the dash of botanical color, President Roosevelt was feeling lousy and in a foul mood to boot. He had been fighting a cold to the point of having had to cancel his appointments the day before. Now he was awaiting Vice Admiral Ross T. McIntire, White House Physician and Surgeon General, to give him the OK to proceed with two important engagements later that day.[2] McIntire had known Franklin Roosevelt for more than twenty years.

They had met during World War I when Roosevelt was assistant secretary of the navy and McIntire was a navy surgeon. Roosevelt brought the physician to the White House in 1933 as his personal doctor, and they spent a great deal of time together. McIntire traveled with the President, fished and played poker with him, and treated the president's sinus problems on an almost daily basis. McIntire found his petulant patient still in bed.

"Well, how are you feeling today?"

"I'm fine thank you very much, and I have already taken my own temperature. It's just 99.4 degrees."

"Hope you don't mind if I check for myself?" The doctor took the president's temperature and sighed, knowing his medical opinion was not going to sway the president from going ahead with his plans.

Roosevelt was to give a radio address that afternoon to an international audience participating in the Christian Foreign Service Convocation. The primary meeting was taking place at the Waldorf Astoria Hotel in New York City, but local events were taking place at hundreds of locations worldwide. Later in the evening he was to be the featured guest at the annual White House Correspondents Association Dinner, and he had no intention of missing out on the fun. Dr. McIntire gave the okay, and FDR began preparing for his speech.[3]

Radio technology had advanced such that segments of a broadcast could originate from settings anywhere, which appealed to secular and religious institutions hosting regional gatherings. The sweet and inspiring voice of opera star Marian Anderson singing "Ave Maria" came over the airwaves from a church in Calgary, Canada.[4] The Tuskegee Institute Choir sang "Oh Morn of Beauty" by Finnish composer Jean Sibelius from the chapel on the Tuskegee campus in Alabama. The Sibelius selection resonated powerfully, as an outnumbered Finnish Army had recently fought a courageous, if ultimately futile, battle against an unprovoked Russian invasion.[5]

President Roosevelt entered the radio room in the White House basement at 3:15 P.M. His audience consisted of Christian religious and political leaders as well as various sects' missionaries. He began by relating a history of proselytizing:

"Before the advent of the Christian era, messengers and missionaries had traveled throughout the known world—they were commonly traders or soldiers seeking advantage for themselves, or agents of conquerors carrying notice of invasion to come."[6]

His voice a little hoarse, his delivery slow and deliberate, he extolled the virtues of the Christian message of brotherhood and spoke of the early feudal days of fief against fief, of powerful kingdoms against smaller, weaker ones, informatively and entertainingly arriving at his point.

"Today we seek a moral basis for peace," FDR said. "It cannot be a real peace if it fails to recognize brotherhood. It cannot be a lasting peace if the fruit of it is oppression, or starvation, or cruelty, or human life dominated by armed camps. It cannot be a sound peace if small nations must live in fear of powerful neighbors. It cannot be a moral peace if freedom from invasion is sold for tribute. It cannot be an intelligent peace if it denies free passage to that knowledge of those ideals which permit men to find common ground. It cannot be a righteous peace if worship of God is denied. On these fundamentals the world did not have a true peace in those years between the ending of the World War and the beginning of present wars."

Roosevelt's words offered a stark contrast, some might say a rebuke, to an article by Lindbergh in the current issue of *The Atlantic*. Under the headline "What Substitute for War?" he put forth a seemingly reasonable and articulate argument that Germany was simply doing what England and France had done to expand their empires.

"We in America have a tendency to look on this war in Europe as a conflict between right and wrong, with right represented by the 'democracies' and wrong represented by the 'totalitarian' countries,"[7] Lindbergh wrote. "But the motives and causes of war are not so easily caged. If one looks at Europe objectively, neither side seems to have a monopoly of right—except the kind of right which is judged by its own particular and rather momentary standards. Even this type of right frequently changes when it is applied to the opposing side."

Lindbergh's assertion that "neither side seems to have a monopoly of right" in the context of Nazi Germany's brutal treatment of Jews and indiscriminate bombing of civilians seems incredible. But that statement reflects his point of view, and it challenged the core of Roosevelt's argument that the war was one between right and wrong.

"For instance, one of the banners which 'democratic' peoples follow is called 'Equality of Opportunity,'" Lindbergh's essay continued. "But this flag now waves before the German legions in their demand for equality of opportunity in the influence and possessions of the world today, while the 'democratic' armies of England and France stand defending empires of conquered and hereditary wealth. So that we find 'equality of opportunity' *within* a nation called 'democratic' and 'right' by the same people who call the demand for 'equality of opportunity' *among* nations 'totalitarian' and 'wrong.'"

Lindbergh saw no moral difference between Hitler's actions and Queen Victoria's. His defense of Germany's invasion of Poland amounted to the claim that the British and French did something similar years ago. In light of Hitler's persecution of the Jews, Lindbergh's position hinted at unspoken but ardent antisemitism.

"The English and French claim they are right in fighting to maintain their possessions and their ethics, and the status quo of their last victory," Lindbergh wrote. "The Germans, on the other hand, claim the right of an able and virile nation to expand—to conquer territory and influence by force of arms as other nations have done at one time or another throughout history.

"This problem is not new; it has always existed. We have never found a way of agreeing on the rights of nations or of men. The 'rights' of one generation are often built upon the 'wrongs' of a previous one. Drake was a successful pirate, so he was knighted by Queen Elizabeth. Washington led a successful revolution and changed his status from that of an English traitor to that of an American hero."

Roosevelt apparently made no direct public response to Lindbergh's article. But the president's closing comment to his global religious audience, whose ranks were horrified by Hitler's brutality, made FDR's position clear.

"The active search for peace which the early Christians preached meant meeting and overcoming those forces in the world which had set themselves against the brotherhood of man and which denied the equality of souls before the throne of God," the president said. "In those olden days they faced apparently unconquerable force—and yet were victorious."[8]

HYDE PARK, NEW YORK

Springwood, the Roosevelt family estate in Hyde Park, was quiet on Sunday morning, April 7, 1940. The Hudson River was running high from heavy rains and snow melt in the Adirondack Mountains. Spring had not yet come to the Hudson Valley and a chill hung in the air.[9] The president was in bed, waylaid by the severe illness that had been plaguing him for nearly a month. The windows in Franklin's bedroom looked out over the hillside descending to the river, and he could see the train bridge high above the Hudson connecting Poughkeepsie and Highland. His mother Sara was on her way to the Sunday service at St. James's Episcopal Church a few miles down the road. He hoped to be well enough later that day to inspect progress on his Presidential Library, which was nearing completion just a hundred yards from where he lay.[10]

Franklin Roosevelt was born at Springwood and spent his youth wandering the estate's hundreds of acres of woodland along the east bank of the Hudson. His parents filled the house with books, art, and portraits of his ancestors. Dark mahogany walls set off the magnificent Ming dynasty porcelain his grandfather Warren Delano brought back from

China in the nineteenth century. His mother joked that he was successful because he was a Delano and despite the fact that he was a Roosevelt.

The Delano family made and lost fortunes in maritime shipping, including the opium trade in China. As a child Franklin was fascinated by his mother's family history of shipbuilding, whaling, and foreign adventures. His uncle Fred Delano gave young Franklin the definitive volume on naval strategy, *The Influence of Sea Power Upon History*, by Alfred Thayer Mahan. Franklin devoured Mahan's book and soon began to collect what would become a library with thousands of books and historic documents on naval history. His lifelong study of sea battles in the *Age of Fighting Sail* guided him when he became commander in chief of the largest navy the world had ever known. But devouring stories of seafaring captains and privateers were only one of his childhood hobbies.

Bird specimens he had collected and preserved as a child filled a glass bookcase taking up an entire wall in the grand foyer. There were also binders filled with hundreds of thousands of stamps from his famous collection. After he contracted polio, he spent hours working on the stamps as an escape from the pressures of his life.

The first Roosevelts had come to New York from the Netherlands in the late 1600s and made their fortune in sugar, banking, and real estate. FDR's great-great-grandfather Isaac Roosevelt helped finance the Revolutionary War and was a partner with Alexander Hamilton in the founding of the Bank of New York. Hardworking and savvy investors, they prospered and split into two branches. One branch established a base on Long Island and produced Theodore Roosevelt and his niece Eleanor. The other Roosevelts moved upriver to the Hudson Valley. Growing up, Franklin had as neighbors along the great river other families able to trace their heritage to the colonial era, including Vanderbilts, Livingstons, and Astors. In fact, FDR had lunch with his old friend Vincent Astor, one of the richest men in the world, when he finally got out of bed that early spring day.[11]

His father James bought Springwood in 1867 and lived the life of a gentleman farmer. After his first wife died, he married the much younger Sara Delano. Franklin was their only child. James died in 1900, and Springwood and the Roosevelt fortune passed to Sara. She was a strong-willed and intelligent woman who instilled a confidence in Franklin that helped him through his most difficult days, when he was struggling to rebound from polio. Although Eleanor and Sara had a difficult relationship, her grandchildren adored Sara, and she was beloved by many, especially her son.

After an informal lunch with his old friend Vincent, Franklin toured the nearly completed building that would one day house his presidential papers. The first presidential library given to the National Archives; FDR's facility served as the basis for today's presidential library system. Roosevelt's vision for "his" library was grander than just a repository for official papers and state gifts. He wanted a home for his collections of ship models, paintings, rare manuscripts, and more than 22,000 books. He hoped other pillars of his administration would donate their papers, enabling historians to study how his government worked and learn from its successes and failures. The president hoped to open the library in June 1941, after he completed his second term and left the White House. He expected in retirement to organize his papers and write his memoirs. At this moment he had no desire to violate a longstanding American tradition and seek a third term. But that was about to change.

Early in the morning of Tuesday, April 9, 1940, German forces attacked Denmark and Norway, a devastating blow to those hoping peace would prevail. Denmark capitulated in only hours. Norway put up a fight, and England sent the Royal Navy and troops to help—to no avail, as the Germans eventually took control, forcing Norway's royal family to flee. Crown Prince Olav joined his father and the Norwegian government in exile in London. Olav's wife Princess Martha and their children sought safety in the United States. Martha became a confidant and close friend of Franklin Roosevelt. Some whispered that their relationship was more intimate than a friendship, but no one knows what happened behind closed doors.

The day after the German attacks the president boarded his special Pullman railcar at the Highland Station and left at 1:00 P.M. for Washington, D.C. An hour into the trip he invited reporters traveling with him into the ornate observation car bringing up the rear of the train. Many of the reporters had been up all night, monitoring the latest news of the invasions.

George Durno, of the International News Service, asked the first question.

"Can you make any comment on the foreign situation, sir?"

"No." the president answered brusquely.

"You have been in touch with Washington, today?"

"Yes, a number of times."

"Any steps to be taken to see what can be done about our neutrality law and its application in the present situation?"[12]

"That is up to the State Department," the president said, shifting his tone as he went on to explain his thinking.

"There are two questions involved. First is a neutrality proclamation in regard to Denmark—because as far as we can tell . . . there hasn't been any fighting," he said. "Secondly, in the case of Norway, we probably won't know anything about that until tonight, as to the legal status of it."

The president moved on to a more complicated and delicate issue, that of preventing American ships from entering the conflict area.

"The zone of warfare has been extended north of the line which was drawn last September and would, therefore, call for a new proclamation," he said.

A reporter began, "With Germany claiming Iceland and Greenland . . ."

"Iceland is an independent nation," Roosevelt snapped. "And Denmark has got sovereignty over Greenland. The events of the past forty-eight hours will undoubtedly cause a great many more Americans to think about the potentialities of the war."

Roosevelt warned his audience about making more of that statement than they should and ending by saying, "It is a damn good thing for Americans to think about the subject and not take everything for granted."[13]

WASHINGTON

When the president arrived in Washington at 9:00 P.M., Secretary Hull and Sumner Welles were waiting for him at Union Station. During the drive to the White House, they briefed him on the latest developments. Thursday was a whirl of meetings, executive orders, and proclamations of neutrality. At 5:30 P.M. Treasury Secretary Henry Morgenthau and Assistant Secretary of State Adolf Berle met with Roosevelt in the oval office. Their first order of business was freezing Norwegian and Danish financial assets in the U.S. Morgenthau brought the president up to date.

"We froze the balances for both Denmark and Norway, and we are holding all ships in ports which would be sailing for Scandinavia, on a twenty-four-hour basis. What I cannot understand is that the Germans had taken Oslo," Morgenthau said, "To let them walk in quietly and take it seems ridiculous. After all the Germans had fifty ships to go up there and where was the English blockade?"[14]

Normally calm in even the worst crisis, President Roosevelt was furious. "The thing that has made me hopping mad is where was the British fleet when the Germans went up to Bergen and Oslo? It is the most outrageous thing I have ever heard of. I am just hopping mad."[15]

Berle brought up the need for FDR to sign Executive Order 8389 freezing the assets and limiting shipping, and Morgenthau handed the president the final draft for his signature. Brandishing his favorite fountain pen Roosevelt uncapped it and signed the order with an angry scrawl. Norway had a total of $88 million in gold and Denmark $52 million in American accounts; those reserves were now frozen. All banks and stock exchanges would have to withhold all transactions unless the Treasury Department specifically gave approval.[16]

"The Danish minister was just here, he wanted to know what would happen if the Danish government, now under complete control of the German military, recalled him and sent someone else in his place," said Roosevelt "Which of the two would we recognize? I told him we should undoubtedly take the factor of duress into consideration and would not recognize any appointee of the now captive government of Denmark until such time as it became a free agent again."

Roosevelt wanted to do more, much more, but the Neutrality Act had him boxed in. The Germans had bulldozed Norway with professional precision and speed, previewing the style of warfare that would define the coming years. The German High Command was demonstrating effective multiservice coordination, its air, land, and sea forces working in perfect synchrony. In the first effective use of paratroopers in war[17] a battalion floated out of the sky, and facing light opposition seized control of airfields at Oslo and Stavanger. Nazi infantry, in a Trojan Horse–attack, hid in the holds of Norwegian transports normally loaded with coal, landing unseen and unmolested. In only hours, the Germans had control of every airfield in Norway, and that nation's most strategic ports. The mighty Royal Navy scored a few successes, sinking four German cruisers, four troopships, and a number of destroyers. But His Majesty's navy was soon put in check by the fearsome Luftwaffe whose fighters and bombers now controlled the Scandinavian skies. The British managed to land troops on the coast, but they were infinitely inferior to the better trained and better armed Germans. Most British troops were driven back or killed by Wehrmacht tanks and Luftwaffe fighters. Massive casualties and incompetent leadership forced the Britons to withdraw, causing much consternation in Parliament and on the front pages of English newspapers.[18] Prime Minister Chamberlain tried to cast the debacle as a positive, but the tides of political fortune had turned, and his days as prime minister appeared to be foreshortened.

Prime Minister Winston Churchill inspects a "Tommy gun" while visiting coastal defense positions near Hartlepool on July 31, 1940.

5

THE FALL OF FRANCE, THE RISE OF CHURCHILL

THE LOW COUNTRIES—MAY 1940

Along Belgium's border with Germany, farmers and townspeople woke to a dreadful sound. The noise began as a low distant rumble, a growl of massed predators seeking their prey. As the sound drew closer its volume became deafening, a throaty mechanical roar moving rapidly from east to west, originating on high. In the dark early hours of May 10, 1940, a thousand planes of the German Luftwaffe crossed the Our River, violating Belgian air space. Protected by Messerschmitt fighters, Stuka dive bombers and Junker Ju-52 transports full of paratroopers, dropped their deadly payloads on towns and villages all along the lowlands. On the ground German panzers penetrated the Ardennes Forest, catching French and Belgian troops there by surprise. Within hours Luxembourg, along with portions of Belgium and France adjoining Germany, had fallen to an incomprehensibly large force—a thousand tanks and two million soldiers comprising 136 divisions. The columns of men and machines stretched back a hundred miles. England and France sent troops to the front, and battles raged across Holland, Belgium, Luxemburg, and France. Interweaving air power, infantry, and armor, Hitler's blitzkrieg tactics bowled over the disorganized Allied troops. Despite his pledge to avoid civilian targets, the Luftwaffe bombed dozens of cities and towns.

Missy LeHand woke President Roosevelt around midnight and told him the news.[1] He began what became a furious round of telephone calls with political leaders at home and abroad. News reports were chaotic and often inaccurate, but there was no doubt that the Reich's latest offensive was proving unstoppable. Upon completing his calls Roosevelt slept a few hours and rose with the sun. At 10:30 A.M. he met with his top diplomatic and military advisors. They discussed the status of the American military, the cost of enlarging the army from 227,000 men to 280,000, the national inventory of antiaircraft artillery and ammunition, and how to boost production of warplanes, armored vehicles, and other military hardware. A disquieting realization—that the United States was woefully unprepared for war—arose.[2]

Just before noon, a weary and frustrated Roosevelt gave the nod to let a horde of reporters impatiently waiting in the lobby into his office. Earl Godwin being absent, Tom Reynolds from United Press was that day's senior correspondent. "This is probably the biggest crowd you ever had," Reynolds said.

"And probably less news!" Roosevelt said. "Why don't you sit down in the chair," he added, referring to Godwin's usual perch.[3]

"I hope you had more sleep than I did," the president said as the last of the reporters squeezed into the room. "I guess most of you were pretty busy all night. There isn't much I can say about the situation. I think it speaks for itself."

"Mr. President, would you care to say at this time what you think the chances are that we can stay out?" Once again, the question on everyone's mind was will America stay neutral?

"Well, I think that would be speculative. In other words, don't say that that means we may get in. That would be writing yourself completely off on the limb and sawing it off!"

Roosevelt's unusually harsh tone reflected his lack of sleep and frustration at the crisis he now faced. For years he had been trying to convince the American public that the United States needed to prepare for war, while at the same time promising not to send American boys into battle on foreign soil. Opponents constantly accused him of conspiring to fight the Germans, and while he denied these charges, he was secretly doing all he could to support the Allies. This dilemma shaped his ongoing war of words with isolationists, who as yet had public opinion on their side.

Several days later,[4] Harry Hopkins joined Roosevelt for a reunion dinner at the White House. Hopkins had had to absent himself from Washington for many months to deal with a life-threatening illness. His care required an extended stay at the Mayo Clinic that included surgery for stomach cancer. Though he was gaunt, frail, and miserable, Hopkins's return was fortuitous, as the president needed a trusted stalwart to help shoulder his growing burdens. Franklin Roosevelt invited his old friend to spend the night at the White House. Hopkins agreed and eventually ended up residing in the executive mansion for three and a half years. He became FDR's closest confidant and personal envoy, operating completely outside the federal bureaucracy and its rigid strictures. He met with Churchill and Stalin before the president did and provided firsthand impressions of the two fearsome leaders. Most importantly Hopkins forged a close friendship with Winston Churchill, laying the foundation for the twentieth century's most important political alliance.[5]

LONDON

On the other side of the Atlantic, Churchill was contemplating his own set of burdens. Ending Neville Chamberlain's disastrous term as prime minister, King George VI had asked Churchill to form a government.[6] But achieving his lifelong ambition to move into 10 Downing Street meant grappling with the worst crisis in the empire's history. That first day, confidence reigned; surely the combined armies of Great Britain and France would contain the German onslaught. But poor planning, outdated equipment, and incompetent leadership brought disaster. Within days German forces were on the outskirts of Paris. The French army's ignominious collapse shocked the world, and the British king, prime minister, and people feared they were next.[7]

The scale and scope of that spring's German rampage challenge comprehension. An inventory of Allied losses between May 10 and May 28 offers grim perspective:

- Belgium: 8,000 killed, 15,000 wounded, 200,000 captured.
- France: 90,000 dead, 200,000 wounded, 1,900,000 captured.
- Britain: 68,000 killed, wounded, or captured.

Those figures would have been significantly higher but for the heroic improvised rescue of more than 330,000 Allied soldiers from Dunkirk. "Now at last the slowly gathered, long-pent up fury of the storm broke upon us," Churchill wrote later. "Four or five millions of men met each other in the first shock of the most merciless of all the wars of which record has been kept."[8]

Three days after becoming prime minister, Winston Churchill stood before the House of Commons to ask for a vote of confidence in his new national government. Among his own party, the Conservatives, many members would have preferred to keep Chamberlain. Circumstance had brought Churchill to this moment. In the first in a series of spectacular wartime addresses that inspired a nation, Churchill launched his own war of words against the propaganda of Adolf Hitler and his plans for a "Thousand Year Reich."

"I would say to the House, as I have said to those who have joined this government, I have nothing to offer but blood, toil, tears, and sweat," Churchill said. "We have before us an ordeal of the most grievous kind. We have before us many, many months of struggle and suffering. You ask, what is our policy? I will say: it is to wage war, by sea, land, air, with all our might and with all the strength God can give us. That is our policy."[9]

Among history's great orators, Winston Churchill towers astride the twentieth century. His wartime speeches stand as some of the most motivational words a political leader has ever spoken. Those he delivered during that dark, disheartening spring of 1940 stand above all others.

Listening to Churchill speak, Franklin Roosevelt perhaps felt a hint of hope. This man might be the partner he was seeking—a kindred spirit who could help shift American public opinion through the example of dogged determination, bravery, and eloquence. Perhaps the "Last Lion" of the British Empire might help solve the president's dilemma. Churchill wielded the English language as one might a sword, with unparalleled power and deftness; he and his oratorical skill would be mighty additions to Roosevelt's arsenal in his own war of words with American isolationists.

On May 15, the French generals realized they could not stop Hitler's blitzkrieg and began to retreat. The French collapse horrified Churchill, who now realized that Britain's only salvation lay across the Atlantic. Franklin Roosevelt might be the partner *he* sought—and American resources and industrial might could be capable of reinforcing and enlarging Britain's arsenal in her actual war with the Axis. Churchill sent his first message as prime minister to Roosevelt as French troops were fleeing the battlefield. In a stark and desperate message, he pleaded for the use of forty to fifty U.S. Navy destroyers for Britain to use in fending off a cross-Channel invasion:

"Confidential and Personal. President Roosevelt from Former Naval Person.

"Although I have changed my office, I am sure you would not wish me to discontinue our intimate, private correspondence. As you are no doubt aware, the scene has darkened swiftly. The enemy have a marked preponderance in the air, and their new technique is making a deep impression upon the French. The small countries are simply smashed up, one by one, like matchwood. We expect to be attacked ourselves in the near future . . . But I trust you realize Mr. President, that the voice and force of the United States may count for nothing if they are withheld too long."[10]

President Roosevelt responded immediately. "I am, of course, giving every possible consideration to the suggestions made in your message," he wrote. "With regards to the loan of forty or fifty of our older destroyers, as you know a step of that kind could not be taken except with the specific authorization of the Congress."[11]

Roosevelt went on to offer Churchill access to the latest aircraft, antiaircraft equipment, and steel. The revised Neutrality Act allowed England to purchase the military gear, but required it transport the matériel in its own ships.

WASHINGTON

Six days after the latest German offensive, rain-soaked Secret Service agents and grim-faced police officers formed a cordon of silent sentinels around the Capitol. President Roosevelt's limousine arrived at the lower-level entrance at 12:58 P.M. Onlookers crowding the edge of the grounds wore grave expressions on tired faces.[12]

Accompanied by Secretaries Hull and Morgenthau and Attorney General Robert Jackson, the president went directly to House Speaker Bankhead's private office. There Roosevelt waited to address another special joint session of Congress. Wearing a blue pinstriped suit and holding on to the arm of General "Pa" Watson, he walked to the rostrum and stood at a podium bristling with microphones.[13] Though sustained and enthusiastic applause greeted him, reflecting a sense of national unity, the mood in the great room was solemn. The president set the tone.

"These are ominous days—days whose swift and shocking developments force every neutral nation to look to its defenses in the light of new factors: The brutal force of modern offensive war has been loosed in all its horror," Roosevelt told the nation. "New powers of destruction, incredibly swift and deadly, have been developed; and those who wield them are ruthless and daring. No old defense is so strong that it requires no further strengthening, and no attack is so unlikely or impossible that it may be ignored."[14]

Franklin Roosevelt left no doubt that modern weaponry eliminated whatever lines of defense oceans east and west had once provided. He warned of a "fifth column" of traitors and spies lurking among ordinary Americans. He asked Congress for an astounding $1.1 billion in emergency military appropriations and vowed to raise production of military aircraft from 6,000 planes a year to 50,000. He also spoke directly to those who believed that Germany represented a dynamic and vibrant future and that the Reich would prevail over tired European democracies.

"There are some who say that democracy cannot cope with the new techniques of government developed in recent years by some countries—by a few countries which deny the freedoms that we maintain are essential to our democratic way of life," he said. "That I reject. I know that to cope with present dangers we must be strong in heart and mind; strong in our faith—strong in the faith in our way of living."

Besides more funds for arms and dramatic growth in the armed forces, he asked for an intangible. He asked Americans to rise to the challenge before them, to find the spirit of freedom within themselves, to have faith in that freedom and to fulfill their destiny.

"Our security is not a matter of weapons alone. The arm that wields them must be strong, the eye that guides them clear, the will that directs them indomitable," the president said. "These are the characteristics of a free people, a people devoted to the institutions they themselves have built, a people willing to defend a way of life that is precious to them all, a people who put their faith in God."[15] Once again Roosevelt was trying to rally America's foundational soul. Much of the press and the public responded with enthusiasm, as did Congress. Both House and Senate moved to introduce bills to meet the president's request for more than $1 billion in new defense spending.

But the chorus of support was not unanimous.

LONG ISLAND, NEW YORK

Charles and Anne Lindbergh lived in a charming three-story farmhouse overlooking Cold Spring Harbor from the village of Lloyd Neck. Their home, which dated to 1714, offered a bucolic retreat from a harsh world gone harsher. In the spring of 1940 Anne was pregnant, and Charles was worried. Writing in her journal, Anne did not blame Hitler entirely for the situation in Europe. The German leader was not some "accidental scourge unconnected to other world events—alone responsible for all," she wrote. "Nazism seems to me scum which happens to be on the wave of the future. I agree with people's condemnation of Nazi methods, but I do not think they are the wave. They happen to be riding on it."[16]

Charles's deep concern regarding current events impelled him to ask CBS for airtime to express his thoughts. On Sunday, May 19—only three days after FDR's appeal to Congress—Lindbergh traveled to Washington, D.C., to broadcast from the CBS studios there. He began speaking at 9:30 P.M.; his theme was "The Air Defense of America."

"In times of war and confusion, it is essential for our people to have a clear understanding of the elements upon which our national safety depends," Lindbergh told fellow Americans. "Aviation has now become one of these elements, and it is about the air defense of America that I speak to you tonight. Air strength depends more upon the establishment of intelligent and consistent policies than upon the sudden construction of huge numbers of airplanes."[17]

This was a direct criticism of Roosevelt's policies and his plan to build 50,000 warplanes a year. Lindbergh then laid out the many reasons why America was in no danger of actual attack: two vast oceans, a wealth of resources, a large population. His voice calm, controlled, and reasonable, he claims that what endangered the United States was the current administration's determination to take sides.

"We are in danger of war today not because European people have attempted to interfere with the internal affairs of America, but because American people have attempted to interfere with the internal affairs of Europe," he said. "Our danger in America is an internal danger. We need not fear a foreign invasion unless American peoples bring it on through their own quarreling and meddling with affairs abroad. Years ago, we decided to stay out of foreign wars. We based our military policy on that decision. We must not waver now that the crisis is at hand."

Lindbergh reduced Roosevelt's cautious support of England and France against the Nazi terror as "meddling." Nearing the end of his twelve-minute address, Lindbergh once again delivered a trope commonly used to refer to ostensible Jewish control of the media, hinting at more blatant antisemitism to come.

"The only reason that we are in danger of becoming involved in this war is because there are powerful elements in America who desire us to take part," Charles Lindbergh said. "They represent a small minority of the American people, but they control much of the machinery of influence and propaganda. They seize every opportunity to push us closer to the edge."[18]

Lindbergh's reference to unnamed parties who "control much of the machinery of influence and propaganda" became a refrain of his, accepted and effective because so many people agreed with it. His remarks reverberated, inspiring letters to flood the little farmhouse in Lloyd Neck; they ran twenty-to-one in favor of his position.[19] His carefully constructed argument gave a powerful voice to isolationist views. Hugely popular Roman Catholic "radio priest" Father Charles Coughlin strongly supported Lindbergh. Coughlin was a controversial media figure, who had been effectively forced off the air by new radio regulations. But a national tabloid newspaper Coughlin controlled, *Social Justice*, continued to spew his anti-Roosevelt and antisemitic diatribes. In the wake of the CBS speech *Social Justice* ran Lindbergh's photo on its cover.[20]

A May 20 *New York Times* page one headline read: LINDBERGH DECRIES FEARS OF INVASION. "MEDDLING" HELD A PERIL. But that day's editorial page criticized Lindbergh. Of his statement dismissing what he called "hysterical chatter" about the danger of Nazi victory, the editors wrote, "Colonel Lindbergh is a peculiar young man if he can contemplate this possibility in any other light than as a calamity for the American people. He is an ignorant young man if he trusts his own premise that it makes no difference to us whether we are deprived of the historic defense of British sea power in the Atlantic Ocean. He is a blind young man if he really believes that we can live on terms of equal peace and happiness 'regardless of which side wins this war.'"

Roosevelt administration figures dismissed Lindbergh's speech; Secretary of State Cordell Hull was quoted as saying that "world events during the last few years had fully justified the program urged by the president."[21] At lunch with Henry Morgenthau the day after Lindbergh's broadcast, Roosevelt stopped eating, put down his fork, and told his old friend, "If I should die tomorrow, I want you to know this. I am absolutely convinced that Lindbergh is a Nazi."[22]

LONDON

The same day CBS carried Lindbergh's latest speech, Winston Churchill delivered another radio address to the people of the British Empire, continuing his historic run of wartime broadcasts. These soliloquies strengthened the fortitude for which the British are so well known. He never turned his back on ugly truths, or lost faith in his country's ultimate victory. In those Sunday afternoon remarks he started with a frank description of the situation facing Britons.

"A tremendous battle is raging in France and Flanders," he said. "The Germans, by a remarkable combination of air bombing and heavily armored tanks, have broken through the French defenses north of the Maginot Line, and strong columns of their armored vehicles are ravaging the open country."[23] His vivid imagery of valiant soldiers fighting the forces of evil contained both horror and hope. But his faith was clear.

"Our task is not only to win the battle—but to win the war," he continued. "After this battle in France abates its force, there will come the battle for our Island—for all that Britain is, and all that Britain means . . . behind the Armies and Fleets of Britain and France—gather a group of shattered states and bludgeoned races: the Czechs, the Poles, the Norwegians, the Danes, the Dutch, the Belgians—upon all of whom the long night of barbarism will descend, unbroken even by a star of hope, unless we conquer, as conquer we must, as conquer we shall."[24]

Hard-pressed by the advancing Germans, the Allied armies split into two, backs to the edge of the Atlantic. President Roosevelt, encaged by the Neutrality Act, could do nothing. Already he was looking to the future, and the need for America to rearm and build the weaponry Churchill needed to survive. Two weeks later FDR asked Congress for $1.2 billion more, then another $1 billion. By early June 1940, Congress, convinced of the need to upgrade the American military, had approved $3.3 billion for defense—the equivalent of 50 percent of the total military budget for the past six years!

The French Army's disintegration and the velocity of the German advance astonished Churchill. Members of his government implored him to negotiate with Hitler to prevent an invasion and what threatened to be the annihilation of the bulk of the surviving British expeditionary force now trapped on the beaches at Dunkirk. Churchill ordered Operation Dynamo, using small vessels and naval ships to evacuate 330,000 soldiers in one of the most remarkable retreats in history. On June 4, the evacuation successful, Churchill rallied his supporters and volleyed at would-be appeasers in a speech bristling with stubborn resistance. "We shall fight on the beaches, we shall fight on the landing grounds," he told Britons. "We shall fight in the fields and in the streets, we shall fight in the hills; we shall never surrender."

CHARLOTTESVILLE, VIRGINIA

On June 10, Benito Mussolini ordered the Italian army to invade France, brazenly attempting to claim a share of the glory achieved by Hitler's stunning victories. That day President Roosevelt was to address the class graduating from the University of Virginia Law School, whose ranks included his youngest son, John. A violent rainstorm forced relocation of the event from an outdoor amphitheater to the gymnasium. The president wore formal robes and a cap and gown. Due to the weather delay, distribution of diplomas paused so Roosevelt could deliver his remarks at the scheduled time of 6:15 P.M.[25]

Standing before the graduates and their families and friends, Roosevelt unleashed a tirade against isolationists' refusal to acknowledge that the country faced terrible danger.

"Some indeed still hold to the now somewhat obvious delusion that we of the United States can safely permit the United States to become a lone island, a lone island in a world dominated by the philosophy of force," he said. "Such an island may be the dream of those who still talk and vote as isolationists. Such an island represents to me and to the overwhelming majority of Americans today a helpless nightmare of a people without freedom—the nightmare of a people lodged in prison, handcuffed, hungry, and fed through the bars from day to day by the contemptuous, unpitying masters of other continents."[26]

The president then focused his ire on the Italian tyrant, using words he had written over strong objections from the State Department.[27]

"The Government of Italy has now chosen to preserve what it terms its 'freedom of action' and to fulfill what it states are its promises to Germany," Roosevelt said. "In so doing, it has manifested disregard for the rights and security of other nations, disregard for the lives of the peoples of those nations which are directly threatened by this spread of the war; and has evidenced its unwillingness to find the means through pacific negotiations for the satisfaction of what it believes are its legitimate aspirations. On this tenth day of June, nineteen hundred and forty, the hand that held the dagger has struck it into the back of its neighbor." Listeners jumped to their feet, clapping and cheering in support of the president's powerful condemnation.

"The hand that held the dagger has struck it into the back of its neighbor" was an extraordinary statement for the leader of a neutral nation to use in characterizing another nation's leader. Roosevelt used this Shakespearean imagery, the bloody dagger in the hands of a villain, to express outrage and disgust at a cowardly act of betrayal. For Franklin Roosevelt, the law school address marked a turning point. With another election in the wings and his role in that election as yet unsettled, he made the decision to speak his mind and trust the American public to accept their duty to help defend democracy.

Writing after the fact, a number of FDR's closest advisors claimed this was the context in which Roosevelt, who had been contemplating the possibility for months, finally decided to seek an unprecedented third term.[28] The French Army's disintegration and the very real threat that Hitler would invade and conquer England ended his indecision, according to these observers. At that summer's Democratic convention Roosevelt insisted that the delegates "acclaim" him their candidate, a status he would not actively seek. But there was no doubt he would run again.

The Nazis entered Paris on June 14, 1940, and Hitler posed for a photograph standing before the Eiffel Tower. Four days later Churchill entered the House of Commons, smoking a cigar and wearing his trademark dark suit and bowler hat. Striding into the chamber with the pages containing the text of his speech in his clenched fist, he made his way to the speaker's podium.[29] Standing before Parliament in what appeared to be the war's darkest moment, he exhorted all inhabitants of the globe-spanning British Empire to prepare to defend their homeland. "Let us therefore brace ourselves to our duties, and so bear ourselves that, if the British Empire and its Commonwealth last for a thousand years, men will still say, 'This was their finest hour,'" he said.

France formally surrendered on June 22, 1940, leaving only Great Britain to stand against Hitler and his plan for world domination by his Thousand Year Reich. The dictator's forces were coiled to strike across the English Channel and complete his conquest of Europe. That same day President Roosevelt asked Congress for another $4.8 billion for defense. He got it.

The summer of 1940 was a desperate time for Britons. Prime Minister Winston Churchill used every linguistic tool he possessed as he struggled to persuade President Roosevelt to send destroyers and planes. But Roosevelt was still hamstrung by the Neutrality Act. On July 31 Churchill again pleaded for destroyers. "Mr. President," he wrote, "with great respect I must tell you that in the long history of the world, this is a thing to do now."[30]

PART TWO

A HELPING HAND

President Roosevelt at the White House on January 30, 1940, his fifty-eighth birthday.

6

DESTROYERS, DECEIVERS,

AND DECISIONS

WASHINGTON—JUNE 1940

On the day after Churchill's "finest hour" speech Franklin Roosevelt was facing a multitude of challenges. The French army's collapse and Hitler's existential threat to England were uppermost in his mind. But the Democratic party convention was only weeks away, and he had still not announced his intentions regarding the fall election. Even greater than his concern about whether to take the radical step of running for a third term was the threat posed by Charles Lindbergh's emergence as a highly effective advocate for the isolationist cause and a potential disrupter in November. Germany's brutal aggression had persuaded some Americans to endorse arming and provisioning England, provided the government sent no military personnel into combat. Roosevelt so far had failed to convince citizens of the United States that Hitler's war endangered them and that they needed to embrace their role as citizens of the world. FDR's stance regarding aid to the allies was fast becoming a political issue that the Republicans intended to use against him in the coming election.

In a politically brilliant but controversial maneuver, on June 19, 1940, President Roosevelt appointed two Republicans to key Cabinet posts. Frank Knox, the Republican vice-presidential candidate in 1936, became Secretary of the Navy. Henry Stimson became the secretary of war, a position he had held under Republican President William Howard Taft, before becoming Herbert Hoover's secretary of state. He and Knox had expressed staunch support for aiding England and France and for massive increases in defense spending.

The Republicans nominated Wendell Willkie as their candidate for president. A former Democrat, Willkie had headed a Southern power company and opposed implementation of Roosevelt's Tennessee Valley Authority and Rural Electrification projects, though he agreed with the president's international policies. Boyish good looks, a shock of unruly hair, and reasonable policies helped Willkie attract moderate Republicans and moderate Democrats, which made him the most serious political rival Roosevelt had yet faced on the presidential campaign trail.

Chicago

The 1940 Democratic National Convention in Chicago is legendary for its drama and intrigue. Roosevelt's decision to run for a third term caused great controversy, breaking as it did a seemingly inviolable tradition of a two-term limit on American presidents. Opponents accused FDR of planning to install himself as a dictator in order to drag the country into the conflict in Europe. The United States was still resolutely isolationist; a Gallup poll showed that 64 percent believed the U.S. should stay out of the war. But Roosevelt was the strongest candidate in the Democratic Party and was still immensely popular with the people.

After the party gathering's initial days of confusion and debate, on July 18 Franklin Roosevelt was re-nominated with nearly 90% of the delegates supporting him on the first ballot. Yet, his choice of running mate nearly ripped the party in two. Roosevelt wanted Henry Wallace, his secretary of agriculture and a strident liberal. Southern conservatives vehemently opposed Wallace, and floor fights broke out between the two factions. Every mention of Wallace's name filled the stadium with boos and catcalls. The situation was so fraught that the president asked his wife to go to Chicago to calm things down. Eleanor had been following the convention from Val-Kill, her tranquil home in Hyde Park, and reluctantly agreed after several people, including Frances Perkins, begged her to come.[1]

Mrs. Roosevelt came onstage at 10:30 P.M. amid a battle raging on the convention floor. As it dawned on delegates who was approaching the podium, hundreds cheered and shouted. She was wearing a simple blue grey dress, and a straw hat with little blue flowers around the edge.[2] She waved to the crowd, and many people described a noticeable change in the stadium's mood. However heated the debate ignited by her husband's choice for VP, the party faithful loved and respected Eleanor. As she prepared to speak, the crowd fell silent with anticipation.

"I know and you know that any man who is in an office of great responsibility faces a heavier responsibility perhaps than any man has ever faced before in this country," she said. "Therefore, to be a candidate of either great political party is a serious and a very solemn thing. You cannot treat it as an ordinary nomination, in an ordinary time. We people in the United States have got to realize today that we face now a grave, a serious situation."[3]

The First Lady spoke with a steady, calm voice. She was not a great orator, nor a particularly talented wordsmith. But she had a spontaneity and a sincerity that connected with people. In fact, she did not write this speech out in full, instead relying on a half-page of notes to guide her through one of the most important speeches of her life. The delegates felt her earnest desire to resolve the conflict and bring the party together, as only she could.

"You must know that this is the time when all good men and women give every bit of service and strength to their country that they have to give," she continued. "This is a time when it is the United States that we fight for. We cannot tell from day to day what may come. This is no ordinary time. No time for weighing anything, except what we can best do for the country as a whole."

Her line "this is no ordinary time" emerged from that speech as a perfect description for the international situation. It does not appear in her notes. She ends with a simple call to duty: "This is only carried by a united people who love their country and who will live for it to the fullest of their ability with the highest ideals, with the determination that their party shall be absolutely devoted to the good of the nation as a whole and to doing what this country can to bring the world to a safer and happier condition."

In her Pulitzer Prize–winning book *No Ordinary Time*, Doris Kearns Goodwin described the speech this way: "By the time she finished, the prevailing emotion of the crowd had been transformed. Genuine applause erupted from every corner of the room. Trivial hurts and jealousies subsided as the delegates recalled why they had chosen Roosevelt in the first place. All along they had simply wanted some sign of appreciation for what they were doing, and now the first lady was giving it to them."[4]

As Eleanor was leaving the podium, there was a moment of silence. The organist began playing "God Bless America" and the thousands present began a vigorous ovation, clapping and cheering.[5] In averting a crisis, Eleanor again rose to the occasion and delivered for her husband when he needed her most. As she walked offstage someone draped a large garland of flowers around her neck, and she joined her son Franklin in the wings. The convention then voted to nominate Henry Wallace for vice president.[6]

The president accepted his nomination in a nationwide radio address from the Oval Office the following evening: "It is with a very full heart that I speak tonight. I must confess that I do so with mixed feelings—because I find myself, as almost everyone does sooner or later in his lifetime, in a conflict between deep personal desire for retirement on the one hand, and that quiet, invisible thing called 'conscience' on the other. During the spring of 1939, world events made it clear to all but the blind or the partisan that a great war in Europe had become not merely a possibility but a probability, and that such a war would of necessity deeply affect the future of this nation."[7]

Roosevelt's voice boomed from speakers scattered throughout Chicago Stadium. The 20,000 people on hand listened in silence as he explained why he had decided to seek a third term, and what he had been doing to prepare the country for the dangerous world it now faced. He claimed he would not campaign in any traditional way because the burdens of his office demanded his constant attention. But he offered a carefully reasoned caveat. "I shall never be loath to call the attention of the nation to deliberate or unwitting falsifications of fact," he told Americans.

Continuing his powerful peroration, he made his intentions clear. "I do not recant the sentiments of sympathy with all free peoples resisting such aggression or begrudge the material aid that we have given to them," he said. "I do not regret my consistent endeavor to awaken this country to the menace for us and for all we hold dear. I have pursued these efforts in the face of appeaser fifth columnists who charged me with hysteria and warmongering. But I felt it my duty, my simple, plain, inescapable duty, to arouse my countrymen to the danger of the new forces let loose in the world. So long as I am President, I will do all I can to ensure that that foreign policy remain our foreign policy."

The delegates rose as one, cheering and shouting support, shaking the stadium with the volume of their voices. The ovation lasted six minutes and the band played "Hail to the Chief" over and over.[8] Listening to radios at home and elsewhere millions nationwide were moved by his words and candor. Though he did not change committed isolationists' minds, he did engage the moral imperative of aiding people fighting fascism and totalitarianism.

Two weeks later, on the morning of August 4, 1940, a distinctly different group was preparing to meet. The weather was hot and humid, and the front page of the *Chicago Tribune* declared in bold type: PEACE RALLY TO HEAR LINDBERGH TODAY. The drop line said THE ANTI-WAR AMERICANS, BEING IN THE MAJORITY, HAVE A RIGHT TO BE HEARD. Beneath the headline a large political cartoon showed Uncle Sam pointing at Soldier Field with a sign that read "Gigantic Peace Rally Today" and listed the day's speakers, with Charles Lindbergh headlining.

The *Chicago Tribune* was owned by Robert McCormick, a conservative Republican, fierce critic of President Roosevelt, and anti-war crusader who funded isolationist politicians and organizations. McCormick also owned WGN, a powerhouse radio station popular with listeners across the Midwest. The rally was sponsored by the Citizens Committee to Keep America Out of War, with financial and promotional support from McCormick.

When Charles Lindbergh arrived at Chicago Municipal Airport aboard a TWA plane, McCormick's personal chauffeur picked him up.[9] A crowd of 40,000 enthusiastic isolationists filled the stadium. There were a number of speakers that day but when Lindbergh approached the podium the crowd exploded in cheers and raucous applause. Wearing a blue suit and tie Lindbergh smiled and waved at the crowd waiting for them to settle down. In a calm, patient voice, he explained to the audience that the pressure to enter the war was growing, and he felt he needed to create a "strong and immediate opposition to the trend toward war."[10]

"We are often told that if Germany wins the war, cooperation will be impossible, and treaties no more than scraps of paper," Lindbergh said.

"I reply that cooperation is never impossible when there is sufficient gain on both sides and that treaties are seldom torn apart when they do not cover a weak nation. I would be among the last to advocate depending upon treaties for our national safety. I believe that we should rearm fully for the defense of America, and that we should never make the type of treaty that would lay us open to invasion if it were broken."

Lindbergh went on to claim he was speaking as a private citizen and that he knew he would be criticized for what he said. And he made clear he saw no preference for England over Nazi Germany.

"But if we refuse to consider treaties with the dominant nation of Europe, regardless of who that may be, we remove all possibility of peace. There are still interests in this country and abroad who will do their utmost to draw us into war," he said. "Against these interests we must be continuously on guard.

"Both political parties have declared against our entry into the war. People are beginning to realize that the problems of Europe cannot be solved by the interference of America; we have at last started to build our own continent. By these acts, our eyes turned once more in the direction of security and peace, for if our own military forces are strong, no foreign nation can invade us, and, if we do not interfere with their affairs, none will desire to.

"Let us offer Europe a plan for the progress and protection of the western civilization of which they and we each form a part. If we refuse to consider treaties with the dominant nation of Europe regardless of who that may be, we remove all possibility of peace."[11]

Waves of applause repeatedly interrupted him. He left the stage to a standing ovation that lasted several minutes.

WASHINGTON

Hanging above the fireplace in the oval study on the second floor of the White House was an oil painting that held special meaning for President

Roosevelt. It showed the USS *Dyer*, a World War I destroyer anchored in the harbor of Ponta Delgada in the Azores.[12] Franklin Roosevelt had been Assistant Secretary of the Navy when he commissioned the painting, which depicts his arrival in the Azores on July 16 1918, on his way to an inspection tour of U.S. naval facilities supporting the war in Europe.

Most naval art that Roosevelt collected captured the glory days of fighting sail, but a few pet images reflected more recent events. Lately the president had been thinking a lot about World War I–era destroyers. He knew Britain was the last bulwark against Hitler's complete domination of Europe and the Middle East. Without American aid, specifically destroyers, Britain would crumble beneath the treads of the German war machine. Roosevelt's Ambassador to Great Britain, Joseph Kennedy, had recently told FDR in a memo that Britain's surrender was "inevitable."[13] Churchill had written to the president telling him the situation was desperate, and that without destroyers and arms England could fall.[14]

At 2:15 P.M. on August 13, President Roosevelt met in the oval study with Treasury Secretary Henry Morgenthau about a variety of issues. Roosevelt had proposed to institute a peacetime draft, which Congress was debating, and he was concerned about the political fallout.

"I think I should say something about the draft bill in my press conference on Friday," he told Morgenthau. "There's a good chance Willkie might say something and tie up the draft and the tax bill. It might take the wind out of his sails if I come out for $30 a month for the soldiers."[15]

Morgenthau feared the first peacetime draft in American history would alienate voters. "I still think the draft is a bad idea," he said. "We should stick to the all-volunteer system."

"I like the volunteer system as well," FDR said. "I would have liked to have a selective draft for the boys in the CCC. We need to get this done."

Morgenthau changed the subject to Churchill's plea for more ships. "What are you going to do about the destroyers?" he asked.

"Don't know yet. I'm meeting with War, Navy, and State in a few minutes."

"Do you mind if I sit in?" Morgenthau asked. As Treasury Secretary he had a direct interest in the sale or transfer of arms.

"Yes of course."

Several minutes later Henry Stimson, Frank Knox, and Sumner Welles entered the office. There was a wide range of issues to discuss but working out a way to get Churchill the destroyers he needed was the top priority. The team weighed in with several ideas and expressed concern about the difficulties the Neutrality Act presented. Roosevelt suggested a way to get around the congressionally mandated limits.

"We can't just give them the ships, but if they gave us land in Newfoundland, Bermuda, and Trinidad where we could build naval bases, it might work," he said. "We could give them those PT boats, and some long-range bombers."

"Should we give them the bombsights as well?" Morgenthau asked, referring to a newly introduced advanced aiming device for warplanes.

"No, no, no. absolutely not."

Knox, Stimson, and the president all opposed the idea. The Norden bombsight, said to greatly increase bombing accuracy, was a top-secret development and they wanted to keep it that way.

"Should I make the deal with Churchill first and then tell Congress, or tell Congress first?"

"You should tell Congress first," Morgenthau replied quickly.

Roosevelt pondered a moment, but consensus was that he should make the deal before bringing Congress into the conversation. They began drafting a memo to send Churchill proposing the trade.

That day, August 13, 1940, Luftwaffe bombers hit Royal Air Force bases and civilian targets in southern England. French harbors along the English Channel, now under German control, were crowded with landing barges and troop transports. Tens of thousands of German soldiers moved relentlessly toward the coast, preparing for what seemed to be the inevitable crossing of the English Channel. The Battle of Britain had commenced, and in subsequent weeks squadrons of German bombers ravaged Britain. The "Blitz" made infernos of neighborhoods and killed thousands of civilians. But rather than crushing the English spirit, the weight of the destruction intensified Briton's resolve.

Responding to Churchill's plea for obsolete U.S. Navy destroyers, on August 30, President Roosevelt bypassed the Neutrality Act with an Executive Order, using a loophole that allowed the military to dispose of surplus war matériel deemed unnecessary for the defense of the United States. On September 2, Secretary of State Cordell Hull approved the deal, and Admiral Harold Stark certified the destroyers were not vital for American security. The U.S. Navy transferred fifty World War I–era destroyers to the Royal Navy in exchange for ninety-nine-year leases on British naval and air bases along the Atlantic coast and the Caribbean. The arrangement just barely skirted the Neutrality Act's legal edges, but it gave Churchill hope. He sent a secure triple priority message "Personal for the President from Former Naval Person."[16] "I need not tell you how cheered I am by your message or how grateful I feel for your untiring efforts to give us all possible help," Winston told Franklin. "You will, I am sure, send us everything you can, for you know well that the worth of every destroyer that you can spare to us is measured in rubies."

FDR had to tread carefully to win reelection, and he proclaimed that the acquisition of these strategic bases was "the most important action in the reinforcement of our national defense since the Louisiana Purchase."

The deal was surprisingly popular with the public, which saw the value of these new bases. Before the deal was announced in August, a Gallup poll had Willkie and the president in a close race, FDR leading with 51 percent to 49 percent. After the destroyers-for-bases deal was announced, FDR's lead grew to ten points. In response Willkie changed tactics and began attacking Roosevelt as a would-be dictator and a warmonger, accusing the incumbent of having secret agreements in place and proclaiming, "You may expect war by April 1941 if he is elected."[17] This new strategy worked, and Willkie's popularity soared.

Harry Hopkins, convinced that Willkie was gaining on Roosevelt, said the time had come for the president to start campaigning. After spending Labor Day weekend at home in Hyde Park, FDR headed south for two events meant to highlight his accomplishments. His first stop was Chattanooga, Tennessee.

TENNESSEE

The men of the U.S. Army 6th Cavalry Regiment lined the streets around Chattanooga's Terminal Station as the presidential train pulled up. Red, white, and blue bunting hung from lampposts, railings, and windows, and thousands of people strained to glimpse Franklin Roosevelt. In a convertible with the top down, the president and entourage made their way to the recently completed Chickamauga Dam, part of Roosevelt's cherished Tennessee Valley Authority program which was bringing affordable electricity to millions. Onlookers had come from all over the state, and 50,000 sat and stood along the stone and earth banks of the impressive structure.[18] The president's car drove along the top of the dam and pulled up to a custom radio hookup consisting of microphones attached to a metal arm that swung into the car. Sitting in the back seat under a blazing sun, the president waved to the crowd and began his remarks at 10:00 A.M.

"I am glad to come here today, especially because I took part in the laying of the cornerstone of this dam some years ago," he said.

Roosevelt praised the workers who had built this monument to American engineering, acknowledging Labor Day as the perfect time to pay tribute to them. Not only would this mountain of concrete and steel prevent floods and irrigate crops, but it would also generate electricity to power homes and businesses. Amid all the celebratory huzzahs, however, Roosevelt had to acknowledge the crisis facing the nation overseas.

"Today, my friends, we are facing a time of peril unmatched in the history of the nations of all the world," he said. "Because we are undertaking the total defense of this nation of ours, the Tennessee Valley region has assumed, in addition to its own domestic betterment, its share of responsibility for national defense. We are seeking the preparedness of America, not against the threat of war or conquest alone, but in order that preparedness be built to assure American peace that rests on the well-being of the American people. Let us therefore, today, on this very happy occasion, dedicate this Dam and these lakes to the benefit of all the people, to the benefit of the prosperity that they have stimulated, the faith they have justified, the hope that they have inspired, the hearts that they encourage—the total defense of the people of the United States of America."[19]

Roosevelt was just getting started. From Chattanooga the president headed to the Great Smoky Mountains National Park which he created. There, at Newfound Gap, he was helped from the car to a podium draped with bunting. The spectacular view before him encompassed the border between Tennessee and North Carolina and a cascading set of ridgelines that are often wrapped in a blue glow that makes them unforgettable. In one of the most magnificent and beautiful sites for any of his thousands of speeches, he summoned the spirit of the pioneers.

"Here in the Great Smokies, we have come together to dedicate these mountains, streams, and forests, to the service of the millions of American people," he said. "There are trees here that stood before our forefathers ever came to this continent; there are brooks that still run as clear as on the day the first pioneer cupped his hand and drank from them."

Invoking the toil and trouble those ancestors faced to carve a living out of wilderness, he focused on the need to count on your neighbor. "The dangers were many," he said. "The rifle could never be far from the axe. The pioneers stood on their own feet, they shot their own game and they fought off their own enemies. In time of accident or misfortune they helped each other, and in time of Indian attack they stood by each other. Today we no longer face Indians and hard and lonely struggles with nature—but today we have grown soft in many ways. If we are to survive, we cannot be soft in a world in which there are dangers that threaten Americans—dangers far more deadly than were those that the frontiersmen had to face. The arrow, the tomahawk, and the scalping knife have been replaced by the airplane, the bomb, the tank, and the machine gun. Their threat is as close to us today as was the threat to the frontiersmen when hostile Indians were lurking on the other side of the gap." His glorification of white settlers as they forcibly expelled indigenous people reflects the commonly accepted myth of that time of American exceptionalism and "manifest destiny." While this narrative is offensive to many today, the white audience he was addressing was taught this view of history throughout their schooling.

A fundamental issue of the race was the peacetime draft FDR had initiated. Republicans used the program like a hammer to bludgeon Roosevelt as a warmonger. But he stood his ground.

"It is not in every case easy or pleasant to ask men of the nation to leave their homes, and women of the nation to give their men to the service of the nation," he said. "But the men and women of America have never held back even when it has meant personal sacrifice on their part if that sacrifice is for the common good. That there is a danger from without is at last recognized by most of us Americans. That such a danger can no longer be met with pitchforks and squirrel rifles or even with the training or the weapons of the war of 1917 and 1918, is equally clear to most of us Americans.

"The pioneers survived by fighting their own fight and by standing together as one man in the face of danger. If we, their descendants, are to meet the dangers that threaten us, we too must be ready to fight our own fight and stand together as one man. In hours of peril the frontiersmen, whatever their personal likes or dislikes, whatever their personal differences of opinion, gathered together in absolute unity for defense. We, in this hour, must have and will have absolute national unity for total defense.

"The winds that blow through the wide sky in these mountains, the winds that sweep from Canada to Mexico, from the Pacific to the Atlantic—have always blown on free men. We are free today. If we join together now—men and women and children—to face the common menace as a united people, we shall be free tomorrow. So, to the free people of America, I dedicate this park."

Looking out over the pristine wilderness he had preserved for future generations Franklin Roosevelt savored the moment and embraced the challenges that lay ahead. He had led America out of the Great Depression. Now all he had to do was convince the citizens of the United States that the time had come to use the power of American manufacturing to save the world. And win reelection. Standing in his way was a network of Nazi sympathizers and isolationists, including senators and congressmen.

LOVETTSVILLE, VIRGINIA

Loudon County's lush green farmlands were whipped by violent winds and blinding lightning strikes on the afternoon of August 31, 1940. The thunderstorm raged across a vast swath of Virginia fifty-some miles west of Washington, D.C. The Pennsylvania Central Airlines DC3 scheduled to fly from Washington to Pittsburgh was delayed for twenty-eight minutes, but finally took off at 2:18 P.M. heading west. Buffeted by gale force winds, the pilot radioed at 2:31 that he was over Herndon "normal and climbing." Residents of Lovettsville heard the DC3's twin engines above the roar of the storm as it passed overhead at 2:50. An explosion rent the air and bystanders rushed to the crash scene. Bodies were scattered for half a mile around the crater left by the plane, whose remnants indicated that the aircraft struck the ground at a 45-degree angle at full speed. All twenty-five people aboard died instantly.[20] [21]

A lightning strike was suspected as the cause and federal authorities investigated but no explanation for the crash has ever been determined.

Some asked if it might have been a bomb. Among the fatalities was Senator Ernest Lundeen (R-Minnesota). When police officers recovered his body, they found the text of a speech he was to give that weekend. That text, and the suspicious circumstances of Lundeen's death, led to one of the most shocking scandals to hit Congress in many years. Also aboard the doomed plane were three FBI agents, and rumors soon began circulating around the capital that Lundeen had been under surveillance and was the subject of a federal inquiry.

It would take the FBI years to reveal all the details, but Senator Lundeen was part of a propaganda campaign funded and controlled by the German government to undermine American support for Great Britain. At the hub of the affair was a Nazi agent named George S. Viereck. And Senator Lundeen was not the only elected official collaborating with Viereck. A Justice Department investigation would eventually reveal that more than twenty members of Congress were involved. These coconspirators included Senator Burton Wheeler (D-Montana) who would go on to be an important leader in the America First Committee, and Representative Hamilton Fish III (R-New York), one of Franklin Roosevelt's neighbors in the Hudson Valley as well as one of FDR's most aggressive opponents.[22]

George Sylvester Viereck was a poet and propagandist. Born in Munich, Germany, he immigrated to the U.S. as a boy in the 1890s. He worked for Germany in both World War I and World War II. Charming and ruthless, with a receding hairline and round glasses, he was an accomplished author and journalist who traveled in high society. He met Hitler several times and was a featured speaker at the notorious 1934 "Friends of the New Germany" rally at Madison Square Garden, during which he encouraged his audience to support Hitler and Nazi Germany. By the late 1930s he was Hitler's top agent in the United States, and he hatched a Machiavellian plan that succeeded beyond anyone's expectations. The scheme had three objectives: Convince Americans that England was doomed to defeat; turn public opinion against entering the war in Europe; protect trade between the U.S. and Germany.[23]

Viereck began publishing German propaganda under his own name through contacts in the media but his primary focus was on recruiting well-known public figures and isolationists in Congress and using them to help disseminate Nazi talking points. He generated content for congressional allies that he could send out under official imprint. Once he realized that federally elected officials enjoyed a privilege known as "franking" allowing them unlimited free postage, his activities went into high gear. The Reich paid him $120,000, equivalent today to $1.2 million, in untraceable cash. In the secret war he was waging Viereck had ammunition in the form of words and weapons—newspapers, radio, and the U.S. mail—wielded by his commandos: politicians and celebrities firing volley after volley of pro-German, anti-British propaganda written by Nazis.[24]

In 1937 Lundeen, a newly elected senator from Minnesota and outspoken isolationist, was a prime target for Viereck. The Nazi operative ingratiated himself with the fervent isolationist and the two men soon became good friends and coconspirators. Viereck would write the speeches and Lundeen would deliver them, sometimes on the Senate floor, automatically appearing in the Congressional Record, whose contents were in the public domain and could be reprinted endlessly. Lundeen helped Viereck recruit fellow isolationists, and House member Hamilton Fish III helped him gain access to franked envelopes bearing a Capitol Hill return address in which Viereck mailed Nazi propaganda to millions of unsuspecting Americans.

Not content to rely on established media outlets, Viereck bought Flanders Hall, a publishing company in New Jersey that he used to print and distribute English-language translations of German books. Flanders Hall's oeuvre overflowed with antisemitic rants, vile lies about the British Empire, and sometimes the texts of speeches by his verbal commandos—all paid for by the German embassy.

In the lead up to the 1940 election, Viereck used Senator Wheeler's franking privilege to mail a million anti-Roosevelt postcards.[25]

Senator Lundeen worked with Viereck on remarks he planned to deliver during a Labor Day event back home in Minnesota. The speech was to kick off a major campaign mocking Roosevelt and praising Germany and Hitler.[26] Viereck delivered the final version to Lundeen the morning of August 30, a day before the airplane crash.

British intelligence agents knew all about Viereck and monitored him closely. They shared much of the evidence that accumulated with the FBI. One crucial source of this intel came courtesy of Franklin Roosevelt's old friend, Vincent Astor. Working independently from American law enforcement, Astor developed a strong working relationship with British intelligence operating out of Manhattan.[27]

Astor had been convening a select group of powerful New York business executives initially known as "The Club" and later "The Room." Participants included J. P. Morgan Jr. and Nelson Doubleday. This secret society met regularly in a nondescript apartment at 34 East Sixty-Second Street in Manhattan to exchange information about financial transactions of foreign powers. Astor shared that information with Roosevelt. Astor also owned the *Newsweek* building at 152 West 42nd Street; he rented offices there to Nazi agents who used them to conduct business. The Nazis did not know that Astor had given the room next door to the FBI, whose agents monitored every deal the Nazis made, filming many of them. When war broke out, the FBI arrested all of the Nazi agents, and questioned their collaborators.[28]

Astor's most important contribution involved his ownership of Western Union and his estate in Bermuda. England had arranged to have all diplomatic mail from the Americas routed through Bermuda. Astor set up a massive interception operation that opened Axis embassies' diplomatic pouches, sieved the contents for information, then resealed the pouches and sent them on their way. Thus, the British could read German embassy reports on Viereck's work even before his Nazi handlers could.

Viereck's operation was exposed when a grand jury subpoenaed him in September 1941. He was indicted on five counts of failing to register as a foreign agent. His case went to the Supreme Court; he was convicted and sent to prison. Hamilton Fish's staff member George Hill, who had assisted Viereck in the use of franked envelopes and other abuses of congressional privilege, also testified before the grand jury. When he denied assisting Viereck he was charged with perjury, convicted, and sent to prison in 1942.

It is impossible to tally the number of people affected by the coordinated attacks on Roosevelt policies that Viereck set in motion. The propaganda he circulated was one small part of a massive effort by many people, including Henry Ford, Father Coughlin, and Robert McCormick. For reasons altruistic as well as malicious, these and other isolationists believed America should stay out of the war and that Germany would make a better partner for the United States than Great Britain. They and their ilk arrayed themselves against Franklin Roosevelt in the fall of 1940 as he was seeking a third term in the White House.

WASHINGTON

The president was also facing a serious challenge to his candidacy from Black leaders who were demanding an end to discrimination in the defense industry and segregation in the military. The First World War had offered new opportunities for Black Southerners to move north and escape the injustices of the Jim Crow South, known as the Great Migration. Again, this time in 1940, the United States' reviving economy had inspired a second great migration. Weary of racist oppression, Jim Crow laws, lynchings, and lack of opportunity and jobs, Black Americans had begun moving north and west to cities beginning to bustle after years of depression. The burgeoning defense industry on the West Coast and in Midwestern metropolises only enhanced the attraction of trying life anywhere but in the South.

Since the turn of the century a Black consciousness movement had taken root. Two of its prominent voices were Asa Philip Randolph, president of the Brotherhood of Sleeping Car Porters, and Walter White, head of the National Association for the Advancement of Colored People.

The 18,000-member Brotherhood of Sleeping Car Porters, a potent force in the Black community, was one of only a few national unions representing Black workers, who were becoming an important voting block for Democrats.[29] Randolph presided over the union's annual convention at the Harlem YMCA on September 16, 1940, the day Roosevelt signed the Selective Training and Service Act, America's first peacetime draft. America's Armed Forces were historically segregated, and Black units served under white officers. The new Selective Service Act enshrined the armed forces' historic racist skew by allowing use of discriminatory tests and preserving a tradition of segregated units. Military leaders and Civil Rights advocates furiously debated how to incorporate Blacks into the draft. But the War and Navy departments refused even to consider integration.[30]

Randolph knew well the dismal conditions facing most Black Americans—75 percent of adults had not completed high school, and those in the work force earned less than 40 percent of what white Americans in similar jobs were paid. Many employers openly refused to hire Black people. Defense contractor North American Aviation's stated policy was "We will not employ Negroes." In an unusual interplay between labor and management, white unions refused Blacks admission and white-owned companies prohibited Blacks from nonunion jobs as well.[31]

At their 1940 convention in Harlem the railroad porters passed a resolution calling on the federal government to end systematic discrimination against Black people in the defense industry and armed forces. Eleanor Roosevelt wrote a letter to her husband pleading with him to meet with Randolph and White and consider the political consequences if he did nothing.[32] Opponent Wendell Willkie was gaining in the polls, and Republicans were far more supportive of Black civil rights than

Democrats, who made up the 'Solid South' on which that party relied. Even arch-conservative Hamilton Fish III had cosponsored an amendment to outlaw discrimination in the draft. As a U.S. Army Captain, Fish commanded Company K of the all-Black 369th Infantry Regiment, the Harlem Hellfighters, to great success in World War I. They fought with the French Army because the rigidly segregated U.S. Army did not allow Blacks to serve with white troops.

On September 27, 1940, at 11:30 A.M., Asa Philip Randolph, Walter White, and T. Arnold Hill of the National Urban League walked into President Roosevelt's executive office.[33] Waiting with the president were Secretary of the Navy Frank Knox and Assistant Secretary of War Robert Patterson. Henry Stimson, the Secretary of War, had refused to participate, claiming it was beneath him to interact with Negroes. That morning Germany, Italy, and Japan had announced the Tripartite Pact, creating a global alliance of Fascist totalitarians. In addition to the looming war, Roosevelt was dealing with a strong challenge in the November election.

The president had recently installed an audio recording system given him by David Sarnoff of RCA. The mechanism, a newly developed technology, etched audio waves onto film stock. Only the president knew the recorder was on during the meeting. Presenting his usual cheerful self, the president warmly welcomed his guests. A cordial Randolph got right to the point.

"Mr. President, it would mean a great deal to the morale of the Negro people if you could make some announcement on the role Negroes will play in the armed forces of the nation, in the whole national defense set-up," the union president said.[34]

Roosevelt responded on a positive note. "I did the other day!" he exclaimed. "We did it the other day when my staff told me of this thing [the meeting]."

"If you did it yourself, if you were to make such an announcement, it would have a tremendous effect on the morale of the Negro people all over the country."

"Yeah, yeah, yeah, yeah, yeah," FDR said, interrupting Randolph by characteristically saying what a visitor wanted to hear so that he could move onto his next meeting. "Now, I'm making a national defense speech around the twentieth of this month about the draft as a whole, and the reserves, and so forth. I'll bring that in . . ."

Understanding exactly what Roosevelt was doing, Randolph politely but firmly cut him off. "It would have a tremendous effect because, I must say, it is an irritating spot for the Negro people," he told the president. "They feel that they are not wanted in the various armed forces of the country, and they feel they have earned their right to participate in every phase of the government by virtue of their record in past wars for the nation. And consequently, without regard to political complexion, without regard to any sort of idea whatever, the Negroes as a unit, they are feeling that they are being shunted aside, that they are being discriminated against, and that they are not wanted now."

"The Negro is trying to get in the army!" White exclaimed in frustration.

"Of course, the main point to get across in building up this draft army, the selective draft, is that we are not, as we did before so much in the World War, confining the Negro into the non-combat services," a defensive Roosevelt replied. "We're putting him right in, proportionately, into the combat services. We feel that's something."

The president's comment that he was not "confining the Negro to non-combat services" was not strictly true.

"Colonel Knox, as to the navy, what is the position of the navy on the integration of the Negro in the various parts?" Roosevelt asked Knox, who vehemently opposed Blacks serving in the navy. "You have a factor in the navy that is not present in the army, and that is that these men live aboard ships," Knox said. "And if I said to you that I was going to take Negroes into a ship's company . . ." He mumbled under his breath, then continued, "this sort of thing won't do. And you can't have separate ships with a Negro crew, because everything in the navy now has to be interchangeable."

Adopting a professional military man's tone, Knox said, "I agree with, however, with the president's suggestion on some way of providing, in the words of the message of the Negro patriotic leaders, to serve the nation without raising the question that comes from putting white men and Black men living together in the same ship."

White raised the idea of a Black adviser working with the Secretary of the Navy. "An assistant responsible to the secretary, he said, to Knox adding, "I want to see you about that." Knox said nothing. He stared stonily at Randolph. "He's giving you what you call the silent treatment!" Roosevelt told White. "Ha, ha, ha!"

Randolph and White, increasingly agitated, made their case, and President Roosevelt responded with his usual charm and smile, nodding and agreeing to look into the matter. Missy LeHand came into the room and held the door open, indicating the meeting was over. "Goodbye!" the president said.

White wrote to Mrs. Roosevelt a few days later to say he was satisfied with the discussion concerning the inclusion of Blacks in all branches of the military.[35]

On October 9, 1940, in response to that meeting, Press Secretary Stephen Early released a statement outlining the administration's policy on Blacks in the military. "The policy of the War Department is not to intermingle colored and white enlisted personnel in the same regimental organizations," the statement read, "to make changes would produce situations destructive to morale and detrimental to the preparations for national defense. Therefore, the department does not contemplate assigning colored reserve officers other than those of the Medical Corps and chaplains to existing Negro combat units."[36]

The statement infuriated Randolph and White, especially when newspapers reported that White had approved the statement. The NAACP immediately wrote to the White House demanding a retraction and on

October 12 released a blistering critique entitled, "White House Charged with Trickery in Announcing Jim Crow Policy in Army."

The subhead was no less direct. "NAACP denies approving segregation in wire to the president and declares he used Negro leaders and organizations in attempt to cover up unfair treatment of race in National Defense."[37]

The Black press erupted, and a number of influential Black leaders announced they would be voting for Willkie. The First Lady confronted her spouse about the statement and the danger of losing the Black vote. The informal group known as the "Black Cabinet" put pressure on Roosevelt to do something. A startled FDR appointed a highly respected Black lawyer, Judge William H. Hastie, to be a civilian aide to Secretary Stimson. He also promoted Colonel Benjamin O. Davis Sr. to brigadier general, making him the first Black U.S. Army general in American history.

In a personal letter to White, Randolph, and Hill, Roosevelt expressed regret that "there has been so much misinterpretation" of the policy statement. He urged them to "rest assured that further developments of policy will be forthcoming to ensure that Negroes are given fair treatment on a non-discriminatory basis."[38]

The letter placated no one, and Randolph soon started plotting a public response—a march on Washington by 10,000 Blacks demanding equal treatment in defense industry hiring. This was an incendiary idea. The District of Columbia was a Southern city with Jim Crow laws and a police department known for its racial bigotry and brutality. A gathering of 10,000 angry Blacks would undoubtedly lead to violence.

As the election neared, Roosevelt found himself at odds with a wide range of citizens: isolationists, Southern bigots, Black Americans seeking equality, conservative newspapers, and an outspoken American hero, Charles Lindbergh. The battle lines were drawn, and the stakes could not have been higher.

Charles and Anne Lindbergh, date unknown.

7

LOVE TAKES FLIGHT

MEXICO CITY—DECEMBER 1927

The midday Mexican sun beat down on the endless mass of people surrounding the landing strip at Valbuena Aviation Field ten miles outside Mexico City. President Plutarco Elías Calles had declared a national holiday, the first ever in honor of a North American, but the crowds would have come anyway. More than 150,000 people lined the streets and surrounded the bleachers installed for the arrival ceremony. Hundreds had slept the preceding night on the ground to gain a spot with a view.[1] Workers in overalls, politicians in suits, women carrying children—no one wanted to miss the historic moment when the great aviator hero touched down. Soldiers and half of Mexico

City's police force cordoned off the runway. All eyes strained to catch a glimpse of the *Spirit of St. Louis.*

But mutterings of concern soon were circulating through the crowd. Onlookers had been expecting Charles Lindbergh to arrive from Washington, D.C., at noon. By 1:30 P.M. a sense of foreboding had dampened the celebration. President Calles, in his bunting draped bleacher built against the wall of a giant hanger, waited nervously with his VIP guests, including American Ambassador Dwight Morrow and actor and comedian Will Rogers. Every minute brought a new rumor: "His plane was seen near Toluca." "A plane was seen going into the water!" When a sharp-eyed police officer called out "There he is!" The crowd leapt to its feet only to sag with the realization that the aircraft approaching was a scheduled passenger flight. Finally, at 2:30 P.M., a small form came into view high in the distance. The little aircraft began a slow, graceful approach, and as it neared the airfield the distinctive silhouette of the world's most famous plane came into focus. The crowd erupted in cheers and shouts of "Viva Lindy! Viva Lindy!"

President Calles had been chain-smoking and anxiously tapping his cane on the ground. An aide walked over and whispered in his ear.

"It is Lindbergh!" the man said. "It is positively Lindbergh this time."

The president jumped to his feet, a wide smile creased his face, and he called out, "Bring me a drink!"[2]

The *St. Louis* made a low altitude run over the airfield and buzzed the president's box. Lindbergh pulled back on the stick and began a steep climb, hanging for a moment at the apex, then gracefully descending in a controlled arc toward the concrete runway.

After hours of tension, the crowd pressed against the police line. The officers and soldiers were no match for the power of the people. As soon as his plane came to a stop Lindbergh shut down his engine to stop the propeller before someone was hurt or killed. Motorcycle policemen circled the plane in a futile attempt to ward off the crowd, which surged like a giant wave and crashed upon the plane. As Lindbergh emerged from the cockpit, they chanted "Brava Lindy!"[3]

Ambassador Morrow went out to the plane to greet Lindbergh. The men knew each other well. Morrow had been Lindbergh's financial advisor at JP Morgan before he became Ambassador. Morrow had arranged for the historic flight as a gesture of international goodwill.

The Ambassador escorted Lindbergh to the president's box. Calles was so overcome with joy that besides shaking the pilot's hand, he embraced him with a full bear hug. "You are a guest of our nation, and we are proud to have you here!" he exclaimed.

"I am equally proud and thank you very much," Lindbergh responded humbly.

"You are a very brave man; you have come a long way."

Lindbergh had needed 27 hours and 15 minutes to fly 2,300 miles nonstop from Washington, D.C., to Mexico City, about six hours less than his historic flight from New York to Paris six months earlier. Fog obscured the coastline of the Gulf of Mexico. He had only crude hand-drawn maps, and the mountainous wilderness surrounding the Mexican capital gave few clues as to his whereabouts. Flying low he came upon a sign for the town of Toluca, forty miles west of the capital, and from there made his way to a champion's welcome.

This was Lindbergh's first stop on a tour of Latin America that was to keep him on the move until mid-February. Ambassador Morrow had invited Lindbergh's mother Evangeline to spend the holidays at the Embassy with her son, the first real vacation Charles Lindbergh had had since his record-setting transatlantic flight in May.

Evangeline, a high school science teacher in Minnesota, was an important part of Lindbergh's life. His father, a former congressman who had opposed the U.S. entry into World War I, had died three years earlier. Charles' parents had divorced in 1918 and his mother had helped guide him through his early career.

No one knew at the time, but that Christmas Charles Lindbergh found a gift that he would treasure for the rest of his life. Ambassador Morrow's twenty-one-year-old daughter Anne was also at the embassy for Christmas. The shy aviator, twenty-five, who had never had a serious girlfriend, immediately noticed the beautiful, quiet, self-conscious college student.[4] Anne noticed him as well, and wrote in her diary after their first meeting, "I saw . . . a tall, slim boy in evening dress—so much slimmer, so much taller, so much more poised than I expected. A very refined face, not at all like those grinning 'Lindy' pictures."[5]

As the Christmas holiday went on, Anne watched from a distance. A later diary entry sums up her feelings: "He is taller than anyone else—you see his head in a moving crowd and you notice his glance, where it turns, as though it were keener, clearer, and brighter than anyone else's, lit with a more intense fire . . . What could I say to this boy? Anything I might say would be trivial and superficial, like pink frosting flowers. I felt the entire world before this to be frivolous, superficial, ephemeral."[6]

The Morrows said goodbye to Lindbergh on December 28, and he continued his fifteen-country goodwill tour of Central America and the Caribbean. Upon returning to the United States, he received the Congressional Medal of Honor from President Calvin Coolidge. *Time* magazine chose him as that weekly's first Man of the Year. He took Henry Ford up for a private plane ride, the start of a decades-long friendship.

In the spring of 1928, tired of constant attention and nonstop activity, Lindbergh decided he needed to find balance in his life. His thoughts turned to the intelligent young woman he had met in Mexico. After much awkward back and forth, Charles took Anne flying and they were soon engaged. They married in May 1929 and the following year had a son they named for his father. Baby Charles's murder and the subsequent "trial of the century" are well known. Press scrutiny of the famed pilot and his lovely wife turned toxic as tabloid photographers and reporters hounded the couple. Overwhelmed, in 1935 they departed America for England. During their years abroad Charles made multiple visits to Germany, whose Nazi government invited him to inspect the regime's advanced warplanes. He reported his findings to American military attaché Truman Smith at the U.S. embassy, and his reports reached the highest levels of the Army Air Corps.

Anne wrote several well-received books and traveled with Charles on many of his aerial adventures. She became an excellent pilot and navigator. After *Kristallnacht* in November of 1938, they decided the time had come to depart Europe, and they arrived in America in April, 1939.

LONG ISLAND, NEW YORK

Their return to the United States and Charles's increasingly controversial opposition to American involvement in European conflicts led Anne to write a short book expressing her point of view. In September 1940, as the presidential campaign was heating up, her forty-page *The Wave of the Future: A Confession of Faith* came out.[7]

Anne tried to explain her thoughts in the context of her husband's ardor on behalf of American neutrality. For her, the war was a battle between the "forces of the past" and the "forces of the future." Totalitarianism, despite its horrific abuses, was the future, she said, and democracy's time was passing.

"What was pushing behind Communism? What behind Fascism in Italy? What behind Nazism?" she asked. "Is it nothing but a 'return to barbarism' to be crushed at all costs by a "crusade"? Or is some new, and perhaps even ultimate good, conception of humanity trying to come to birth, often through evil and horrible forms and abortive attempts?"

She closes by saying, "There is no fighting the wave of the future, any more than as a child you could fight against the gigantic roller that loomed up ahead of you suddenly."

The Wave of the Future quickly became the most popular nonfiction book in America—as well as the most criticized and detested book of that period. A review in *Foreign Affairs* summarizes its message: "This is one of the most controversial books to appear in recent years, and one of the most difficult to appraise. In substance, Mrs. Lindbergh's thesis is that the great fact of history, the law of life, is eternal and inexorable change, that we are now in one of the great periods of rapid and profound change, and that it is therefore the better part of wisdom—for Americans as well as for all other peoples—to accept this process, whatever it may be, and not to fight against it. The 'wave of the future,' as it presents itself to Mrs. Lindbergh, is totalitarian, and in her eyes, there is no use in our trying . . . to stem it."

Harold Ickes, Roosevelt's pugnacious secretary of the interior, attacked Anne Lindbergh, calling her a Nazi and labeling her book "The bible of every American Nazi, Fascist, Bundist and Appeaser."[8]

Shocked and troubled by the virulent response to her book, and feeling that critics were deliberately distorting her writing, Anne, who was in the advanced stages of pregnancy, withdrew to the family home and on October 2, 1940, gave birth to a baby girl.

The same month *Wave of the Future* came out, students at Yale University formed the America First Committee. The new organization eventually grew to 450 chapters nationwide enrolling more than 800,000 members. The founders included Douglas Stuart, son of the founder of the Quaker Oats Company, future U.S. President Gerald Ford, future U.S. Supreme Court Justice Potter Stewart, and Sargent Shriver, the first director of the Peace Corps. They chose as their official leader General Robert Wood, CEO of Sears, Roebuck. Financial support came from Joe Patterson, publisher of the New York *Daily News*, Robert McCormick of the *Chicago Tribune*, Henry Ford, and a slew of other wealthy isolationists.

The America First Committee also attracted the patronage of Democratic Senators Burton Wheeler and David Walsh and Republican Senators Gerald Nye and Henrik Shipstead. A range of well-known figures gave their support, including Frank Lloyd Wright, Teddy Roosevelt's daughter Alice Roosevelt Longworth, and Joseph Kennedy.

WASHINGTON, D.C.

Charles Lindbergh initially kept his distance from the group, helping to make connections behind the scenes but not joining publicly. He continued to oppose Roosevelt's campaign and endorse neutrality. On October 14, 1940, he delivered a prime-time radio address on the Mutual Broadcasting Network from their studios in Washington. For the first time, he allowed a newsreel crew to film and record him after the radio broadcast. He had based his previous reluctance to do so on his belief that "because of the Jewish influence in the newsreel and the antagonism I know exists towards me, I take the chance that they will cut my talk badly."[9]

Millions of adoring fans tuned in, and many who disagreed listened as well. The election was three weeks away, and the target of his speech was unnamed but in no doubt.

"I come before you tonight to enter a plea for American independence," Lindbergh began. Asking where the leadership of Washington, Jefferson, and Lincoln was, he launched his most direct attack on the president.

"What we lack today is the type of leadership that made us a great nation; the type that turned adversity and hardship into vitality and success," the isolationist aviator said. "No one doubts that we are in the midst of a world crisis. We do not question the need for rearmament and for reform, for a better economic system. What we do question is the leadership that has brought these conditions upon us. Under their leadership we have alienated the most powerful military nations of both Europe and Asia, at a time when we ourselves are unprepared for action, and while the people of our nation are overwhelmingly opposed to war."[10]

The *New York Times* headlined its story the next day LINDBERGH ASSAILS PRESENT LEADERS. The broadcast drew mixed reviews. The following week Lindbergh was at a Trans-Lux newsreel theater, and when the projectionist rolled footage of him speaking, some in the audience hissed. At the end of the newsreel many people in the theater clapped, demonstrating how divided the country was on the topic.[11]

NEW YORK CITY

With Lindbergh raising the stakes and generating public support for isolationism, Wendell Willkie stepped up his critique, hammering at FDR's ostensible secret plan for war. This line of attack infuriated the president, who rarely backed down from a fight. With the election closing in, FDR needed fresh speechwriters. He turned to the still-recovering Harry Hopkins, temporarily staying at the Essex House in New York City. Hopkins invited Robert Sherwood over for a talk. The six-foot-seven, Pulitzer- and Oscar-winning writer, known for a poetic sense of language and a firm belief in the power of words, had no idea why he was there. Hopkins' small apartment was strewn with clothes and papers. Smoking a cigarette and wearing a wrinkled suit that hung loosely on his skeletal frame, Hopkins appraised Sherwood with experienced eyes.

"The president has to give a speech on Columbus Day," Hopkins said. "It's supposed to be one of those routine State Department speeches about Western Hemisphere solidarity, directed primarily to South America. But the president wants to talk to the America people about Hitler. So far as he is concerned, there is absolutely nothing important in the world today but to beat Hitler."[12]

Hopkins glared at Sherwood, waiting for a response. Not sure what to say, Sherwood remained silent.

"What do you think the president ought to say?" Hopkins pressed.

At a loss for words, and somewhat taken aback, Sherwood replied, "Well, you know, I work with the Committee to Defend America by Aiding the Allies, so I agree with the president's attitude toward Nazi Germany."

"Ok, good. Let's go see Sam Rosenman."

Sam Rosenman, a highly respected New York Supreme Court Justice, had worked with FDR for years. Credited with coining the term "The New Deal" he left the court in 1943 to work for the president full time.[13]

Hopkins and Sherwood walked the short distance from the Essex House to Rosenman's apartment on Central Park West. The pudgy, bespectacled Rosenman was in his dining room. The order and symmetry of the beautifully decorated apartment stood in stark contrast to the disorderly drifts of papers covering the dining room table: news clippings, White House notes, and fragments of a speech that Roosevelt had dictated to Missy LeHand. The three sat around the edges of the pile.

"Can someone tell me why exactly I am here?" Sherwood asked.[14]

"The boss needs a new ghostwriter, some new blood," Hopkins said. "You're it."

After a meandering discussion between the three men about the dismal state of the world and the imminent election, Rosenman, who had been holding a pencil, slammed it down on the table.

"Well, gentlemen—there comes a time in the life of every speech when it's got to be written," he said. "That time for this speech is NOW! So, let's get to work."[15]

A new writing team was born. One that turned out to be a history-changing collective—politically persuasive, linguistically liberal, and always striving to write in Franklin Roosevelt's unique voice. Together Sherwood, Rosenman, and Hopkins helped FDR craft some of the most memorable speeches in American history.

Hopkins and Rosenman were old hands at this alchemy. Sherwood, in contrast, was used to working alone. This trio of scribes would remain FDR's primary wordsmiths for the remainder of his life. They were more than just speechwriters; they were advisors, friends, confidants, each brilliant in his own way.

Harry Hopkins had been orbiting FDR for years, managing New Deal programs and distributing hundreds of millions of dollars in relief aid. He would soon move into one of the upstairs bedrooms at the White House and become FDR's right-hand man during the war.

Putting egos aside, the three spent countless hours working with Roosevelt to find the perfect, potent combination of words for any given situation. Their great challenge was countering the withering "war-monger" attacks from Willkie and the Republicans. But that was not the only challenge.

For smashing the third-term taboo, the press had turned on FDR. The *New York Times,* New York *Daily News,* and the Scripps Howard papers, in the past reliable pillars of editorial support, opposed his latest candidacy. Existing enemies Hearst and McCormick redoubled their efforts to defeat him. Four days after Lindbergh's radio address, the president announced that he would be winding up his campaign by delivering five major speeches.

Philadelphia

At exactly noon on October 23, Franklin Roosevelt and his coterie boarded the presidential train and headed to Philadelphia. Traveling with FDR were his inner circle—Missy LeHand and Grace Tully, Steve Early and Pa Watson, presidential doctor Ross McIntire, and naval aide Daniel Callaghan.[16] All hands understood how important this expedition was—the Roosevelt presidency was on the line, and it was up to the seasoned campaigner to resurrect the old magic. Lately he had not been himself as ill health and the stresses of the war in Europe had taken a toll. After a brief stop in Wilmington, Delaware, the train arrived at Philadelphia's 30th Street Station. The president's secret service detail helped him into his limousine for an inspection tour of nearby shipyards working overtime to build the warships Roosevelt had ordered. Thousands lined the streets, waving flags and shouting his name. Iconic cigarette holder clenched in his teeth, FDR took off his lucky fedora and waved back.[17]

After dinner thousands more came out of their houses and lined the streets leading to Convention Hall where the president was to speak. Catching sight of the motorcade they shouted "Yeah!" in a joyous outburst. When the tour had passed through the central city to its destination, 20,000 spectators surrounding the hall greeted Roosevelt with a deafening roar. A band played "God Bless America" as aides helped the president out of the car and into the cavernous building.

Emerging onto the stage President Roosevelt walked slowly toward the podium, holding Captain Callaghan's arm with a firm grip. The audience gave him a standing ovation with gusto and FDR stood for several long minutes waiting for the crowd of 15,000 to calm down so he could speak.[18]

Roosevelt began by explaining his pledge in July not to campaign because of the heavy burden of governing in a time of crisis. He reminded them of his one caveat. "Last July I also said this: 'I shall never be loath to call the attention of the nation to deliberate or unwitting falsifications of fact,' which are sometimes made by political candidates. The time has come for me to do just that."[19]

His supporters cheered, glad to see a reprise of the fighting spirit that had first propelled him to the White House eight years ago. His voice gaining strength and resolve, with a hint of angry outrage, he acknowledged the legitimacy of some criticism, but exposed Willkie's most outrageous statements for what they were.

"It is an entirely different thing for any party or candidate to state . . . the unemployed are going to be driven into concentration camps, or that social security funds . . . will not be in existence when the workers of today . . . apply for them, or that the election of the present government means the end of American democracy within four years," FDR said. "I think they know, and I know we know, that all those statements are false! I consider it a public duty to answer falsifications with facts. I will not pretend that I find this an unpleasant duty. I am an old campaigner, and I love a good fight."

Gaining momentum and confidence, FDR took the fight to the hidden forces behind Willkie. Roosevelt knew of the Nazi-funded misinformation campaign against him and made specific reference to it.

"Certain techniques of propaganda, created and developed in dictator countries, have been imported into this campaign," he said. "It is the very simple technique of repeating and repeating and repeating falsehoods, with the idea that by constant repetition and reiteration, with no contradiction, the misstatements will finally come to be believed. They are used to create fear by instilling in the minds of our people doubt of each other, doubt of their government, and doubt of the purposes of their democracy."

In closing Roosevelt directly addressed the most effective barb of Willkie's attack line—that the president had a secret plan to enter the war. "We are arming ourselves not for any purpose of conquest or intervention in foreign disputes," he said. "I repeat again that I stand on the platform of our party: 'We will not participate in foreign wars, and we will not send our army, naval or air forces to fight in foreign lands outside of the Americas except in case of attack.' It is for peace that I have labored; and it is for peace that I shall labor all the days of my life."

Roosevelt's appearance in Philadelphia was an unqualified success. Democratic party leaders were ecstatic. The "Champ" was back and in fighting form. And this was but the first of FDR's five campaign star turns.[20]

One accusation from Willkie's campaign was particularly grievous—that FDR had been delinquent in preparing a national defense. Considering the many times Republicans in Congress had opposed FDR's requests for additional funds for the military, this was a charge he would not let go unanswered. At Madison Square Garden on October 28, he worked in a reference to a popular old vaudeville song "The Daring Young Man on the Flying Trapeze" to characterize his opponents' ever-changing position.

"In those days, they thought that the way to win votes was by representing this Administration as extravagant in national defense, indeed as
hysterical, and as manufacturing panics and inventing foreign dangers.
But now, in the severe days of 1940, all is changed! Not only because
they are serious days, but because they are election days as well. On the
radio these Republican orators swing through the air with the greatest
of ease; but the American people are not voting this year for the best
trapeze performer! Outside the halls of Congress, eminent Republican
candidates began to turn new somersaults. At first, they denounced the
bill; then, when public opinion rose up to demand it, they seized their
trapeze with the greatest of ease, and reversed themselves in mid-air!"[21]

The line—a classic example of Rooseveltian wordplay—brought
cheers and applause. The construction is simple—expose the hypocrisy
and deliver a punchline both familiar and devastating. Jutting his chin,
he let the punchline ring as the audience laughed and jeered. "They
seized their trapeze with the greatest of ease and reversed themselves
in mid-air."

But that was not even the best line in the speech. Three right-wing
Republican Congressmen had opposed FDR's every effort to bolster
national defense, including repeal of the arms embargo allowing for
cash and carry delivery of arms to England. The offenders were Joseph
Martin from Massachusetts, Bruce Barton representing Manhattan, and
Hamilton Fish III, the Hudson Valley scion and anti-FDR diehard, who
had been working with the Nazi Viereck to distribute Third Reich propaganda. While drafting the speech, Rosenman and Sherwood decided the
trio's names could be spoken as a syncopated neologism: Martin, Barton,
and Fish. At the White House the following day they gave their draft
to Roosevelt, who liked to read each version aloud to test it in his mouth
and in front of a live audience. As he worked his way through the draft,
Rosenman and Sherwood said nothing, stealing a glance at each other
as FDR neared their pet phrase.[22]

"The following Republican leaders, among many others, voted against the Act: Senators McNary, Vandenberg, Nye, and Johnson, and Congressmen Martin, Barton, and Fish."

Roosevelt's eyes twinkled. He looked up from the page with a big smile, then looked down and repeated, "Martin, Barton and Fish—Martin, Barton and Fish." He repeated it again, changing the cadence to put emphasis on his neighbor and nemesis. "Martin, Barton—and FISH." The writers laughed at having guessed correctly. "I think we are going to have a lot of fun with that one," the Boss said. "I'm tickled pink!"[23]

Having warmed up the crowd with the daring young man on the flying trapeze, Roosevelt again worked his magic. When the president came to the topic of the opposition to his repeal of the arms embargo, he indeed had fun.

"But how did the Republicans vote on the repeal of that embargo?" he asked. "In the Senate, the Republicans voted fourteen to six against it. In the House, the Republicans voted one hundred and forty to nineteen against it. The Act was passed by Democratic votes, but it was over the opposition of the Republican leaders. And just to name a few, the following Republican leaders, among many others, voted against the Act: Senators McNary, Vandenberg, Nye, and Johnson; now wait, a perfectly beautiful rhythm—Congressmen Martin, Barton, and Fish."

The audience did howl with laughter, and a few lines later, he reprised the line: "Great Britain and a lot of other nations would never have received one ounce of help from us—if the decision had been left to Martin, Barton, and FISH."

The crowd joined in on "Martin" and shouted, "Barton and Fish!" Three days later, the same response happened in Boston. With that phrase, FDR draped all the pro-Nazi, anti-British, reactionary rhetoric of the right wing around Willkie's neck. Willkie later admitted, "When I heard the president hang the isolationist votes of Martin, Barton and Fish on me, and get away with it, I knew I was licked."

WASHINGTON

On October 28 Henry Morgenthau received a top secret message from Winston Churchill for the president regarding Great Britain's dire situation and specific needs for shipping, aircraft, and military supplies. The prime minister described the imminent German invasion, estimating sixty divisions of hardened troops, an overwhelming force of Luftwaffe fighters and bombers, and an increasing number of deadly U-Boats operating out of French ports all along the English Channel. His plea was urgent, his language bleak.[24]

"You will see, therefore, Mr. President how very great are our problems and dangers," Churchill wrote. "We feel, however, confident of our ability, if we are given the necessary supplies, to carry on the war to a successful conclusion. And anyhow we are going to try our best. You will, however, allow me to impress upon you the extreme urgency of accelerating delivery of the programme of aircraft and other munitions which has already been laid before you. The equipment of our armies, both for home defense and overseas, is progressing, but we depend upon American deliveries to complete our exiting programme which will certainly be delayed and impeded by the bombing of factories and disturbances of work. The world cause is in your hands."

Churchill had already placed orders for 11,000 warplanes, 27,000 engines, 68,000 tons of explosives, and 2,000 tanks. Only a fraction of these had been delivered, and some shipments had been sent to the ocean bottom by German torpedoes.

The next day the president presided over the opening lottery under the Selective Service Act, the first peacetime draft in American history. Surprisingly, Willkie supported the draft, and ignored his advisors who urged him to use it as a cudgel against FDR. To mark the occasion Roosevelt delivered a brief radio message after the lottery numbers had been drawn. He never mentioned the word "draft" but harkened back to the republic's early days by using the term "muster," invoking thoughts and images of colonial patriots on the Concord green.[25]

"We are mustering all our resources, manhood, and industry and wealth to make our nation strong in defense," he said. "For recent history proves all too clearly, I am sorry to say, that only the strong may continue to live in freedom and peace. Ever since that first muster, our democratic army has existed for one purpose only: the defense of our freedom."

As soon as the president finished the radio address he went to his bedroom, where he welcomed Morgenthau at 12:35 P.M.[26]

"Here is the message Churchill sent," the treasury secretary said. "It's not good." Morgenthau handed the message and the pages of reports detailing what had been ordered, what had been delivered, and what the Brits still needed.

"Did you send a copy to Hull?" the president asked as he was reading.

"Yes."

When FDR finished reading, Morgenthau handed him another piece of paper.

"Here is a draft of the statement for the Boston speech," he said. Military intelligence had composed this version, and it provided an overview of the purchase and delivery of aircraft and weapons to Great Britain. "The details are in attachments marked I-A and I-B."

"Okay, I've seen most of this already," the president said, scanning through the pages.

"The English aren't too crazy about you releasing the actual numbers, they fear they might be useful to the Nazis."

"Well, I might use some of it in Boston," FDR said. "Lots of talk out there about not getting Winston what he needs."[27]

At 11:00 P.M. that night Roosevelt and team left Washington headed for Boston and one of his last campaign events before the election. The train made many stops, and telegrams kept coming in warning the president that if he did not make a definitive statement about keeping

America out of the war, he might lose the election to Willkie. At the Boston Garden, he repeated a version of a pledge he had made dozens of times.[28]

"And while I am talking to you mothers and fathers, I give you one more assurance," he said. "I have said this before, but I shall say it again and again and again. Your boys are not going to be sent into any foreign wars." Only this time he left out the qualifying phrase "unless we are attacked."

President Roosevelt delivered his last campaign speech in Cleveland on November 2, three days before Americans voted. Sam Rosenman called it FDR's best. The text covered all his accomplishments, his vision for America, his disdain for his opponents, and his belief in democracy. Facing the most aggressive challenge in his political career, he rose to the moment.

"The surge of events abroad has made some few doubters among us ask: Is this the end of a story that has been told?" Franklin Roosevelt asked. "Is the book of democracy now to be closed and placed away upon the dusty shelves of time?"

The audience shouted "NO!" almost in unison.[29]

"My answer is this: All we have known of the glories of democracy—its freedom, its efficiency as a mode of living, its ability to meet the aspirations of the common man—all these are merely an introduction to the greater story of a more glorious future," he continued. "We Americans of today—all of us—we are characters in this living book of democracy. But we are also its author. It falls upon us now to say whether the chapters that are to come will tell a story of retreat or a story of continued advance. I believe that the American people will say: 'Forward!'"

Roosevelt's voice was strong and confident, his delivery filled with gusto and humor.[30] His rhythm and cadence were driving his message forward, constructing a roadmap for the future. He promised that Americans would keep their freedoms and set the stage for the historic State of the Union speech he was to deliver in a little over two months.

"But we have learned that freedom in itself is not enough," he said. "Freedom of speech is of no use to a man who has nothing to say. Freedom of worship is of no use to a man who has lost his God. Democracy, to be dynamic, must provide for its citizens opportunity as well as freedom. We of this generation have seen a rebirth of dynamic democracy in America in these past few years. The American people have faced with courage the most severe problems of all of our modern history."

As he neared his finale, he seemed to gain physical stature at the podium. The audience was enthralled, and he rewarded that rapture with a quintessentially Roosevelt conclusion: "There is a great storm raging now, a storm that makes things harder for the world. And that storm, which did not start in this land of ours, is the true reason that I would like to stick by these people of ours until we reach the clear, sure footing ahead. We will make it—we will make it before the next term is over. We will make it; and the world, we hope, will make it, too."

That expression of confidence while acknowledging the enormous challenges ahead was a hallmark of Franklin Roosevelt's political speeches—from the most intimate fireside chats to the bellowing belligerence of a campaign rally before 50,000 people.[31]

Roosevelt's robust response to the Republican's blistering attacks that he wanted to become a dictator and was violating the two-term limit established by George Washington himself, had Biblical overtones of Noah saving his tribe—"There is a great storm raging now . . . and that storm . . . is the true reason that I would like to stick by these people of ours until we reach the clear, sure footing ahead."

Were his words compelling enough to move "these people of ours" to stick with him hoping for that sure future footing? Like Noah, he had preached to the public about the dangers ahead, despite condemnation and scorn. He had taken on the burden of building an ark of military preparedness and determined allies. He had foreseen the great flood of violence and tyranny bearing down, and he had devised a plan to reach the clear sure footing of a peaceful postwar world. Now he had to endure the torture of waiting to see if he had convinced the people to follow his lead.

Thirty years later, FDR's eldest son James wrote about a private conversation right before the election.[32] James asked his father about "the dishonesty of his stand on the war." FDR's reply is telling: "Jimmy, I knew we were going to war. . . . I had to delay until there was no way out of it. I knew we were woefully unprepared for war, and I had to begin a buildup for what was coming. But I couldn't come out and say a war was coming because the people would have panicked and turned from me. I had to educate the people to the inevitable, gradually, step by step, laying the groundwork for programs which would allow us to prepare for the war that was drawing us into it. If I don't say I hate war, then people are going to think I don't hate war! . . . Sometimes you have to deny your political opposition the paint they need to present the public the picture of you they want to show. You can't feed your enemies ammunition.

"I would have loved to have said that as president I was in a position to know what was happening in the world . . . and I can see we are going to have to go to war sooner or later with the fascist forces. But I couldn't say that because the public and congressmen didn't want to hear it, and so wouldn't have believed it and would have turned on me. So, you play the game the way it has been played over the years, and you play to win."

Springwood, the home of Sara Roosevelt in Hyde Park, NY, 1941.

8

A NIGHT TO REMEMBER

HYDE PARK, NEW YORK—NOVEMBER 1940

Franklin Roosevelt arrived at Hyde Park Town Hall with his mother Sara, Eleanor, and Missy LeHand shortly after noon on Election Day 1940. As the president was entering the polling place, a group of reporters and photographers in the balcony above called out to him.

"Mr. President, can you look up here at us?"

"All you're going to get is my bald spot!" the president exclaimed. "I don't think the election officials should allow that."[1]

Holding on to Eleanor's arm, steel braces cinched tightly around his legs, FDR laboriously made his way into the voting booth, and spent just over a minute behind the worn green curtain. When he emerged, he instructed an election worker, "Give me a report as soon as you can."

On the sidewalk outside a group of locals had gathered to see their most famous neighbor. The newshounds were there as well.

"Can you wave at the crowd?" a photographer called out.

"Oh no, I gave that up years ago. I only wave at trees that have leaves on them. Besides . . ." he said, laughing, "I have a crick in my neck." FDR did however wave at the crowd with his lucky fedora as Eleanor and Missy were helping him into the car. The group headed back to Sara's home, Springwood, where the rest of his party waited.

The president and his entourage had arrived the day before, and Roosevelt enjoyed a grand tour of nearby towns including Kingston, Beacon, and Newburgh. This part of the Hudson Valley was reliably Republican, but party aside, locals took immense pride in their native boy. It was a sentimental journey for FDR; he had traveled this course the day before each election he was on a ballot, back to 1910. Roosevelt made a point of visiting the counties represented in Congress by Hamilton Fish III, and gave short, amusing talks from the back seat of his car. At each stop on this trip, he admitted he might be making the rounds a final time.

"As you know, obviously, this will be the last time I come as a candidate on this kind of trip."

"No!" the crowd shouted.

"I hope the newspapermen will note the fact that this is the biggest crowd that has ever turned out in any of my trips!"[2]

The main living room at Springwood is a large, beautiful space, its dark wooden walls decorated with a remarkable collection of rare books, paintings of famous naval battles, and museum-quality Chinese ceramics. A portrait of Franklin's father James hung above the sizeable fireplace at one end of the room, his grandfather's likeness above the hearth at the other end. A table had been set up and FDR, Hopkins, Pa Watson, and Ross McIntire settled down to pass the time with a friendly game of poker. Eleanor went to Val Kill, her home up a hill about a mile from the Big House, as the family called Springwood.

As evening settled in everyone except the president and his mother went up to Val Kill for an informal dinner of creamed chicken and rice. Eleanor was not a great cook but the beautiful grounds surrounding her home and her cozy rustic retreat made everyone feel comfortable. People listened to the early returns on the radio, and then they went back to the Big House. They found FDR already at the dining room table tabulating votes.[3] This was a tradition with him. He loosened his tie, discarded his jacket, and wielded a pencil with the skill of a surgeon.

In the small smoking room off the kitchen, UPI, AP, and INS teletype machines were clacking away with the latest news. The president's two youngest sons, Franklin Jr., and John, joined him along with Missy. Harry Hopkins would wander in and out, until he retreated upstairs to his bedroom to rest. Sara and her friends chatted and knitted in the little room off the main hall known as "the snuggery." The rest of the gang—Pa Watson, Doc McIntire, Sam Rosenman, Henry Morgenthau, and various friends and family members—clustered around radios in the main living room.

Early returns unexpectedly favored Willkie—Roosevelt's great fear had been that the relentless campaign of lies against him would push voters into the Republican's camp. Eleanor moved gracefully from room to room, delivering snacks and tidbits of news. She never showed her true feelings, that she dreaded another four years in the White House fishbowl. By 11:00 P.M. the tide had shifted, it was becoming clear that Roosevelt had won a third term. By midnight, locals had assembled in front of Springwood, carrying torches and signs that read "Safe on Third" and "Keep the Fireside Chats burning." A local band played "The Old Grey Mare" and the president and his family made their way onto the front porch to greet them and say thanks.[4]

"One of the things that makes me very happy about this thing is the fact that we have won a very great victory in these three counties of

Dutchess, Putnam, and Orange!" Roosevelt declared delightedly. "Even though our present congressman may have been reelected by a very small majority, we are all proud of the splendid fight his opponent has made." This was the first time FDR had won his home district of Dutchess County in a presidential election.

"My heart has always been here," he said. "It always will be. Thanks ever so much and I am going to be back here, as you know, just as much as the government of the United States will let me."

FDR triumphed by his smallest margin yet—54.7 percent of the popular vote versus Wendell Willkie's 44.8 percent. He had won an unprecedented third term at an unparalleled moment in history. The campaign of 1940 illustrates Roosevelt's mastery of the language of persuasion and his ability to read human emotion. FDR targeted every word he spoke at a particular listener, every phrase either a reminder of progress made, a condemnation of opponents' hypocrisy, or an alarm about dangers facing America. The people's appreciation for the president's success in ending the depression were unlikely to carry over into his foreign policy. Roosevelt knew the great task facing him was almost impossible. He needed to change the minds of a majority of Americans, help them see their better angels and come to the aid of the millions suffering under the boot heels of Adolf Hitler and his Nazi minions. Returning to the White House after his historic victory, the president was now the last great hope of the free world.

WASHINGTON, D.C.

As the open-air Packard was pulling out of Union Station, Franklin Roosevelt looked at Eleanor, smiled, and said, "Isn't this just *grand*, Babs!" She nodded in reluctant agreement, resigned to four more years as First Lady. Vice president elect Henry Wallace, sitting next to the president, looked out to see 25,000 people lining the street, waving and cheering.

The sight was an extraordinary show of love and support for the president, whose unprecedented reelection to a third term energized local residents.

Despite his exhaustion FDR reveled in the adulation. The presidential limousine drove out into the plaza and stopped at a cluster of microphones wired to loudspeakers. Putting his arm around Wallace, Roosevelt smiled and leaned into the mics.

"My old friends of Washington, this means a great deal to me, Mrs. Roosevelt, and Mr. and Mrs. Wallace, because it isn't as if we are new to Washington. Your turning out this way means that we get along together pretty well!"[5]

The crowd cheered and Franklin beamed his famous smile, while Mrs. Roosevelt and the Wallaces sat, silent spectators to a truly historic moment. "You all know how very much we like farm life, but in all the cities in the world we would rather live in Washington than anyplace else," he said. The crowd cheered again and pushed into restraining lines the Metropolitan Police Department had set up. "Thank you all from the bottom of our hearts. We are glad of the results from two days ago, and of the prospect of staying here just a little longer. Thank you again!"

Waving, President Roosevelt and his companions drove out of the plaza, headed toward the White House. Nearly 200,000 people lined the mile-long route between Union Station and 1600 Pennsylvania Avenue NW, a crawl that took twenty minutes as the exultant but tired president basked in his fans' enthusiasm.

The following day, at 12:10 P.M., the door to the executive office in the White House was flung open and more than a hundred reporters rushed into the room. The president's first post-election press conference began with a buzz of excitement.

Earl Godwin, the avuncular morning radio newscaster, called out, "Catch some sleep?"

"I got a load of it; I'm going to catch up some more next week," FDR said. "I need a lot more. Don't you need some more? You do have the worst hours of anybody I've heard of."[6]

"I know it. All night long on the New York thing. That was tough."

The press secretary called out "All in!" to let the president know that the journalistic horde was fully assembled. The reporters asked a miscellany of questions and toward the end of the colloquy one, referring to Churchill's order for 12,000 planes, asked, "Is there any movement along that line now?"

Roosevelt shifted in his chair and leaned back, as he often did when about to veer off onto a topic he wanted to talk about.

"I will tell you, there is one thing which you might as well print," he began. "I think it is all right. I am very often called 'The rule of thumb man.' Quite a long while ago, about three weeks, four weeks ago, there came a question about munitions of various kinds for Canada and Great Britain, as they came off the line, where we both needed the same thing. And I laid down a rule of thumb, which is only a general rule and, of course, is absolutely subject to exceptions. And the rule is a 50-50 rule. In other words, we take half; they take half."

The reporter followed up. "Does that apply to the large bombing planes, the Flying Fortresses?" he asked. "Would it apply to planes that are now coming off the lines?"

The other reporters grew still, knowing this was a sensitive topic on which the president disagreed with Army Chief of Staff General George Marshall and Secretary of War Henry Stimson.

"Yes and no," Roosevelt said. "In other words, we might need more than the fifty per cent for a while, or there might be some article that we needed less than fifty per cent for the next few months. But, as I say, it is only a rule of thumb, subject to many exceptions in the case of an individual article."[7]

Secure in his new term, the president could begin to use his office, and his persuasive voice, to shift public opinion to support Great Britain and embrace the idea of supplying Churchill the weapons he needed, even if congressional opposition persisted.

The day after the election the British prime minister sent FDR a congratulatory cable. "I did not think it right for me as a foreigner to express my opinion upon American politics while the election was on, but now I feel you will not mind my saying that I prayed for your success and that I am truly thankful for it," Churchill wrote, describing his fear of "a protracted and broadening war . . . that will be remembered as long as the English language is spoken in any quarter of the globe."[8]

Churchill knew that Britain's only hope for survival was American support and eventual entry into the war. Using all his skill in crafting a message that found the elusive line between sycophancy and partnership, he concluded with a vow: "The people of the United States have once again cast these great burdens upon you, I must avow my sure faith that the lights by which we steer will bring us all safely to anchor."

Franklin Roosevelt did not reply. No longer concerned about reelection, FDR still had to live within the straitjacket of the Neutrality Law "cash and carry" mandate on arms sales—a grave worry for a British Empire whose treasury was nearly depleted.

LONDON

The small elevator reeked of cigar smoke as Chief Inspector Thompson gently placed the steel helmet on Winston Churchill's head. Wearing his Royal Air Force greatcoat over his grey-blue jumpsuit, Churchill muttered "damn Huns." The elevator doors opened on the top floor of Number 10 Annex, in the Board of Trade Building. Churchill burst forward like a tiger freed from a cage. He could hear the banshee cry of air raid sirens as he made his way up the winding staircase to the roof. He flung a door open and stepped out as a massive explosion nearby shook the building.[9]

"I'm sorry to take you into danger, Thompson," the prime minister said as the two approached the roof's edge. "I would not do it, only I know how much you like it."

"I am not at all sure about that, sir," Thompson said. "But what I am concerned about is your safety. I do think that you should stop going on the roof and risking your life unnecessarily!"

Blowing out a puff of cigar smoke, Churchill replied gruffly. "When my time is due it will come," he said.[10]

England's situation was dire. Fleets of Luftwaffe raiders had been bombing London nightly for months, inflicting massive damage and loss of life. On November 14, Coventry, a hundred miles northwest, was swarmed by five hundred German bombers whose crews dropped explosive and incendiary payloads, destroying vast swathes of that city. A firestorm ravaged Coventry Cathedral, reducing that fourteenth-century Gothic masterpiece to flaming rubble. Five hundred and sixty-eight civilians were killed and many more wounded.[11]

Prime Minister Churchill's gravest concern, however, came not from above but below. Packs of the Kriegsmarine's sleek, sinister grey wolves prowled the cold dark waters of the North Atlantic, seeking prey—merchant ships bound for Great Britain bearing desperately needed food and military supplies. In a single week, U-boat torpedoes sent more than 160,000 tons of shipping to the bottom of the sea. On the day Franklin Roosevelt was reelected president the 500th ship was lost.

Even more distressing to the beleaguered prime minister was the severe budgetary crisis squeezing his nation. England, at war for more than a year, had exhausted its cash reserves. Knowing he soon would not be able to pay for the weapons Roosevelt was providing, Churchill summoned his Ambassador to the United States, Lord Lothian, to assist him in drafting a letter to the president outlining the situation. They worked in secret, carefully constructing a powerful plea for aid. Standing in the underground Cabinet Room facing his closest advisors, Churchill explained the tightrope his message had to walk.

"If the picture is painted too darkly, elements in the United States would say that it was useless to help us, for such help would be wasted and thrown away," he said. "If too bright a picture was painted, then there might be a tendency to withhold assistance."[12]

His war ministers approved the letter.

Lord Lothian flew to the United States aboard an Atlantic Clipper, landing at LaGuardia Airport on November 23. The press was there to greet him. Normally a most diplomatic speaker, Lord Lothian thanked the president for his pledge of "50-50" and warned there was a tough year ahead. He described England's financial situation as "becoming urgent." Newspapers quoted him as saying, "Well boys, Britain's broke, it's your money we want."[13]

Washington, D.C.

Two days later Secret Service agents escorted Lord Lothian to the waiting room outside the President's office.[14] Missy LeHand greeted him and commented that he had certainly stepped in it. At 2:00 P.M. she walked into Roosevelt's office to tell him the ambassador had arrived. As Missy led Lothian into the office, he and FDR both knew they were in for a difficult conversation. The two had met during World War I and were good friends. Lothian had been instrumental in securing the "Destroyers for Bases" deal. But Lothian's comments at the airport had created a furor, outraging Treasury Secretary Henry Morgenthau, who exploded that Lothian's jabber "did not help one damn bit!" Isolationists in Congress raised alarms about allowing Britain to order military supplies while its finances were murky.[15]

After a tension filled interval, the door to the Oval Office opened, Lord Lothian strode out and headed straight for a gaggle of reporters in the hallway, leaving his hat behind.[16]

"What did you and the president talk about?" a reporter called out. "Did you ask for money?"

"The President and I never mentioned finances," Lothian said. "The President wanted to know about the war and what is going on in England. I told him all I know."

"Any more details?" the reporter pressed.

"My discussion on conditions was optimistic, providing we can get some more help from you," the ambassador said. "The President made no promises of any sort. However, ships and planes are high on our list of needed material."[17]

"Does your definition of ships include warships?"

"I used the word 'ships.'"

And with that Lord Lothian retrieved his hat and left the White House.

The German press had a field day, calling Lothian's meeting with the president "the cry for help of a beggar."[18] The jibe was not far from the truth.

The Royal Navy, in dire straits, needed yet more destroyers and transports to keep food and matériel flowing across the Atlantic. Churchill was short on fighter planes and bombers to counter the relentless Luftwaffe's nighttime raids.

At a press conference the day after FDR and Lord Lothian met, a reporter directly asked the implicit question "Did the British Ambassador present any specific requests for additional help?"[19]

Leaning back into his most genial self and lifting his chin, the president referenced one of his favorite childhood poems, Lewis Carroll's "The Walrus and the Carpenter."

"I am sorry, I will have to disappoint quite a number of papers," he said. "Nothing was mentioned in that regard at all, not one single thing—ships or sealing wax or anything else."

Laughter filled the room as once again Roosevelt deftly sidestepped a query he did not want to answer. For the president, the time had not come to talk of many things, at least not yet.

Behind the scenes at the White House, pressure was intensifying. Military and treasury officials were feverishly analyzing British financial data but coming up with no solution to the payment problem. The law was punitively specific: Britain had to pay for any military equipment from the United States. That harsh equation was the backdrop as the president and his small band of advisors set out December 2 to cruise the Caribbean aboard the cruiser USS *Tuscaloosa*, visiting locales being considered for naval bases and enjoying a much-needed vacation from the cold, grey streets of Washington, D.C.

President Franklin D. Roosevelt fishing from the USS Tuscaloosa
as it passes through Mona Passage en route to the Bahamas.

9

THE CRUISE THAT LAUNCHED
A THOUSAND SHIPS

FLORIDA—DECEMBER 1940

The wood-paneled interior of the ornately decorated observation room in the president's Pullman car smelled of cigarettes and sea air. Raised shades and open windows admitted passing views of the Florida coast and a bright blue sky on a warm December morning.[1] Franklin Roosevelt sat in a comfortable chair at one end of the cabin and pulled the cigarette holder from his mouth. "OK Pa, let 'em in," he said with a smile. "It's noon."

General "Pa" Watson opened the railcar's forward door. A gang of reporters and photographers flowed into the room, gently elbowing one another as each tried to gain the best view of the president. They sur-rounded Roosevelt in a friendly and familiar manner.

"Couldn't you tell us where you are going?"

Roosevelt took a drag on his cigarette and smiled. "I wish I knew," he said. "Well, I'll tell you. The last time we started I told you about some phony islands that were on the map. This time I won't deceive you at all. We are going to Christmas Island to buy Christmas cards, then we are going on to Easter Island to buy Easter eggs."

"Are you going to arrive there on Christmas Day?"

"We have to get there before then to get the cards off."

The joking was a familiar ritual with the newshounds who dogged him. They knew that only a select few pool reporters would be accompanying him on his planned cruise around the Caribbean to visit the British naval bases he had obtained in exchange for destroyers. Roosevelt raised his chin. "I wish we could have arranged it so that outside of the Three Musketeers the rest could have gone along to justify expenses at Miami," he said.

His literary reference was to Thomas Reynolds of the United Press, president of the White House Correspondents Association, George Durno of the International News Service, and Douglas Cornell of Asso-ciated Press. They would be supplying their employers and the rest of the White House press corps pool reports chronicling the president's journey.

A reporter shouted, "Is the dog going aboard?" referring to Roosevelt's newly acquired Scottish Terrier Fala.

"Yes, and he is very good, too," FDR said. "We had him on the *Potomac* the other day and he was just as good as gold. The chief trouble was to keep the crew from feeding him!"

"You have the same trouble with Pa Watson, don't you?"

The room rang with laughter at the presidential advisor's expense. Pa stood off in a corner of the rolling press room, smiled, happy to play the foil for the president's adept handling of the press. He moved forward and ushered the reporters from the observation car and across the platform connecting to the next car.

The presidential train pulled into the Seaborne Air Line Railroad station near downtown Miami at 1:00 P.M. on the mark.[2] Naval aide Captain Daniel Callaghan pushed the president in his wheelchair to the back of the train, where a special lift lowered the seated president to the ground. Callaghan carefully lifted Franklin into the back seat of the open top limousine. As the car made its way toward Municipal Pier No. 3, Roosevelt waved to crowds lining his route. Warm winter sunshine bathed the Miami streets, now filled with happy throngs, including clusters of schoolchildren dismissed early to welcome the president. People cheered and applauded as the motorcade passed, a pleased FDR beaming in the back seat.[3]

Hundreds of sailors in dress whites lined the railings of the *Tuscaloosa* as the president pulled up alongside the 588-foot *New Orleans*–class cruiser. Once Watson and Callaghan had helped lock Roosevelt's leg braces, Secret Service agents got him to his feet and out of the automobile. Gripping Watson's arm to maintain his balance, FDR moved slowly toward a specially constructed gangplank with railings on both sides, leaning from one side to the other in his well-practiced trademark gait. The president stopped to shake hands with the warship's officers. Besides Watson and Callaghan, FDR's party included Harry Hopkins and Rear Admiral Ross McIntire, the president's physician.[4]

More than a thousand people stood shoulder to shoulder on the pier as the *Tuscaloosa* prepared to cast off. Wearing a suit and tie and his famous fedora, Roosevelt leaned against the railing and waved to well-wishers. Newsreel camera operators and press photographers recorded the ship's departure for the open sea. This was FDR's third cruise aboard *Tuscaloosa*, now customized for him with the installation of an elevator that let him move between decks in his wheelchair. Other modifications included ramps, widened doorways, and a screened veranda affording him privacy on deck.

As *Tuscaloosa* was clearing the harbor at 2:14 P.M. the ship's captain ordered a 21-gun salute. Two escort destroyers assumed defensive anti-submarine positions, and *Tuscaloosa* set a course for Guantanamo Bay, Cuba, at 27.5 knots—full speed ahead.[5]

Despite the British payment crisis, FDR eased into floating vacation mode, fishing and sunbathing during the day, poker, movies, and drinking at night. Harry Hopkins described this routine as "refueling."[6]

Tuscaloosa arrived off the south coast of Cuba at 1:15 P.M. December 4 and was soon moving slowly five hundred yards offshore. Almost immediately FDR and companions had their poles out and were trolling from the rear deck. Ross McIntire hooked a four-pound barracuda, taking the daily fishing derby prize with what may have been the only fish ever caught off so large a ship while that vessel was underway. At 3:30 P.M. the ship docked at Guantanamo Bay Naval Station in berth twenty-five.[7]

Under clear skies and amid delightfully warm weather, the travelers adopted a relaxing routine. Over several days, they visited Jamaica, Beata Island, St. Lucia, and Martinique, exploring harbors that were candidates for conversion into naval bases, meeting with local leaders, and whenever possible fishing from *Tuscaloosa*'s motorized whaleboats.

On December 7, Prime Minister Churchill finished the final text of the letter he and Lord Lothian had been drafting, an impassioned 4,000-word plea to the president explaining in grim detail the global military situation and describing England's empty coffers. Churchill called the missive "one of the most important of my life."[8]

On the morning of December 9, *Tuscaloosa* was anchored in seven fathoms of water in St. John Harbor off Antigua.[9] Navy patrol seaplane 54-P-1 came in low along the ship's port side to land perfectly a hundred yards away.[10] Sailors in a whaleboat shuttled to the seaplane and picked up a mail pouch containing reports the president needed to sign, along with top secret military documents. As Roosevelt, Watson, and Hopkins sorted the pouch's contents, FDR picked out a thick envelope marked as coming from Prime Minister Churchill. The president and Hopkins exchanged knowing looks. FDR opened the envelope to find Churchill's brutally honest and exceptionally persuasive letter.

"The moment approaches when we shall no longer be able to pay cash for shipping and supplies," Winston wrote. "I believe you will agree that it would be wrong in principle and mutually disadvantageous in effect if at the height of this struggle Great Britain were to be divested of all saleable assets, so that after the victory was won with our blood, civilization saved, and the time gained for the United States to be fully armed against all eventualities, we should stand stripped to the bone."[11]

In his seven months as prime minister Churchill had inspired the King's subjects and free people worldwide with his stubborn bravery and eloquent oratory. But his letter's candid expression of desperation and his unblinking admission of his Empire's vulnerability affected Roosevelt deeply.

Sitting on the cruiser's deck in the Caribbean sun, Roosevelt read and reread the letter, contemplating his next move. He held no meetings with advisors nor read any briefing books, but simply sat staring into the horizon for extended periods.[12] Then he would suddenly insist on fishing or taking in a topside boxing match between young sailors as a part of his "refueling." All the while his mind was racing, thinking, plotting—seeking a solution to an impossible dilemma.

That evening Roosevelt and his guests dined in the wardroom mess with the ship's officers. After dinner Callaghan wheeled FDR to the main deck to join the crew for a screening of the recent screwball comedy *I Love You Again*, starring Myrna Loy and William Powell. The evening's show began with a newsreel entitled "Hobby Lobby" and featuring Mrs. Roosevelt extolling the virtues of hobbies.[13]

That evening, back in Washington, Lord Lothian was in the midst of a vicious kidney infection; a convert to Christian Science, he refused medical treatment. Two days later he died.

Tuscaloosa was cruising through the British West Indies when Roosevelt learned of Lothian's death by way of an urgent radio dispatch sent by Secretary of State Cordell Hull. The president immediately drafted a message of condolence to King George VI.[14]

"I am shocked beyond measure to hear of the sudden passing of my old friend and your Ambassador, the Marquis of Lothian," Roosevelt wrote. "Through nearly a quarter of a century we had come to understand and trust each other. I am very certain that if he had been allowed by Providence to leave us a last message, he would have told us that the greatest of all efforts to retain democracy in the world must and will succeed."

Lothian's death lent an intensely personal dimension to the contents of Churchill's letter. Lothian had provided a critical connection between the president and the prime minister, who had not yet met face to face as the leaders of their countries.

The following day Roosevelt received His Royal Highness, the Duke of Windsor, Governor of the Bahamas. The duke, pushed out of England after his 1936 abdication, was a Nazi sympathizer. On the cruiser's communication deck over a buffet lunch of mushroom soup, fruit salad, and kingfish, Windsor told FDR of England's desperate need for more destroyers, and the men discussed possible locations for a naval base in the Bahamas.[15]

After lunch, the duke agreed to speak to the reporters, and the president held his first press conference with the Three Musketeers since leaving Miami.

Tom Reynolds of United Press brought up military cooperation.

"Your highness, I suppose since you became Governor of the Bahamas you have given some thought to the question of mutual defense of the islands?"[16]

"We have not organized any defense," Windsor said. "There are no British defenses here. In what way do you mean?"

"Mutual defense."

"Surely. You know about how you would use your bases here in connection with our problem at the present time. Whatever the President wants we will give him the best we have."

Saying he hoped the British would emulate Roosevelt's Civilian Conservation Corps in the Bahamas to provide jobs for the local unemployed young men, he excused himself. Leaving the reporters puzzled, the Duke of Windsor departed the *Tuscaloosa* to board a seaplane bound for Miami.

Roosevelt took center stage, launching into a discussion of fishing.

"I went out this morning and caught a little yellow fish that long," he said, holding his hands a few inches apart. "General Watson caught a fish and Harry Hopkins caught a fish that I think is the record fish of the trip!" The Three Musketeers pressed him.

"After your tour here of the four bases, I think the country would be very interested in having any report or reaction you might have."[17]

Roosevelt explained the importance of protecting the Panama Canal. When George Durno produced a nautical map of the Caribbean, the president pointed out the significance of Bermuda, the Bahamas, and Puerto Rico to defending the North American coast. His deep knowledge of various harbors and navy requirements impressed the reporters, as did his grasp of most Caribbean islands' dismal economies. Roosevelt concluded by telling his interlocutors that the next afternoon the *Tuscaloosa* would be docking at the Charleston, South Carolina navy yard from which he would be heading to Warm Springs, Georgia, before returning to Washington.

It is impossible to know exactly how Franklin Roosevelt's mind worked. He was always operating on multiple levels. He had long since learned to maintain an amiable carapace of charm, confidence, and good humor. But he also had an inner dimension, darker, more closed and secretive. This duality allowed him to compartmentalize his many stressors and inner demons, which he kept hidden. One such compartment had undoubtedly been working nonstop on how to finesse the Neutrality Act's strictures and help Churchill. Finally, something clicked. The inspiration might have been his inspections of naval bases he had obtained in exchange for that flotilla of obsolete destroyers, or a flash of awareness arriving as he was fishing with his close friends, or even Lord Lothian's death. But right around this time the president had a conversation with Harry Hopkins that marked the emergence of a brilliant, history-changing idea embodied in two words: Lend-Lease.

"I didn't know for quite a while what he was thinking about, if anything," Hopkins later recalled. "I began to get the idea that he was refueling, the way he so often does when he seems to be resting and carefree. So, I didn't ask him any questions. Then, one evening, he suddenly came out with it, the whole program. He didn't seem to have any clear idea how it could be done legally. But there wasn't a doubt in his mind that he'd find a way to do it."[18]

President Roosevelt speaking at a campaign stop at the entrance to Midtown Tunnel, Oct. 28, 1940.

10

WORDS THAT CHANGED THE WORLD

WASHINGTON, D.C.—DECEMBER 1940

Like a chess master planning twenty moves ahead, FDR returned to Washington rested and ready to rescue his beleaguered British compatriot. Thus began a series of pronouncements, genuinely extraordinary even for Franklin Roosevelt. The sequence started with a press conference, expanded to a fireside chat and then the State of the Union, and finally his third inaugural address, all in just thirty-four days. Roosevelt took command of the English language, wielding words as weapons to save democracy. These four events underpinned the grand alliance that went on to win World War II and guide the post-war world to a lasting peace. FDR's first move was subtle, like a chess player moving a pawn forward on an open board.

Washington, D.C., was hunkering down against gale force winds as day broke on December 17, 1940. In the 30° chill, the capital's workers wrapped scarfs tightly against the battering gusts. At midday the Washington *Evening Star*'s front page reported that Britain would be unable to buy more weapons unless Congress approved additional financial aid.

At 4:00 P.M., President Roosevelt was in the Oval Office, seated behind his large desk, surrounded by his favorite naval paintings and ship models. On his desk was a miniature menagerie of donkeys and elephants along with mementos of his political career. Outwardly relaxed, he signaled to his press secretary to admit the reporters jostling on the other side of the door. Looking "tanned, exuberant, and jaunty," the president began innocently.[1]

"I don't think there is any particular news, except possibly one thing that I think might be worth my talking about," he said.

The president then lectured the reporters about why America should help Britain. Weapons in the hands of English soldiers were more effective than in storage, he explained, adding that factories producing war matériel were key to America's economy.

"And the more we increase those facilities—factories, shipbuilding ways, munition plants, et cetera, and so on—the stronger American national defense is," he continued.

To make his point he offered a folksy analogy. "What I am trying to do is eliminate the dollar sign," he said. "Get rid of the foolish old dollar sign."[2] The experienced reporters in the room perked up, knowing something was coming.

"Suppose my neighbor's home catches fire, and I have got a length of garden hose four or five hundred feet away . . . [if] he can take my garden hose and connect it up with his hydrant, I may help him to put out his fire," FDR said. "Now, what do I do? I don't say to him, neighbor, my garden hose cost me \$15, you have got to pay me \$15 for it. What is the transaction that goes on? I don't want \$15—I want my garden hose back after the fire is over."

Brilliant. Simple. Generous. Persuasive. Something every person could understand and agree with. Who *wouldn't* lend a hose to a neighbor whose house was on fire? He explained that if the hose were damaged, the borrower would replace it.

"In other words, if you lend certain munitions and get the munitions back at the end of the war, if they are intact, haven't been hurt—you are all right," the president said. "If they have been damaged or have deteriorated or have been lost completely, it seems to me you come out pretty well if you have them replaced by the fellow to whom you have lent them."

The reporters pressed him on details of the process and Congress and the Neutrality Act. James L. Wright of the Buffalo *Evening News* asked whether the arrangement described was more or less likely to get the United States into the war. Like a grandmaster, Roosevelt moved his king to safety, easily avoiding knotty queries. Roosevelt cautioned his audience that what he was saying was on what he called "background," meaning they could not attribute his remarks to him. He was moving his pieces into position on the chessboard. The front page of the next day's *New York Times* read ROOSEVELT WOULD LEND ARMS TO BRITAIN.

Twelve days later, on Sunday, December 29, a black limousine pulled up at the main entrance to the White House. Out stepped Hollywood royalty, the glamourous Carole Lombard and Clark Gable, her dashing husband. Mrs. Roosevelt greeted the movie stars and escorted them into the Diplomatic Reception Room.[3] Along the curved wall at the back, radio technicians sat at small tables covered with equipment. Lights, newsreel cameras, and cables were everywhere in the room, crowded with Washington's most powerful people, including the secretaries of State, War, Navy, Treasury, and Agriculture and the U.S. Attorney General. Mrs. Roosevelt and her celebrity guests sat in the front row before a large desk holding an array of microphones emblazoned with the alphabet soup of network names: CBS, NBC, MBS.

From Maine to San Diego, people pulled up chairs and sat close to their radios. Americans knew this was going to be a significant speech, one that would set the nation's course for years. Every network carried that night's broadcast, heard by 50 to 80 million domestic listeners and millions more abroad.[4]

At 9:25 p.m. President Roosevelt entered the room in his wheelchair, waving at his friends and guests. He was lifted into the chair behind the desk. Those present knew this was a historic moment, and Roosevelt delivered as only he could. He spoke not just to the American people but to the entire world, especially Winston Churchill and Adolf Hitler. His words still reverberate. Wearing a black dinner jacket and black bow tie, he began solemnly. "This is not a fireside chat on war," he said. "It is a talk on National Security."[5] At that very moment German planes were bombing London.

"If Great Britain goes down, the Axis powers will control the continents of Europe, Asia, Africa, Australia, and the high seas—and they will be in a position to bring enormous military and naval resources against this hemisphere," Franklin Roosevelt told his global audience. "It is no exaggeration to say that all of us, in all the Americas, would be living at the point of a gun—a gun loaded with explosive bullets, economic as well as military. There can be no appeasement with ruthlessness. There can be no reasoning with an incendiary bomb."

The statement "there can be no reasoning with an incendiary bomb" is simultaneously cold hard logic, and emotionally searing. British newspapers had been reporting on infernos ignited there by German incendiaries, describing the stench of flesh burning and the charred remains of women and children. Photographs documenting the aftermath of German attacks appeared nearly every day, etching themselves into the psyche of even the most ardent isolationist. Famed CBS radio reporter Edward R. Murrow had been describing the horror of the nightly bombings for months during his "This . . . is London" broadcasts. During one raid he went into an underground shelter and in his deep baritone voice said "I saw a man laboriously copying names in a ledger, the list of firemen killed in action during the past month. There were about one hundred names."[6] Roosevelt's words skillfully evoked the horror of Hitler's plans.

"The Nazi masters of Germany have made it clear that they intend not only to dominate all life and thought in their own country, but also to enslave the whole of Europe, and then to use the resources of Europe to dominate the rest of the world," FDR said. "In a military sense Great Britain and the British Empire are today the spearhead of resistance to world conquest. And they are putting up a fight which will live forever in the story of human gallantry." This juxtaposition of enslavement against heroic gallantry and resistance poised listeners for his denouement, which put into motion changes in American foreign policy that continue to this day.

A stern expression on his face, a firm conviction in his voice, Roosevelt declared, "We must be the great arsenal of democracy. For us, this is an emergency as serious as war itself. We must apply ourselves to our task with the same resolution, the same sense of urgency, the same spirit of patriotism and sacrifice as we would show were we at war."

"We must be the great arsenal of democracy." This is the centerpiece of FDR's long-term strategy, a clear path forward that builds on American industrial might without drawing on the nation's most precious resource—young lives. Having won reelection, President Roosevelt was no longer reluctant to speak his truth, and, for the first time, he predicted victory for Britain.

"I believe that the Axis powers are not going to win this war. I base that belief on the latest and best of information," he said. "We have no excuse for defeatism. We have every good reason for hope—hope for peace, yes, and hope for the defense of our civilization and for the building of a better civilization in the future. I have the profound conviction that the American people are now determined to put forth a mightier effort than they have ever yet made to increase our production of all the implements of defense, to meet the threat to our democratic faith."[7]

"Arsenal of democracy" came not from FDR or even his talented speechwriters. Jean Monnet, a French diplomat, had spoken the phrase in a conversation weeks before with Supreme Court Justice Felix Frankfurter. Frankfurter urged Monnet to let the president be the first to use it publicly, and the words made their way into an early draft of the speech. The first time he read it, FDR exclaimed, "I love it!"[8]

President Roosevelt's remarks reached an estimated 75 percent of Americans, whether on radio or in newspapers.[9] Telegrams and messages inundated the White House, and press secretary Steve Early claimed messages were running 100 to 1 in favor of the president's speech.[10]

Critics reacted immediately. Democratic Senator Burton Wheeler, a balding, cigar-smoking political insider and leader of the isolationists in Congress, derided the new policy in a radio broadcast the following night. "If we lend or lease war materials today, we will lend or lease American boys tomorrow," Wheeler said. Even so, the *New York Times* reported, Newspapers are Unanimous in their Support of Defense Call.

Assuming the role of the arsenal of world democracy was an aggressive vision for an isolationist America, summoning as it did images of Uncle Sam flexing new militaristic muscles and using the nation's natural resources and manufacturing base to stand up to the fascist forces laying waste to peaceful countries. Those words truly set America on a new course, birthing a military-industrial complex that continues to dominate U.S. foreign policy to this day.

Dwight D. Eisenhower, Supreme Commander of the Allied Expeditionary Force and 34th President of the United States, warned in his 1961 farewell address that "In the councils of government, we must guard against the acquisition of unwarranted influence, whether sought or unsought, by the military-industrial complex. The potential for the disastrous rise of misplaced power exists and will persist. We must never let the weight of this combination endanger our liberties or democratic processes. We should take nothing for granted."[11]

Franklin Roosevelt's pledge and its implementation changed our manufacturing base, our economic policies, our foreign policies, and our self-image. And as he promised, so he delivered. America became the great arsenal of democracy. And eventually the great arsenal of the world. Since WWII's conclusion in 1945, the United States has been the world's number one arms exporter, in 2022 selling more weapons than the next ten countries combined.

No country benefited more from this policy than Great Britain. In his history of World War II, Winston Churchill looked back on 1940 and wrote, "This small and ancient island . . . had proved itself capable of bearing the whole impact and weight of world destiny. Alone, but upborne by every generous heartbeat of mankind, we had defied the tyrant at the height of his triumph."[12]

OVAL OFFICE

Friday, January 3, 1941, was a busy day in Washington, D.C. Returning from its Christmas recess, Congress met in the Capitol to begin its 77th session, teeing up significant issues concerning war and taxation. The president held his first press conference of the new year at the White House. Reporters strolled in at 11:38 A.M. Earl Godwin, leader of the pack with a special reserved seat at the front, was absent.

"Where's the big boy?" Roosevelt asked.

"He decided he better go up to the Hill this morning," said Tom Reynolds of United Press.[13]

"Sit down yourself."

Reynolds sat in Godwin's chair. "Thank you," he replied.

"I think you rate it."

Another reporter piped up, "He's been sitting down all morning!"

The president looked at Reynolds with concern. "Been sitting down all morning?"

"Yes, but I had a hard night!" Reynolds said to a round of laughter as the press secretary called "All in."

Roosevelt announced that he had two topics he wanted to address. He first summarized a new proposal to build shipyards capable of delivering two hundred merchant ships, noting that with so many transports being sunk there would soon be a shortage. The other matter involved personnel.

"I expect next week to send to the senate a name for the ambassador to Great Britain but in the meantime, I am asking Harry Hopkins to go over as my personal representative for a very short trip to the other side . . . just to maintain personal contact between me and the British government," FDR said. Hopkins had already departed aboard a Yankee Clipper to stand in for the departing Joseph Kennedy, who had resigned over sharp differences with FDR regarding support for England. The president was surreptitiously sending Hopkins to give Winston Churchill a close once-over and decide whether the prime minister was up to the challenge of defeating Hitler. During the considerable time he spent with Churchill as German bombers blitzed London night upon night, Hopkins developed enormous respect for him, seeding what grew into a deep and affectionate friendship with Churchill and his wife Clementine. Hopkins's temporary venture into diplomacy led to one of the most important connections, and friendships, of World War II. But for the moment Roosevelt said nothing of his advisor's secret assignment.

"Will he have any mission to perform?" a reporter asked.

"He's just going over to say, 'How do you do' to a lot of my friends."

Reporters smiled knowingly. There was more to this than the Boss was letting on.

That evening Judge Sam Rosenman arrived at the White House, and after dinner he and the president spent hours honing the text for the State of the Union address FDR was to deliver in three days. Franklin

Roosevelt's verbal strategy to remake America into a nation ready for war was moving toward the endgame.[14]

January 6 began for the president as most days did. Missy LeHand came into his bedroom while he was still in bed, calling out "Morning, FD!" as she handed him mail and newspapers. He had his standard breakfast of eggs, coffee, and toast. Valet Arthur Prettyman helped him dress and shifted him to his wheelchair. From his bedroom he went to the oval office, where at 11:00 A.M. he welcomed Senator Robert Wagner (D-New York) to discuss pending tax legislation.[15]

Shortly after noon the Oval Office began to fill. The small gathering included Eleanor, Norway's Princess Martha and husband Crown Prince Olav, Sam Rosenman and wife, Grace Tully, Missy LeHand, and several Roosevelt family friends. On the front driveway the group broke up as members boarded a convoy of black limousines. The cars turned east onto Pennsylvania Avenue, headed toward the Capitol.

Days earlier, Adolf Hitler had delivered his New Year's Order of the Day to the German armed forces.[16] He thanked his fighting men for their great achievements and reveled in the sweet prospect of victories to come.

"According to the will of the warmongering democrats, and of their capitalist and Jewish allies, this war must be continued," the dictator said. "The representatives of the crumbling world hope that in 1941 it may be perhaps possible to do that which was impossible in the past. We are ready. We find ourselves at the beginning of 1941, armed as never before . . . Soldiers of the National Socialist Armed Forces of Greater Germany, the year 1941 will bring us, on the Western Front, the completion of the greatest victory of our history."

While Hitler was planning for all-out war, some leading Americans were continuing their fervent advocacy on behalf of isolationism. The president's fireside chat had comforted Winston Churchill and the British people, but delivered no weapons—and also enraged legions of America Firsters. Powerful men, now waiting at the Capitol for the President's arrival, were poised to enlist those legions' support as part of their campaign to thwart an impending Roosevelt proposal they regarded as naked warmongering.

Roosevelt was an avid poker player, and he held a strong hand as he prepared to deliver his third inaugural address. So Charles Lindbergh upped the ante, thinking he held a powerful trump card: an old friend who hated FDR—Henry Ford. Besides being one of the richest industrialists in the country, Ford owned multiple businesses in Germany, had also received the Grand Cross of the German Eagle from the Nazis, and once published a virulently antisemitic newspaper, the *Dearborn Independent.*

Clutching his son's arm, Franklin Roosevelt made his way slowly toward the House podium, watched by friend and foe alike. Every inch of the great chamber was filled with expectant faces. Arriving, he stood for a moment, waiting for the assembly to still itself. When the president did speak it was in a low voice, devoid of his usual humor and warmth. The subject was danger.

"I address you, the members of the 77th Congress, at a moment unprecedented in the history of the Union," he said. "I use the word 'unprecedented,' because at no previous time has American security been as seriously threatened from without as it is today."[17]

Step by step, he built a compelling narrative of American military involvements through history, detailed the current threats, and described the massive efforts to rebuild the Army and Navy. The most important immediate concern was the urgency to enhance weapons production.

"To change a whole nation from a basis of peacetime production of implements of peace to a basis of wartime production of implements of war is no small task," he said. "And the greatest difficulty comes at the beginning of the program, when new tools, new plant facilities, new assembly lines, and new shipways must first be constructed before the actual matériel begins to flow steadily and speedily from them."

He stressed Great Britain's existential need for those munitions. Then he explained the proposed supply-chain arrangement that quickly became known as "Lend-Lease" and which sought to solve the Britons' dilemma with what, depending on the beholder's perspective, was either real-world practicality or political and fiscal legerdemain.

"The time is near when they will not be able to pay for them all in ready cash," FDR said. "We cannot, and we will not, tell them that they must surrender, merely because of present inability to pay for the weapons which we know they must have. I do not recommend that we make them a loan of dollars with which to pay for these weapons—a loan to be repaid in dollars. For what we send abroad, we shall be repaid within a reasonable time following the close of hostilities, in similar materials, or, at our option, in other goods of many kinds, which they can produce and which we need."

Murmurs threaded through the audience as isolationists shifted uncomfortably in their seats. Their underlying fear was that, for America, unrestrictedly arming Great Britain inevitably signaled a prelude to direct participation in the war. Subtly addressing these critics, the president encouraged cooperation and derided those who spurned their responsibilities as citizens of the world.

"The best way of dealing with the few slackers or troublemakers in our midst is, first, to shame them by patriotic example, and, if that fails, to use the sovereignty of government to save government," he said.

Then Franklin Roosevelt transcended his familiar litany regarding dictators, war, and oppression. He now spoke with passion on behalf of the pillars of a successful democracy—fair wages, equal opportunity, civil liberties, social security, and medical care. The ideals of the New Deal recast. From the people's pulpit, he began to preach a sermon about divinely conferred freedoms in need of safeguarding against the encroaching forces of darkness:

"In the future days, which we seek to make secure, we look forward to a world founded upon four essential human freedoms. The first is freedom of speech and expression—everywhere in the world. The second is freedom of every person to worship God in his own way—everywhere in the world. The third is freedom from want—which, translated into world terms, means economic understandings which will secure to every nation a healthy peacetime life for its inhabitants—everywhere in the world. The fourth is freedom from fear—which, translated into world terms, means a worldwide reduction of armaments to such a point and in such a thorough fashion that no nation will be in a position to commit an act of physical aggression against any neighbor—anywhere in the world."[18]

Based on the Bill of Rights and expanded to embrace everyone, these words were Roosevelt's alone. During a speechwriting session on the third draft of this speech, the president indicated he had an idea for a "peroration" or summation. At this his collaborators Hopkins, Sherwood, and Rosenman stopped talking and waited. FDR leaned back in his swivel chair and, after a long pause, began speaking in a clear, slow manner. Rosenman later described how "the words seemed now to roll off his tongue as though he had rehearsed them many times to himself."[19]

He unhesitatingly dictated the entire passage, whose final version differed from the original only by a few words. When finished he turned to his accomplices for their reaction. Looking askance at the president and skeptical of FDR's inclusion after the first two freedoms of people "everywhere in the world," Harry Hopkins said, "That covers an awful lot of territory, Mr. President. I don't know how interested Americans are going to be in the people of Java."[20]

"I'm afraid they will have to be some day, Harry," Roosevelt said. "The world is getting so small that even the people in Java are getting to be our neighbors now."

The depth of his feeling for that phrase later impelled Roosevelt to append "everywhere in the world" to all four freedoms in the final pass. When battle-weary soldiers far from home asked why they were fighting and dying in strange lands, the Four Freedoms answered. When religious minorities were enduring the horrors of concentration camps, they placed their hope in the promise of these four freedoms. When world leaders met and plotted the destruction of the Axis and the creation of a new global order, they used these four freedoms as a compass to navigate past differences and defeats. Four simple ideas—freedom of speech and worship, freedom from want and fear—these are conditions that all people sought, but so few had achieved. This maxim, "everywhere in the world" was integral to changing how Americans saw themselves in the world—and how the world could be.

It is rare indeed to be able to trace a direct link between the words of a speech and world-changing events, but in this case that connection is clear. After the war, the United Nations Universal Declaration of Human Rights, championed by Eleanor Roosevelt, echoed those words. Those words have inspired the constitutions of many countries. An annual Four Freedoms Award has been bestowed upon such world leaders as the Dalai Lama, Coretta Scott King, Mikhail Gorbachev, Harry Truman, John Lewis, and Elie Wiesel. The beautiful Four Freedoms Park at the southern point of Roosevelt Island in New York's East River spreads a mere hundred yards from the gleaming tower of the United Nations building alongside FDR Drive. And, of course, four paintings by Norman Rockwell represent the spirit of the four freedoms with a visual style placing them in the rarified company of world-renowned works of art. Franklin Roosevelt's State of the Union address to Congress on January 6, 1941, ranks among the most significant ever given. The following morning's *New York Times* banner headline read:

ROOSEVELT ASKS ALL OUT AID TO DEMOCRACIES;

TO SEND THEM SHIPS, PLANES, TANKS, AND GUNS

PART THREE

FIGHTING FOR THE SOUL OF AMERICA

The Roaring Lion, a portrait of Winston Churchill by Yousuf Karsh, 1941.

11

NEITHER A BORROWER
NOR A LENDER BE

LONDON—JANUARY 1941

I n the British capital, the first week of January 1941 was bitterly
cold, icy blasts of wind making life even more miserable for those
unhoused by relentless nighttime bombing. Coal, food, and wool were
in short supply. But as the prime minister climbed into bed in the early
morning hours of January 7, dressed in his nightshirt, a sidearm on the
bedside table, he was in a surprisingly good mood.[1] His forces in North
Africa had scored an important victory against the Italians and taken
the fortress city of Tobruk in Libya. More significantly, he had listened

to President Roosevelt deliver his State of the Union message laying out his Lend-Lease plan. Churchill particularly prized Roosevelt's choice of terms when he affirmed that "the future and the safety of our country and of our democracy are overwhelmingly involved in events far beyond our borders." He would have preferred to hear FDR declare war on Germany, but the Lend-Lease proposal offered the possibility of a godsend, and declared it "made him feel that a new world had come into being."[2]

Churchill had no illusions about the political battle about to commence in the American Congress, nor regarding the stubborn resilience of that body's faction of anti-British isolationists. But he took special pleasure in knowing that the president was sending his friend and advisor, Harry Hopkins, to London as his personal representative. This was the opening Churchill had been waiting for, a back door into the deepest recesses of the White House and a potential ally in his quest to bring America into the war. A man he called "the closest confidant and personal agent of the president."[3]

Harry Hopkins entered 10 Downing Street the morning of January 10 haggard and jaundiced, his scant frame threadbare. Still recovering from serious ailments and debilitating surgery for stomach cancer, he nonetheless had made the arduous journey, arriving the night before at Claridge's Hotel amid particularly intense bombing and anti-aircraft fire. Wearing an overcoat that hung limply from his shoulders, unlit cigarette dangling from his mouth, he seemed a sad sack. Though he was but fifty years of age, an English official described him as "so ill and frail that a puff of wind would blow him away."[4]

If Hopkins at first did not impress his hosts, neither did 10 Downing Street bowl over Harry Hopkins. Ahead of a lunchtime meeting with Churchill, the White House insider got a tour of the residence. His guide was Brendan Bracken, one of Churchill's closest aides. In a message to Roosevelt, Hopkins said the place was "a bit down at the heels because the Treasury next door has been bombed more than a bit." He was being kind. German bombs had left many windows broken or boarded up.

Every floor of the building looked damaged, and cleaning and repair crews were scurrying about.

After the tour, Bracken conducted Hopkins to the dining room in the basement, recently reinforced to prevent its collapse.[5] Bracken poured him a sherry.

Churchill, wearing a short black coat and striped trousers, entered characteristically—clear-eyed, blustery, and walking fast. He extended his hand and in what his visitor called "a mushy voice" said, "Welcome to England." After showing around photos of daughter-in-law Pamela and grandson Winston, the prime minister recounted for Hopkins what he had said on the radio the night before. The occasion was the departure for Washington of Lord Halifax, Britain's new ambassador to the United States and Churchill's envoy to President Roosevelt.[6]

"I hail it as a most fortunate occurrence that in this awe-striking climax in world affairs there should stand at the head of the American Republic, a famous statesman . . . in whose heart there burns the fire of resistance to aggression and oppression, and whose sympathies and nature make him the sincere and undoubted champion of justice and freedom, and of the victims of wrong doing where ever they may dwell," the prime minister had declared.

Hopkins looked Churchill in the eye. "The president is determined that we shall win the war together," he said. "Make no mistake about it. He has sent me here to tell you that at all costs and by all means, he will carry you through—no matters what happens to him—there is nothing that he will not do so far as he has human power."[7]

The men lunched on soup, cold beef, green salad, cheese, and coffee.[8] Hopkins described the scene to FDR and added at the end that they enjoyed "a little wine and port. He took snuff from a little silver box—he liked it."

This encounter began one of the most unlikely and influential friendships of the war, between a plain-spoken former social worker and champion of the New Deal and a conservative, bombastic, and emotional scion of one of England's great families. The bond that grew between Hopkins and Churchill foreshadowed and nurtured the partnership between FDR and Churchill that changed the course of history.

Originally Hopkins had planned on only two weeks in the U.K., but those two weeks turned into six. Circulating in London and traveling extensively beyond, Hopkins interacted with a variety of officials and other Britons as well as resident Americans like popular CBS journalist Edward R. Murrow. At home Hopkins had listened to Murrow's newscasts, which began with his grave signature opening, "This . . . is London." Murrow, one of the most influential Americans in wartime London, is said to have had an affair with Churchill's daughter-in-law Pamela. Murrow's vivid reporting on life under the Blitz had deeply affected Hopkins, and he sought a meeting with the reporter.

Expecting to conduct an interview, Murrow called on Hopkins at Claridge's. He found Hopkin's room cluttered, with top secret documents scattered heedlessly. In a turnabout, it was Hopkins who grilled Murrow.

"I suppose you could say that I've come here to try to find a way to be a catalytic agent between two prima donnas," Hopkins told the journalist. "I want to try to get an understanding of Churchill and of the men he sees after midnight."[9] Murrow candidly assessed the prime minister's closest advisors but insisted Churchill *was* the government and made all the important decisions.

WASHINGTON

On the same day Hopkins arrived in London, January 10, the Lend-Lease bill was formally introduced as HR 1776. The bill proposed to authorize the president to produce weapons, munitions, aircraft, and ships, and to transfer those weapons to any country whose defense the commander in chief deemed "vital to the defense of the United States." The ensuing debate was heated and vicious.

Two days later Senator Wheeler attacked the legislation over the radio, claiming that Roosevelt really intended to ally the U.S. with Great Britain in its war against Hitler. "Lend-Lease would mean ploughing under every fourth American boy," he said, infuriating FDR.[10] The president parried at a press conference the next day, calling Wheeler's statement "the most untruthful, the most dastardly, unpatriotic, rottenest thing that has been said in public life in my generation."

On the campaign trail the previous autumn FDR's opponent Wendell Willkie had startled some fellow Republicans by supporting aid for England, but in Congress plenty of GOPers opposed the plan. So did the isolationist press. A *Chicago Tribune* headline shouted SENATORS TO FIGHT FDR BILL. The lead article's header declared SCHEME CALLED A DICTATORSHIP AND WAR MOVE. In William Randolph Hearst's *San Francisco Examiner*, a banner headline predicted CONGRESS TO PUT LIMIT ON DICTATOR POWER OF FDR. The legislative battle to save Britain abroad, and democracy at home, had begun.

Beneath a winter sun at 11:40 A.M. on January 20, 1941, James Roosevelt wheeled his father to an open-air Packard and helped him into the center of the back seat to leave room for two other passengers. Wearing a black silk top hat and overcoat—the temperature was just above freezing—the president said, "Samuel, how are you?" as House Speaker Sam Rayburn (D-Texas) seated himself to Roosevelt's right.[11] Turning to his left as Senate Majority Leader Alben Barkley (D-Kentucky) climbed in, FDR asked "Alben, can you get in there?" With the wave of a presidential hand the motorcade pulled out of the White House driveway, and into the history books.

Surrounding the Packard rolled thirty-six city policemen astride motorcycles, four armored trucks filled with soldiers and mounting antiaircraft guns, and two sedans with Secret Service agents poised on their running boards. Large and enthusiastic crowds along Pennsylvania Avenue NW cheered on the president and his companions as they made their way to the Capitol and an unprecedented event—an American president taking the oath of office for a third time.

At the Capitol James Roosevelt, now a U.S. Marine Corps captain in dress blues replete with brass buttons and golden epaulets, lent his father a strong arm, making it possible for him to navigate his highly visible passage to the podium. At 12:11 P.M. Franklin Roosevelt spoke the words George Washington had spoken more than 150 years earlier.

"I do solemnly swear I will execute the Office of the President of the United States . . ."

As he was reciting the final words of the oath, the crowd, estimated at 400,000, erupted in cheers and applause.[12] Reveling in a moment of extraordinary accomplishment, Franklin Roosevelt stood and absorbed the adulation that gave him the strength to endure the hardships that led to this moment. Nearly twenty years earlier he had lain paralyzed from the waist down, a broken man unsure of his future: knocked off his feet by polio, unable to walk unaided, living with a burning pain both physical and spiritual. The ensuing years had humbled him, conferring patience, empathy, persistence, and most of all faith, the belief that he had a role to play in the betterment of America.

In his third inaugural address, FDR executed the climatic moves in his campaign to convince Americans that saving democracy and freedom was their destiny. He strove in his message to define the soul of America. In doing so, he put his isolationist opponents in check. His carefully crafted opening connected him to the nation's two most beloved figures.

"In Washington's day, the task of the people was to create and weld together a Nation," FDR told listeners. "In Lincoln's day the task of the people was to preserve that Nation from disruption from within. In this day, the task of the people is to save that Nation and its institutions from disruption from without. The destiny of America was proclaimed in words of prophecy spoken by our first President in his first Inaugural in 1789—words almost directed, it would seem, to this year of 1941: 'The preservation of the sacred fire of liberty and the destiny of the republican model of government are justly considered . . . finally, staked on the experiment entrusted to the hands of the American people.'"[13]

This is what Roosevelt envisions when he seeks to salvage the soul of America. Preserving the sacred fire of liberty (everywhere in the world.) He invokes memories of Washington and Lincoln for a particular reason—each man had faced the horror of war and expressed his belief that if the cause was just, the American people would rise to the challenge. He believed in the justness of intervention and knew that his challenge lay in the still-strong forces of isolationism, represented in no small way by Charles and Anne Lindbergh. The aviator advocate had long since thrown down the gauntlet, daring FDR over the airwaves to respond. Anne Lindbergh in *The Wave of the Future* had declared fascism an inevitability to come and democracy a thing of the past. Some say a president ought not attack the words of a private individual, but this day Franklin Roosevelt struck, and struck hard.

"There are men who believe that democracy, as a form of government and a frame of life, is limited or measured by a kind of mystical and artificial fate that, for some unexplained reason, tyranny and slavery have become the surging wave of the future—and that freedom is an ebbing tide," FDR said. "But we Americans know that this is not true."

Starting with a handwritten draft from the president, Sam Rosenman had collaborated closely this round with the poet, writer, and FDR's Librarian of Congress Archibald MacLeish, investing day upon day in their polishing. Meanwhile he tried to talk Roosevelt out of his insistence on addressing the American spirit, the soul of America. In the end the Boss got his way.[14]

"A Nation, like a person, has something deeper, something more permanent, something larger than the sum of all its parts," he said into the cold Washington air that noontime. "It is that something which matters most to its future—which calls forth the most sacred guarding of its present. It is a thing for which we find it difficult—even impossible to hit upon a single, simple word. And yet, we all understand what it is—the spirit—the faith of America. It is the product of centuries. It was born in the multitudes of those who came from many lands—some of high degree, but mostly plain people—who sought here, early, and late, to find freedom more freely. Prophets of the downfall of American democracy have seen their dire predictions come to naught. No, democracy is not dying. We know it because we have seen it revive—and grow."

Roosevelt dove deep into the Founding Father's words. Quoting George Washington's General Orders of July 2, 1776, he boldly lay claim to that cherished legacy:

"Let us therefore rely upon the goodness of the Cause, and the aid of the Supreme Being, in whose hands Victory is, to animate and encourage us to great and noble Actions—The Eyes of all our Countrymen are now upon us."

But connecting his cause with the nation's founding was not enough. Roosevelt also needed to connect to America's savior, the man who held the country together in its hour of greatest danger. Drawing on Abraham Lincoln's second inaugural address he borrowed one of the Great Emancipator's most beloved phrases:

"With malice toward none; with charity for all; with firmness in the right, as God gives us to see the right, let us strive on to finish the work we are in; to bind up the nation's wounds; to care for him who shall have borne the battle, and for his widow, and his orphan—to do all which may achieve and cherish a just, and a lasting peace, among ourselves, and with all nations."[15]

Roosevelt's eloquent culmination juxtaposed peril and purpose, invoking the spirit of colonial patriots and rallying the people to embrace their destiny:

"In the face of great perils never before encountered, our strong purpose is to protect and to perpetuate the integrity of democracy . . . For this we muster the spirit of America, and the faith of America . . . We do not retreat. We are not content to stand still. As Americans, we go forward, in the service of our country, by the will of God."

As the president released the podium and started to turn away, son James stepped up again to support him. The crowd exploded in thunderous applause and huzzahs, crying out, releasing pent-up anticipation for a new form of leadership, a new direction, cheering for the soul of America.[16]

During his acceptance speech in 1936, FDR had proclaimed, "This generation has a rendezvous with destiny." That destiny was not to retreat, nor to stand by, still of voice and uninvolved, but to go forward in the service of the country and the free world. Few knew the price that such service would command. Having issued a challenge to adversary Charles Lindbergh, the president quickly learned his opponent's strength.

Three days later Lindbergh appeared before the House Foreign Affairs Committee to testify against the Lend-Lease bill. FDR's most rabid congressional detractor, Hamilton Fish, had invited him.

Charles Lindbergh delivering a radio address on CBS, 1940.

12

LINDBERGH VERSUS ROOSEVELT

THE U.S. CAPITOL—JANUARY 1941

January 23, 1941, was unseasonably warm in Washington, D.C. The House Foreign Affairs Committee was meeting to discuss Lend-Lease. Lindbergh arrived early at the Capitol, and as he approached the Ways and Means Committee room in the new House Office Building where he was to testify, he encountered a large crowd. Recognizing him, reporters started shouting his name and running toward him. Capitol Police officers surrounded Lindbergh and escorted him into the committee chamber.[1] An estimated 1,000 people jammed into the hearing room, along with newsreel crews and dozens of journalists. As Lindbergh sat down at the witness table, photographers swarmed him, firing off flashbulbs and calling out questions. Ever since his son's kidnapping and murder, the press had been hunting and haunting Lindbergh. The Chair of the Committee, Sol Bloom (D-New York), instructed the press to stand down, and gaveled the meeting to order.

On the dais before him were twenty-five House members, nearly evenly split between foes and friends of Lend-Lease.[2] A household name and face for fourteen years, Lindbergh, thirty-nine, had lost some of the vitality of youth, hair thinning and visage starting to show signs of age. But he had lost none of his boyish charm, nor his calm, persuasive demeanor. He wore a herringbone blue suit, with a dark blue tie over a light blue shirt.[3]

Lindbergh read a statement outlining his opinions on U.S. Army Air Corps preparedness, the state of aviation technology, and the need for a substantial number of new warplanes and air bases. When finished, he handed committee staff a copy, then spent four hours answering committee members' questions. Onlookers were squarely in Lindbergh's corner, laughing at his jests and booing committee members who asked tough questions. He told the panel he thought it a mistake for the United States to extend aid to Great Britain, and that further aid would only extend a conflict fated to end in a stalemate. He repeated his support for neutrality. The most newsworthy exchange came when Rep. Luther Johnson (D-Texas) interrogated the aviator.

"You are not then in sympathy with England's efforts to defeat Hitler?" Johnson asked.

"I am in sympathy with the people on both sides, but I think that it would be disadvantageous for England herself, if a conclusive victory is sought."

"I think you are evading the question—not intentionally, but the question is very simple, whether or not you are in sympathy with England's defense against Hitler?" Johnson said to a chorus of boos. Lindbergh remained unperturbed.

"I am in sympathy with the people and not with their aims."

"You do not think it is to the best interest of the United States eco-nomically as well as in the matter of defense for England to win?"

"No sir, I think that a complete victory, as I say, would mean prostra-tion in Europe," Lindbergh said. "And would be one of the worst things that could happen there and here. I believe we have an interest in the outcome of the war."

"On which side?"

"In a negotiated peace, we have the greatest interest."

"Which side would it be to our interest to win?"

"Neither."

At the end of the session, Chairman Bloom thanked the witness, and told him "You have made one of the best witnesses that this committee could possibly ever hear."[4] As Colonel Lindbergh stood up to leave, members of the committee rose and applauded him.[5]

The battle over Lend-Lease was fierce. Roosevelt's former vice president, John Nance Garner, opposed the bill, as did Joseph Kennedy, FDR's former Ambassador to England. Senator Robert Taft (R-Ohio), a strident FDR critic, declared, "Lending war equipment is a good deal like lending chewing gum—you certainly don't want it back." The Foreign Affairs Committee reported HR 1776 out on January 30, seventeen in favor, eight opposed. It was Franklin Roosevelt's fifty-ninth birthday.

On February 8, with a House vote imminent, floor debate raged. Multiple Republicans floated amendments intended to undermine the bill or limit the president's authority. Doing all he could to delay or derail Lend-Lease, Representative Hamilton Fish (R-New York), the bill's most aggressive enemy, submitted half a dozen amendments, meanwhile demanding that his colleagues send HR 1776 back into committee where he hoped it would die. The Speaker of the House chastised him. Late in the day the House finally voted on the bill, 260 in favor and 165 opposed. It was a bipartisan victory for FDR, with 24 Republicans voting yes and 25 Democrats voting no. Lend-Lease moved to the Senate for consideration.[6]

LONDON

Londoners shivered in the frigid dark the following night but Britain's prime minister was burning with patriotic fervor. Winston Churchill was preparing to deliver his first radio address since September. His immediate audience was the British people, but the listener he cared about most was in Washington, D.C. The day before Winston had bidden his new friend Harry Hopkins farewell, but not before the pair had spent hours working on the text of that night's speech. Churchill's command of English and his method of pacing the room dictating to a stenographer while gesticulating as if addressing a large audience had fascinated Hopkins.[7]

Churchill's bulldog growl reached American ears that night thanks to a global radio hookup meant to assure that his words reached the farthest outposts of the Empire. The prime minister had much to say, but his main goal was to cheerlead for Lend-Lease.

"Five months have passed since I spoke to the British nation and the Empire on the broadcast,"[8] he said. "We stood our ground and faced the two dictators in the hour of what seemed their overwhelming triumph, and we have shown ourselves capable, so far, of standing up against them alone. Distinguished Americans have come over to see things here at the front, and to find out how the United States can help us best and soonest. In Mr. Hopkins who has been my frequent companion during the last three weeks, we have the envoy of the President, a President who has been newly re-elected to his august office. In Mr. Wendell Willkie, we have welcomed the champion of the great Republican Party. We may be sure that they will both tell the truth about what they have seen over here, and more than that we do not ask. The rest we leave with good confidence to the judgment of the President, the Congress, and the people of the United States."

Besides sending Harry Hopkins to London, Roosevelt had recruited Willkie as an envoy to the U.K. and asked him to report on what he saw and learned. Given the bitterness of the 1940 election, the gesture was a remarkable act of reconciliation, as well as one that delivered bipartisan support for sending military aid to Britain. Churchill was happy to explain the mechanics.

"The other day, President Roosevelt gave [Mr. Wendell Willkie] a letter of introduction to me, and in it he wrote out a verse, in his own handwriting, from Longfellow, which he said, 'applies to you people as it does to us.' Here is the verse:

> Sail on, O Ship of State!
> Sail on, O Union, strong and great!
> Humanity with all its fears,
> With all the hopes of future years,
> Is hanging breathless on thy fate!

"Here is the answer which I will give to President Roosevelt: Put your confidence in us. Give us your faith and your blessing, and, under Providence, all will be well. We shall not fail or falter; we shall not weaken or tire. Neither the sudden shock of battle, nor the long-drawn trials of vigilance and exertion will wear us down. Give us the tools, and we will finish the job."[9]

President Roosevelt had every intention of giving Prime Minister Churchill the tools he needed. Roosevelt could only hope Churchill would finish the job.

Despite intense opposition, the Senate passed Lend-Lease fifty-nine to thirty. On March 11, just two months after delivering his State of the Union address, President Roosevelt signed "An Act to Promote the Defense of the United States—HR 1776" into law. Lend-Lease bestowed on the president remarkable power, allowing him to: "sell, transfer title to, exchange, lease, lend, or otherwise dispose of, to any such government [whose defense the President deems vital to the defense of the United States] any defense article."[10]

Franklin Roosevelt and press secretary Stephen Early in the White House, January 1941.

13

WAITING FOR WAR

WASHINGTON, D.C.—MARCH 1941

The front page of the Washington *Evening Star* on March 15, 1941, included a headline reading U.S. NEWSPAPERMAN HELD BY NAZIS ON ESPIONAGE CHARGE. The official German news agency had announced the arrest of Richard C. Hottelet, a young reporter for the United Press. The paper speculated it might be in retaliation for the arrest of several German citizens who worked for a Nazi propaganda organization in New York, the *Transocean News Service*. Hottelet was released later that year as part of a prisoner swap, and went on to become one of the "Murrow Boys," a legendary team of journalists working in London for Edward R. Murrow and broadcasting their reports on the war for CBS.

At 7:00 P.M. that evening, in the Willard Hotel's luxurious Grand Ballroom, President Roosevelt sat at the head table for the White House Correspondents Association annual dinner. That year the ritual had drawn 650 guests, including most of FDR's Cabinet along with Supreme Court justices, solons from the House and the Senate, publishers, and reporters. Even FBI director J. Edgar Hoover was in attendance. As always, the emphasis was on boozy socializing, starting with preliminary receptions, bonhomie in the ballroom, and a round of after-parties. As was customary, the entertainment poked fun at the president and other political figures, especially those involved in the battle over Lend-Lease.

"My friends, this dinner of the White House Correspondents is unique," FDR said when his turn at the microphone came. "It is the first one at which I have made a speech in all these eight years. It differs from the press conferences that you and I hold twice a week, for you cannot ask me any questions tonight, and everything that I have to say is word for word on the record."

Snapping out of whatever alcohol-fueled haze might have had them in its grip, reporters all around the hall, sensing a newsworthy scoop in the making, scrambled for writing implements and blank surfaces on which to scribble notes. They intuited that the president was going not for laughs from the press corps but to reach a global audience.[1]

"Let not dictators of Europe or Asia doubt our unanimity now," he said. "The big news story of this week is this: The world has been told that we, as a united nation, realize the danger that confronts us, and that to meet that danger our democracy has gone into action. Nazi forces are not seeking mere modifications in colonial maps or in minor European boundaries. They openly seek the destruction of all elective systems of government on every continent, including our own.

"From the bureaus of propaganda of the Axis powers came the confident prophecy that the conquest of our country would be an inside job—a job accomplished not by overpowering invasion from without, but by disrupting confusion, and disunion, and moral disintegration from within. The great task of this day, the deep duty that rests upon each and every one of us is to move products from the assembly lines of our factories to the battle lines of democracy—now.

Never in all our history—have Americans faced a job so well worth-while. May it be said of us in the days to come that our children and our children's children 'will rise up and call us blessed.'"[2]

The journalists and politicians in the room repeatedly interrupted the speech with waves of sustained applause and loud cheers. The *Washington Post* proclaimed that Roosevelt's "voice reached out to every corner of the continent and to the outer-most ends of the earth."

This was no exaggeration; the BBC retransmitted the speech world-wide, translated into dozens of languages. Roosevelt proudly elevated his pledge to become the "arsenal of democracy" as America's number one priority in this speech. Factories across the country already were begin-ning to retool, and defense contractors had started hiring thousands of workers to meet FDR's ambitious matériel goals. Even so, with the world on fire, his grand undertaking at times seemed quixotic, as if he were tilting at Nazi windmills with a wooden sword.

The evening's entertainment highlight was a "burlesque newsreel review," produced by Paramount, entitled "Mr. Big Stays in Washington—(Or Does He?)."[3] The mock-serious "Mr. Big," which sent up potential pretenders to FDR's job, had a narration credited to "The Unknown Historian," whose voice bore a remarkable resemblance to Franklin D. Roosevelt's. Billed as "the outstanding, tremendous unadulterated twaddle of the year," the satirical short did not disappoint. After dinner, performers, including the immensely popular comedy duo Bud Abbott and Lou Costello, kept up the levity.

*Senator Burton Wheeler and Charles Lindbergh raising their hands
at a rally at Madison Square Garden, May 23, 1941.*

14

THE FACE OF FASCISM

CHICAGO—APRIL 1941

Pedestrians began streaming along downtown Chicago's Erie Street late in the afternoon of April 17, 1941, achieving a critical mass at 6:00 P.M. The horde's destination was the Near West Side, where at the corner of Erie and West Madison stood the imposing Chicago Stadium, scene of an event scheduled to start in two hours. When completed in 1929 that facility had been the world's largest indoor arena, home ever since to the Second City's beloved Blackhawks. Tonight, the stadium was hosting a rally booked by the America First Committee and featuring that group's newest spokesperson, Charles Lindbergh. After months of keeping America First at arm's length, the celebrity isolationist had finally reasoned that the nation's many such entities ought to unite under a single banner—the banner of America First.[1]

More than 10,000 people had crammed the enormous hall; loudspeakers outside reached another 4,000 milling partisans. From the high vaulted ceiling hung more than fifty giant American flags and enormous loops of red, white, and blue bunting. Onstage stood portraits of George Washington and large signs reading "Defend America First." Charles Lindbergh came to the podium to ecstatic cheers and applause.[2] Once the ovation dwindled Lucky Lindy explained why he had finally allied publicly with the event's sponsor.

"The America First Committee is a purely American organization formed to give voice to the hundred odd million people in our country who oppose sending our soldiers to Europe again," Lindbergh said. "Our objective is to make America impregnable at home, and to keep out of these wars across the sea. Some of us, including myself, believe that the sending of arms to Europe was a mistake—that it has weakened our position in America, that it has added bloodshed in European countries and that it has not changed the trend of the war."[3]

The audience repeatedly screamed its support as if with one voice, interrupting him thirty-one times, according to the *Chicago Tribune*, whose publisher Robert McCormick was helping to finance America First.

"This war was lost by England and France even before it was declared, and that it is not within our power in America today to win the war for England," Lindbergh went on.

A few hours earlier, London had come under one of the Luftwaffe's most devastating attacks so far, as 46,000 incendiary bombs and 350 tons of explosives fell on the capital city. Among targets severely damaged was St. Paul's Cathedral.[4]

Having joined America First, Lindbergh committed himself to fighting Roosevelt's Lend-Lease program at every opportunity. Six days after his coming out party in Chicago, he headlined an America First rally at the Manhattan Center on West 34th Street in New York. More than ten thousand souls packed the former opera house, and millions more coast to coast tuned in on radio. The once self-effacing Lindbergh took the stage with a swagger akin to that of Germany's and Italy's dictators. The crowd roared approval for three minutes, breaking into chants of "We Want *Lindy!*" That night's audience included members of the American Bund, fanatics from Father Coughlin's Christian Front, and other Hitler supporters.[5] The *New York Times* reported that "German accents were numerous" in the crowd.

Senator Burton Wheeler gave a rousing anti-Roosevelt speech, claiming the president was in thrall to "jingoistic journalists and saber-rattling bankers in New York."[6] When the cavernous hall finally quieted, Lindbergh gave his fellow isolationists the rhetorical red meat they craved.

"I know I will be severely criticized by the interventionists in America when I say we should not enter a war unless we have a reasonable chance of winning," he said. "When history is written, the responsibility for the downfall of the democracies of Europe will rest squarely upon the shoulders of the interventionists who led their nations into war uninformed and unprepared. With their shouts of defeatism, and their disdain for reality they have already sent countless thousands of young men to death in Europe."

Men standing near the front shouted out Lindbergh's name and raised the "Sieg heil!" salute. Repeating his thinly veiled reference to the myth that Jews controlled the media, he brought the crowd back to its feet.

"We have been led toward war by a minority of our people," Lindbergh declared. "This minority has power. It has influence. It has a loud voice. That is why the America First Committee has been formed—to give voice to the people who have no newspaper, or newsreel, or radio station at their command; to the people who must do the paying, and the fighting, and the dying, if this country enters the war."

Inside the hall people were cheering and applauding. As in Chicago, thousands more listened on loudspeakers outside. But there were also

THE FACE OF FASCISM

protesters by the hundreds. Police on horseback struggled to keep the plaza in front of the building clear and to separate the rival crowds. Clogged streets brought traffic to a standstill.

The protest was the doing of Friends of Democracy, a watchdog group whose leader, Leon Birkhead, had warned Lindbergh that America First was being manipulated by Hitler's propaganda machine. The pro-Roosevelt magazine *PM* called the event a "liberal sprinkling of Nazis, Fascists, antisemites, crackpots, and just people, in which the just people seemed out of place."[7]

As the rally was beginning, the Friends of Democracy and allies marched along West 34th Street. In the lead was a young woman and ten men carrying pro-Lend-Lease placards. America Firsters began booing, then rushed their opponents, knocking people down and tearing up their signs as police officers stood by watching. It was an ugly scene, and one that would be repeated as the "great debate" grew in intensity in the coming months. With the popular American hero now on board, America First Committee membership ballooned from 300,000 to 800,000.

At a press conference two days after Lindbergh's New York appearance, popular *Evening Star* columnist Constantine Brown asked FDR, "Mr. President, how is it that the Army, which needs now distinguished fliers, etc. has not asked Colonel Lindbergh to rejoin his rank as Colonel?"[8]

Until now Roosevelt had not made any public statements directly mentioning Lindbergh. His response may have been off the cuff, but it bore the marks of advance consideration. Press secretary Steve Early might even have planted the question.

Invoking the Civil War, FDR specifically references Clement Vallandigham, a leader of Northerners who opposed Abraham Lincoln's efforts to preserve the Union and were known as "Copperheads."

"Well, Vallandigham, as you know, was an appeaser," Roosevelt said, explaining his reference. The reporters laughed and settled in for a story.

"He wanted to make peace from 1863 on because the North 'couldn't win,'" FDR went on. "Once upon a time there was a place called Valley Forge and there were an awful lot of appeasers that pleaded with Washington to quit, because he 'couldn't win.' Just because he 'couldn't win.' See what Tom Paine said at that time in favor of Washington keeping on fighting."

"Wasn't it 'These are the times that try men's souls'?" shouted Earl Godwin.

"Yes, that particular paragraph," the president replied. "In fact, I read it in the *Post* or the *Star* the other day."

"Were you still talking about Mr. Lindbergh?"

"Yes," Roosevelt answered, hoisting his chin and flashing his disarming smile.[9]

Bristling at FDR's characterization, Charles Lindbergh immediately wrote to the president, a letter he made public. "I had hoped that I might exercise my rights as an American citizen, to place my viewpoint before the people of my country in time of peace, without giving up the privilege of serving my country as an Air Corps officer in the event of war," he told Roosevelt. Complaining that since his commander in chief had clearly implied "that I am no longer of use to this country as a reserve officer" he was resigning his Air Corps Reserve commission.[10] Lindbergh sent a formal resignation letter to Secretary of War Henry Stimson.[11]

The Roosevelt-Lindbergh feud became a running media narrative. The *New York Times* chastised both in an editorial: "President Roosevelt spoke impetuously last Friday when he went back three quarters of a century into the bitterness of the Civil War to find a disparaging epithet for Charles A. Lindbergh. Mr. Lindbergh in turn shocked those who believe him to be a loyal American—though a sadly mistaken one—by his petulant action in relinquishing his commission in the Army Air Corps reserve."[12]

Lindbergh gave fiery speeches in St. Louis and Minneapolis, claiming over and over that England could not win the war no matter how many planes and ships the U.S. provided, and that he would continue to speak his truth no matter the consequences.

On May 23, 1941, he returned to New York City for another America First rally. Demand for tickets was so intense that the committee booked the enormous Madison Square Garden. The historic hall filled to its listed capacity 22,000, with another 10,000 outside clamoring to get in. Joining Lindbergh onstage was Senator Wheeler, fast becoming the leading elected voice opposing aid to the Allies. Again, a sizable number of those present had direct ties to pro-Nazi groups.[13] When Lindbergh rose to speak, a tide of chants and cheers greeted him. Tricolor bunting, displays of Old Glory, and abundant expressions of patriotic passion camouflaged the anger, hatred, and antisemitism roiling just below the surface.

Without naming his target, Lindbergh attacked President Roosevelt repeatedly.

"We lack only a leadership that places America first—a leadership that tells what it means and what it says," he said. "Give us that and we will be the most powerful country in the world. Give us that and we will be so united that no one will dare to attack us. We have been led toward war against the opposition of four-fifths of our people."

Harkening to the previous autumn's election, Lindbergh and Wheeler contested the legitimacy of Roosevelt's victory. They claimed he had invalidated his victory by lying that he would not send American boys to fight in Europe.[14]

"We had no more chance to vote on the issue of peace and war last November than if we had been in a totalitarian state ourselves," said Lindbergh. "We in America were given just about as much chance to express our beliefs at the election last Fall, as the Germans would have been given if Hitler had run against Göring."

Comparing Roosevelt and Willkie to Hitler and his field marshal marked a dramatic escalation in the virulence of Lindbergh's critique. The crowd loved it, booing and hissing at his every mention of "leadership" as he worked his way toward an ominous warning.

"From every section of our country a cry is rising against this war. It echoes from the very foundations on which our system of government is built," Lindbergh said. "It asks how this situation came about. It demands an explanation of what happened at the elections last November. Our American ideals, our independence, our freedom, our right to vote on important issues, all depend on the sacrifice we are willing to make, and the action we take at this time."

That action was to support America First and oppose Roosevelt. Wheeler and other speakers joined Lindbergh onstage when he finished speaking. Photos showed them with their arms raised, which critics claimed resembled the Nazi salute affected by many in the audience. Lindbergh later said he was merely waving to supporters.

Two Gallup polls during this period recorded American opinion in this vein. April 26 results showed that only 19 percent of those responding thought America should enter the war in Europe, but 70 percent supported giving military aid to the United Kingdom. A May 9 poll found that 63 percent disagreed with Lindbergh's anti-war policy of withholding aid to England, and only 24 percent agreed with him. Through the months polling showed attitudes constantly changing. A vast majority initially opposed any participation in the war, but gradually more and more Americans came to support giving England needed military equipment. And Winston Churchill desperately needed that equipment, as the British Empire was on the ropes.

Winston Churchill is cheered by workers during a visit to bomb damaged Plymouth on May 2, 1941. The prime minister was accompanied by Lady Nancy Astor on this visit, who can be seen behind Churchill.

15

HIGH STAKES ON THE HIGH SEAS

ENGLAND—MAY 1941

In Plymouth, May 2, on England's south coast, people stood atop the rubble of what had once been a favorite pub. Most of the historic port's downtown had been reduced to piles of wreckage, with shards of glass and bricks shoved and shoveled into small berms of detritus. Hundreds lined the streets as a convoy of black cars crawled through the ruins. Standing next to his beloved wife Clementine in the back of a half-truck, Prime Minister Winston Churchill waved at the resilient residents of their country's second most heavily bombed city.[1] When the convoy stopped in the town center, Churchill stepped to the ground. He set his hat on the tip of his cane and waved it on high so citizens at the far edge of his audience could see where he was. Tears streaming down his cheeks, he shouted, "Your homes are low, but your hearts are high!" Lady Nancy Astor, a member of Parliament who was accompanying the Churchills, acidly commented, "It's all very well to cry, Winston, but you've got to *do* something."[2]

The two had a long and strained history. Astor had sided with Neville Chamberlain. Fencing verbally with Churchill before he replaced the appeaser, Lady Astor once warned him, "Winston, if you were my husband, I'd put poison in your brandy!" Churchill is said to have replied, "And if you were my wife, I'd drink it."[3]

The Luftwaffe had been hammering Plymouth for months to get at the nearby Royal Navy base. By early May 1941 thousands of residents were homeless and the city was barely functioning—yet another of many casualties of a war not going well for England.

In Greece, the Germans had recently thrown back British troops, 16,000 of whom were lost in that defeat. Nearer home, men in German field grey had seized the Channel Islands. General Erwin Rommel and his Afrika Korps were besieging the strategically important city of Tobruk, Libya. In the previous three months U-boats had sunk 142 ships, costing Britain 818,000 tons of war supplies. More than 47,000 British civilians had been killed since Churchill's elevation a year earlier. The prime minister, distraught, cabled President Roosevelt on May 3, 1941.[4] Outlining the severity of the situation, he told FDR the only "decisive counterweight" he could see was if "the United States were immediately to range herself with us as a belligerent power." Roosevelt's reply the following day evaded the impossible request that he declare war, but the president did send good news.

"I have issued instructions that supplies in so far as they are available here are to be rushed to the Middle East at the earliest possible moment," FDR wrote. "Thirty ships are now being mobilized to go within the next three weeks to the Middle East. Our patrols are pushing farther out into the Atlantic, I have just added all of our remaining units of the Coast

Guard to the Navy for the purpose of implementing that patrol. With this message goes my warm personal regards to you."[5]

Domestic critics were flaying Churchill. Deriding his morale-building visits to scenes of bombings, an MP carped that "when the prime minister has to parade himself through every bombed area in the country and has to sit on the back of a wagonette waving his hat on a stick, well it has come to a very sad state of affairs."[6] On May 6 Churchill called for a vote of confidence in parliament.

Members rose to praise and pillory him, and the barbs struck home, especially a salvo from old friend and wartime predecessor David Lloyd George. "We have tremendous havoc among our shipping, not merely in losses but in what has not been taken enough into account, in damage," the aged former prime minister said, demanding "an end to the kind of blunders which have discredited and weakened us."[7]

The vote of confidence went wildly in Churchill's favor, 447 to 3, raising his spirits and confidence. But his elation quickly waned when, two days later, London endured its worst battering yet. And though President Roosevelt was sending as many tanks, planes, and ships as he could, the tide was inexorably turning in Hitler's direction.

There were some British victories amongst the roll call of gloom. In mid-May, under cloudy skies, the German battleship *Bismarck* and heavy cruiser *Prinz Eugen* sneaked out of their home port of Gdynia, Poland—renamed "Gotenhafen" by the occupiers—and headed into the North Atlantic. As a commerce raider and one of the world's most powerful dreadnoughts, *Bismarck*, in tandem with the Reich's submarine fleet, posed an existential threat to British shipping. In its first skirmish, *Bismarck* destroyed the battle cruiser HMS *Hood* and damaged Churchill's beloved new battleship, HMS *Prince of Wales*. *Bismarck* paid dearly as well with severer damage to her fuel tanks. The behemoth limped toward Brest in occupied France for repairs. A multiday chase ensued across the Atlantic. On May 26, British torpedo bombers disabled *Bismarck*'s main rudder and the next day British ships of the line pummeled the enemy vessel until the crew scuttled it. Besides delivering a key naval victory, sinking *Bismarck* bolstered morale and renewed Roosevelt's hope that Churchill could turn the tide.

WASHINGTON

The next night, FDR was forced to put off his seventeenth fireside chat owing to ill health. He had suffered a nearly catastrophic drop in blood hemoglobin that confined him to bed for days and required a blood transfusion.[8] His press secretary tried to minimize the severity of his condition, blaming intestinal trouble. But the president's inner circle knew how close a call the episode had been. The broadcast was rescheduled for Pan-American Day, May 27, marked by an evening lawn party at the White House. Ambassadors, ministers and their families from more than a dozen Latin American republics attended.[9]

The president, in a nearly seasonal white tuxedo and black bow tie, was wheeled into the ornate East Room for the radio transmission, to be heard around the globe in fifteen languages. His guests, formally clad, were already seated on little gilded chairs under the crystal chandeliers. Radio techs and newsreel crews were waiting for their cue. The fickle Washington weather had hit a record 97° that day. The president was sweating even before he began his speech. The heat forced film crews to wait until after the live radio broadcast to turn on their lights; Roosevelt did a second take of selected portions just for the newsreels.[10] In these crucial remarks, he directly addressed the issue of Germany controlling shipping lanes vital to Britain and to the United States.

"The Battle of the Atlantic now extends from the icy waters of the North Pole to the frozen continent of the Antarctic," he explained. "Throughout this huge area, there have been sinkings of merchant ships in alarming and increasing numbers by Nazi raiders or submarines. There have been sinkings even of ships carrying neutral flags."[11]

In draft form, his next sentence had raised complaints, hackles, and demands for its excision at the White House, the War Department, and the State Department. Roosevelt overrode all of them.[12]

"The blunt truth is this—and I reveal this with the full knowledge of the British Government: the present rate of Nazi sinkings of merchant ships is more than three times as high as the capacity of British shipyards to replace them," he said. "It is more than twice the combined British and American output of merchant ships today."[13]

Beaded gowns rustled and expensive shoes shuffled as FDR's guests absorbed the unexpected and highly sensitive revelation. Roosevelt pushed on. "We can answer this peril by two simultaneous measures: first, by speeding up and increasing our own great shipbuilding program; and second, by helping to cut down the losses on the high seas," he said. "We have, accordingly, extended our patrol in North and South Atlantic waters. We are steadily adding more and more ships and planes to that patrol." Roosevelt had let Churchill in on this expanded zone of protection, but until now not the public.

"We shall give every possible assistance to Britain and to all who, with Britain, are resisting Hitlerism . . . with force of arms," he continued. "Our patrols are helping now to insure delivery of the needed supplies to Britain. All additional measures necessary to deliver the goods will be taken. I say that the delivery of needed supplies to Britain is imperative. I say that this can be done; it must be done; and it will be done."

Roosevelt then turned his focus to his isolationist critics.

"There are some timid ones among us who say that we must preserve peace at any price—lest we lose our liberties forever," he said with profound disdain. "To them I say this: never in the history of the world has a nation lost its democracy by a successful struggle to defend its democracy. We must not be defeated by the fear of the very danger which we are preparing to resist. Our freedom has shown its ability to survive war, but our freedom would never survive surrender. The only thing we have to fear, is fear itself." He paused, lining up a shot at the America First

Committee. "There is, of course, a small group of sincere, patriotic men and women whose real passion for peace has shut their eyes to the ugly realities of international banditry and to the need to resist it at all costs. I am sure they are embarrassed by the sinister support they are receiving from the enemies of democracy in our midst—the Bundists, the Fascists, and Communists, and every group devoted to bigotry and racial and religious intolerance.

"It is no mere coincidence that all the arguments put forward by these enemies of democracy—all their attempts to confuse and divide our people and to destroy public confidence in our government—all their defeatist forebodings that Britain and democracy are already beaten—all their selfish promises that we can 'do business' with Hitler—all of these are but echoes of the words that have been poured out from the Axis bureaus of propaganda. Those same words have been used before in other countries—to scare them, to divide them, to soften them up."

His voice now steely, he delivered another shocker: "I have tonight issued a proclamation that an unlimited national emergency exists and requires the strengthening of our defense to the extreme limit of our national power and authority. The Nation will expect all individuals and all groups to play their full parts, without stint, and without selfishness, and without doubt that our democracy will triumphantly survive."

Roosevelt's declaration echoed in theme one Woodrow Wilson had uttered in World War I. The broadcast reached a record audience estimated at 85 million, including some at movie theaters where operators paused projectors and played the radio broadcast live.[14]

After the broadcast, the stunned dignitaries moved into the Rose Garden for dinner and dancing. As they arrived the band played "God Bless America."[15]

Newspaper headlines the next day left no doubt about the chat's import. A *New York Times* headline read ROOSEVELT PROCLAIMS UNLIMITED EMERGENCY; WILL RESIST ANY HITLER EFFORT TO RULE SEAS. Several Republican senators, including Robert Taft (R-Ohio) claimed that the president did not have the authority to declare a national emergency. Their protestations had no effect.

THE WHITE HOUSE

Frustration on many fronts had President Roosevelt in a dreadful mood. Amid his strenuous efforts to put Lend-Lease into action, a domestic crisis had arisen, one that could easily derail his plan to boost support for Churchill. It was just before 2:00 P.M. on June 18, 1941, and the next meeting on the day's schedule was one he wished he could wave away. But if he ducked it, 100,000 "Negroes" demanding justice would paralyze Washington.[16]

This was FDR's second meeting with America's two most prominent Black leaders. A. Philip Randolph and Walter White, were now planning to stage a massive march on Washington in two weeks. The prospect of a confrontation on July 1, 1941, between the racist Metropolitan Police Department and Black protesters was causing FDR much anguish. It was a crisis that had been brewing since before the election, one that he had waved off previously, and was now at a full boil.[17]

The planned March on Washington movement had gained momentum with thousands of young Black activists, and Randolph had upped the ante, calling for 100,000 Black citizens to storm Washington, defiantly declaring, "I call on Negroes everywhere to gird for an epoch-making march."[18] Many Black leaders and Black newspapers were hesitant, even fearful of the idea. The *Pittsburgh Courier* called the scheme "crackpot."[19]

President Roosevelt was deeply concerned about the potential for violence and encouraged Eleanor to write Randolph and ask him to cancel the demonstration. Randolph politely refused. FDR leaned on other civil rights leaders, including his Black Cabinet, again without success.[20]

And now, with the march two weeks off, the Black trailblazers were back. Randolph, White, and fellow activists entered the Oval Office at

2:00 P.M. on that humid June day in 1941. Already seated were Secretary of War Stimson, Navy Secretary Knox, New York City Mayor and Office of Civilian Defense head Fiorello La Guardia, and William Knudsen, chair of the National Defense Council. This time the president skipped the usual small talk, banter, and jokes, bluntly asking Randolph, "Well, Phil, what do you want me to do?"[21]

Randolph repeated his previous suggestion that Roosevelt issue an executive order prohibiting discrimination at factories making war matériel.

"You know I can't do that," an angry Roosevelt replied. "In any event, I couldn't do anything unless you called off this march of yours. Questions like this can't be settled with a sledgehammer."

Randolph stood his ground. The march would go on. For him and many Black Americans the time to "wait quietly" was over.

Leaning forward on his desk the president asked, "How many do you think will come?"

"100,000," Randolph replied without missing a beat. Roosevelt scoffed, turned to Walter White and asked again, "Walter, how many people will *really* march?"

Looking directly into Roosevelt's eyes, White replied, "One hundred thousand, Mr. President."[22]

Franklin D. Roosevelt, President of the United States of America, was not used to being defied. Or being talked to in this manner. "Call it off," he said. "And we'll talk again."

"No," Randolph said.

After a tense silence, Mayor La Guardia offered a way out of the deadlock.

"Gentlemen, it is clear Mr. Randolph is not going to call off the march, and I suggest we all begin to seek a formula," the mayor said.[23]

The tension in the room hung for a moment, then began to subside as the president nodded and leaned back in his chair.

The deal eventually agreed to by all was that White and Randolph would help the president's team draft an Executive Order, on which they started working that day in the Cabinet Room. The result was EO 8802, Fair Employment Practice in Defense Industries, which FDR signed seven days later on June 25, 1941:

"Whereas it is the policy of the United States to encourage full participation in the national defense program by all citizens of the United States, regardless of race, creed, color, or national origin, in the firm belief that the democratic way of life within the Nation can be defended successfully only with the help and support of all groups within its borders; and

"Whereas there is evidence that available and needed workers have been barred from employment in industries engaged in defense production solely because of consideration of race, creed, color, or national origin, to the detriment of workers' morale and of national unity:

"Now, Therefore, by virtue of the authority vested in me by the Constitution and the statutes, and as a prerequisite to the successful conduct of our national defense production effort, I do hereby reaffirm the policy of the United States that there shall be no discrimination in the employment of workers in defense industries or government because of race, creed, color, or national origin, and I do hereby declare that it is the duty of employers and of labor organizations, in furtherance of said policy and of this Order, to provide for the full and equitable participation of all workers in defense industries, without discrimination because of race, creed, color, or national origin."

The Fair Employment Practice Committee was established to enforce the new order. This single line, "there shall be no discrimination in the employment of workers in defense industries or government because of race, creed, color, or national origin" established a new standard for the treatment of Black Americans. Executive Order 8802 has been described as the most significant advance in Black civil rights since the end of the Civil War.[24]

In exchange for that historic concession, an enormous victory for the Black community, Randolph called off the march. Even his critics at the *Pittsburgh Courier* saluted his triumph, announcing plans for a "Double V" campaign pursuing "victory over our enemies at home and victory over our enemies on the battlefields abroad."[25]

Out of the cauldron of wartime change emerged an alternative to the racial dogma of patience and acceptance of glacial progress: the galvanizing realization among Black civil rights advocates that direct action was the engine of equality. The ranks of the NAACP and the more militant Committee of Racial Equality grew significantly in subsequent years.

Acclaimed author and scholar David M. Kennedy describes the impact of Roosevelt's Executive Order in his book *Freedom from Fear*: "Now, for the first time since Reconstruction, the federal government had openly committed itself to making good on at least some of the promises of American life for Black citizens. Coming at a moment that was kindled with opportunities for economic betterment and social mobility, EO 8802 fanned the rising flame of Black militancy and initiated a chain of events that would eventually end segregation once and for all and open a new era for African Americans."[26]

The steadfastness that impelled EO 8802 into existence also begat the famous 1963 March on Washington for Jobs and Freedom, the dramatic backdrop for Dr. Martin Luther King Jr.'s historic "I Have a Dream" speech. That milestone was organized by A. Philip Randolph.

Franklin Roosevelt may have had to be muscled into issuing EO 8802, but regardless of that and regardless of who wrote "there shall be no discrimination in the employment of workers in defense industries or government because of race, creed, color, or national origin," it was Roosevelt's signature and the power of the Presidency that made those words the law of the land and changed the course of American civil rights activism. Although it seems a small skirmish when compared to the massive conflict inflaming the globe, it was an important victory in the broad battle for America's soul, bringing the essence of the Four Freedoms to Black Americans, as well as to people "everywhere in the world."

Four days after the meeting between Randolph and Roosevelt in the Oval Office, Hitler invaded the Soviet Union, causing a seismic shift in the global military conflagration that would soon lead to the industrialized murder of millions of innocent people.

German troops at the Soviet state border marker,
photographed by Johannes Hahle, June 22, 1941.

16

BETRAYAL, LIES, AND
AN ACT OF FAITH

LOS ANGELES—JUNE 1941

Throngs began streaming up Pepper Tree Lane around 6:00 P.M. on June 20, toward the Hollywood Bowl. The clear, warm summer air offered a perfect night for an outdoor event. Soon more than 20,000 people had filled the amphitheater to capacity, and thousands more found seating on the ground of surrounding hillsides. They had come to hear their lanky idol Charles Lindbergh headline an America First rally.[1] To pass the time the crowd sang popular folk songs, laughing and smiling as the sun moved toward the horizon.

The program started at 8:00 P.M. with a series of speakers, including silent film star Lillian Gish and Senator D. Worth Clark (D-Idaho). When Lindbergh was introduced, the enormous crowd leapt to its feet, screaming, shouting, and waving American flags. As Lindbergh stood before a podium dense with microphones, photographers wrestled for sightlines and flashbulbs fired in rapid succession. Lindbergh seemed uncomfortable as he shuffled the pages of his typewritten speech in his hands. When the crowd finally quieted, he began.

"We who opposed America's entrance into this war have one great advantage over the interventionists," Lindbergh said. "We will be successful if we can bring the true facts and issues of the war clearly before the people of our country. We fight with the blade of truth—they use the bludgeon of propaganda."

Lindbergh recited his now-familiar litany of reasons why America was safe from attack, why trying to defend England was a fool's errand, and why a negotiated peace with Hitler was the only reasonable solution.

"The alternative to a negotiated peace is either a Hitler victory or a prostrate Europe, and possibly a prostrate America as well," he said. When he finished the audience gave him an extended standing ovation complete with cheers of "Lindy" and "Our Next President!" Even as he spoke, German troops and tanks massed along the Western border of the Union of Soviet Socialist Republics.

THE RUSSIAN BORDER

The night sky was clear. The weather mild. At 3:15 A.M. on June 22, 1941, seemingly endless squadrons of Luftwaffe bombers crossed into Soviet airspace, heavy with payloads. Columns of tanks began moving forward at first light, their low rumble shaking the earth along an 1,800-mile front stretching from the Baltic to the Black Sea. Marching behind the tanks came an eternity of heavily armed soldiers. Operation Barbarossa,

Hitler's betrayal of Joseph Stalin, was the largest combined land and air force in human history.[2] The Germans crashed into Russia with 150 divisions consisting of three million soldiers, nineteen panzer divisions with 3,000 tanks, and 7,000 artillery pieces. Prowling overhead were 2,500 aircraft. The expeditionary force's mission: destroy the Red Army, kill as many civilians as possible, and capture Moscow.[3]

Marshal Joseph Stalin's generals had repeatedly warned him that the Nazis were planning to invade the U.S.S.R. So had the British prime minister. Stalin believed none of these warnings, and even when it happened could not understand why Hitler had betrayed him. The first few days saw the annihilation of any Russian forces in the latest Blitzkrieg's path.[4]

LONDON

Winston Churchill was awakened at 8:00 A.M. and given the news. Pleased with this apparent reprieve from the threat of invasion that had been hanging over his country, he immediately alerted the BBC that he would be delivering a live radio address that evening.[5] When he made good on that alert, his rhetoric captured the moment and reflected the feelings of so many people around the world.

"Hitler is a monster of wickedness, insatiable in his lust for blood and plunder. Not content with having all Europe under his heel, or else terrorized into various forms of abject submission, he must now carry his work of butchery and desolation among the vast multitudes of Russia and Asia. So now this blood thirsty guttersnipe must launch his mechanized armies upon new fields of slaughter, pillage, and devastation. Poor as are the Russian peasants, workers, and soldiers, he must steal from them their daily bread. He must devour their harvests. He must rob them of the oil which drives their ploughs and thus produce a famine without example in human history."[6]

The man who had railed for two decades against the Soviet Bolsheviks as ungodly totalitarians now warily welcomed them as allies in a holy war against Nazism. Churchill knew that with the bulk of Hitler's forces brutally penetrating the Russian heartland the British Empire had an unexpected opportunity to regroup and reframe the war. Now more than ever, President Roosevelt's actions would determine the next phase. Across the pond, Roosevelt said little about the new front, waiting for the right moment.

HYDE PARK

The faint aroma of roses wafted across the great lawn at Springwood. Sara Roosevelt's rose garden was in full bloom. Bees and butterflies floated through the scented air. An early summer heat wave had triggered a ferocious thunderstorm the night before, and the grass was still wet.[7] Eight days after Hitler's hordes stormed across the Soviet Union's western borders, something unique and new was about to open. A steady stream of people walked up the long tree-lined drive. Their destination—a brand new Dutch Colonial style building that Franklin Roosevelt built to hold his official papers and his vast collection of naval art, replicas of sea faring warships, rare books, and curios given to him by fans and world leaders. It would be the very first Presidential Library, paid for with private donations. The land on which it sat and the precious items it contained given to the people by Franklin Delano Roosevelt.

At 4:00 P.M. a crowd of 2,000 people waited in the hot, humid Hudson Valley afternoon for the president to dedicate this new addition to the National Archives of America. The horseshoe shaped building's front door faced a grassy courtyard filled with friends, family, reporters and newsreel cameras. Sara Roosevelt sat next to Princess Martha of Norway and her two children. Eleanor Roosevelt and her daughter Anna sat beside them. In the audience were Supreme Court Justices, Cabinet members, and the Trustees of the Library who had raised the $350,000 needed to construct the two-story stone archive and museum.[8]

Franklin Roosevelt wearing a white suit and striped tie was helped up from his chair by his son James. Taking a few awkward steps forward, he grasped a lectern crowded with microphones, and looked out at the large crowd. A broad smile spread across his face. He had been working toward this moment for four years, and in the face of war and strife he intended to make a statement to the world.

"It seems to me that the dedication of a library is in itself an act of faith," he said. "To bring together the records of the past and to house them in buildings where they will be preserved for the use of men and women in the future, a nation must believe in three things. It must believe in the past. It must believe in the future. It must, above all, believe in the capacity of its own people so to learn from the past that they can gain in judgment in creating their own future."[9]

Holding his chin high, his voice filled with conviction he declared, "This latest addition to the archives of America is dedicated at a moment when government of the people by themselves is being attacked everywhere." He placed special emphasis on the words "by themselves."

"It is, therefore, proof—if any proof is needed—that our confidence in the future of democracy has not diminished in this Nation and will not diminish," he said. "We hope that millions of our citizens from every part of the land will be glad that what we do today makes available to future Americans the story of what we have lived and are living today, and what we will continue to live during the rest of our lives.

"I am glad that you have come today, because as I suggested at lunch to some of the Trustees, this is the last chance you have got to see this Library free of charge," shifting to a lighter tone and smiling. An admission fee of twenty-five cents would begin the next day.

The crowd moved forward toward the entrance, hoping the inside of the building would offer some respite from the 97° summer heat. Wandering through the galleries they marveled at the remarkably detailed ship models, the large paintings depicting major naval battles, and beautifully rendered portraits of his ancestors. The most popular room was the Gallery of Oddities filled with gifts of state, and dominated by a giant eight-foot papier-mâché bust of FDR as a Sphinx with a cigarette holder in its mouth. A prop at the 1939 annual Gridiron Club dinner, it was part of a skit making fun of the president for his refusal to indicate whether or not he would seek a third term. The *Washington Post* described the performance this way:

"The third-term enigma evoked a skit in which President Roosevelt saw himself portrayed as a massive Sphinx gazing dead-pan over the desert sands upon which a group of assorted Democrats clad as Bedouins debated the third term issue and appealed, without avail, to the Great Stone Face for an answer to the question: 'Is he, or ain't he?'" The president was so amused by the sketch that he insisted the bust be sent to his home in Hyde Park for inclusion in the Franklin D. Roosevelt Presidential Library and Museum.

Roosevelt called the opening of this historic new facility "an act of faith." And that it was, in a deeply personal way. In this stone building, its very design a homage to his Dutch ancestors who settled New York, were his most precious belongings; his families' private papers dating back to the late seventeenth century; rare historic manuscripts from the birth of the republic and the founding of the U.S. Navy; jewelry, mementos, and childhood toys both priceless and irreplaceable; his beloved collection of ship models, paintings, and rare books. All of which he generously gifted to future generations. He believed in the future of America and the future of democracy despite the horrors of the war being waged across Europe and the Far East. Little did he know that the coming months would challenge his faith in ways he could not imagine.

CALIFORNIA

On the same day Hitler invaded the Soviet Union, Lindbergh and his wife left Los Angeles and flew north aboard a United Douglas plane along the beautiful Pacific coastline.[10] They arrived in Medford, Oregon, where they traveled two hours south to Siskiyou County in Northern California and the spectacular Wyntoon estate of William Randolph Hearst.[11] Situated at the foot of Mount Shasta, the property hosted two small villages of Bavarian cottages as well as the main house. Charles and Anne stayed in the Cinderella House. The Lindberghs spent three days with the media tycoon, who shared their isolationist perspective. Hearst papers routinely gave Lindbergh's appearances glowing reviews while attacking Roosevelt's policies at every opportunity. The remote retreat gave Charles and Anne a chance to relax without the belligerent press hounding at their heels. Afterward, Lindbergh wrote Hearst a heartfelt thank you note. "A period of crisis is the real test of character and leadership," he told the magnate. "I believe that you have done something for this country in the crisis we are going through, for which our people will be forever grateful."

The aviator and his wife enjoyed an overnight train back to the Bay Area, arriving on the morning of June 25. They spent several days at the historic Sir Francis Drake Hotel, a Renaissance Revival icon looking out onto Union Square. Charles followed the news of the invasion and worked on his next speech.

He made a grand entrance at San Francisco's Civic Auditorium at 8:00 P.M. on July 1, drawing 15,000 people into the hall, with thousands outside the building. Looking like the shy, awkward aviator of his younger days, Lindbergh spoke slowly, but with strong conviction as he mocked European leaders.[12]

"The longer this war continues, the more confused its issues become," he said. "When it started Germany and Russia were lined up against England and France. Now, less than two years later, we find Russia and England fighting France and Germany!"

As in all his public appearances the crowd cheered and chanted, interrupting Lindbergh after almost every paragraph. There was a particularly loud outburst when he declared, "The record of the interventionists in this war has been a record of abject failure."

His closing remarks made headlines across the country: "An alliance between the United States and Russia should be opposed by every American, by every Christian, and by every humanitarian in this country!"

Lindbergh's role as the spokesperson for the America First Committee had generated a wave of hostility. Public libraries removed his and Anne's books from their shelves. Streets and buildings bearing his name were renamed. Roosevelt's interior secretary, Harold Ickes, made the most public rebuke, one which ended up at the White House.

On July 14, at a Manhattan Center rally celebrating Bastille Day sponsored by the France Forever organization Ickes called isolationists "Nazi scuttle fish who pour ink on the truth in order to blacken out the light of freedom."[13] Despite boos, he continued. "No one has ever heard Lindbergh utter a word of horror at, or even aversion to, the bloody career that the Nazis are following, not a word of pity for the innocent men, women, and children who have been murdered by the Nazis in every country in Europe."[14]

Ickes devoted half his time at the microphone to attacking Lindbergh, calling him a mouthpiece for Hitler and the Nazi propaganda machine. "I have never heard this 'Knight of the German Eagle' denounce Hitler or Nazism, or Mussolini or fascism," he said. The diatribe came to be recognized as the most damaging and direct attack on Lindbergh by any member of the Roosevelt administration. It did not go unanswered.

In his journal, Lindbergh wrote, "Nothing is to be gained by my entering a controversy with a man of Ickes type. But if I can pin Ickes' actions on Roosevelt, it will have the utmost effect."[15]

Lindbergh wrote to President Roosevelt demanding an apology, reminding the president that he had accepted the decoration from Göring "in the American Embassy in the presence of your ambassador." He claimed to have had no contact with the German government since returning to the United States. The letter's contents were leaked to the press before FDR received it, and landed on the front page of many newspapers, including the *New York Times*.

"Mr. President, if there is a question in your mind, I ask that you give me the opportunity of answering any charges that may be made against me," Lindbergh had written. "But, Mr. President, unless charges are made and proved, I believe that the customs and traditions of our country give me, as an American citizen, the right to expect truth and justice from the members of your Cabinet."

Secretary Ickes was thrilled that his target had taken the bait and he responded that had Lindbergh been an "upstanding American he would have returned the decoration long ago regardless of when, where, or how he got it."[16]

In his secret diary, later published as *The Lowering Clouds*, Ickes wrote, "My own feelings and that of others . . . is that Lindbergh has slipped badly. He has now made it clear to the whole country that he still clings to this German decoration. He is now in a position where he is damned if he gives it back and damned if he doesn't . . . For the first time he has allowed himself to be put on the defensive and that is always a weak position for anyone."[17]

PART FOUR

A SPECIAL FRIENDSHIP

Prime Minister Winston Churchill and President Franklin D. Roosevelt standing aboard HMS Prince of Wales. *Supporting Franklin Roosevelt on his left side is his son, Captain Elliott Roosevelt USAAF. A presidential aide stands nearby. August 10, 1941.*

17

SECRET MEETINGS

WASHINGTON—JUNE 1941

The summer of 1941 was a bloody one, and President Roosevelt closely followed every detail of every military engagement. Battles were raging in the Mediterranean, North Africa, the Middle East, Norway, China, and Southeast Asia as well as in Russia. The British Empire was staggering under the fierce assault. In 1941 the U-boat wolfpacks prowling the North Atlantic sank 4.3 million tons of shipping. That almost doubled to 7.8 million tons in 1942.

Hitler ordered the concentration camp at Auschwitz expanded, and SS death squads known as *Einsatzgruppen* ("Special Action Groups") prowled the Polish and Russian countryside murdering Jews at every opportunity. Imperial Japan marched into French Indochina, imposing ruthless domination.

The Red Army stopped the Germans just short of Moscow, beginning a murderous stalemate. A debate raged in America over whether Lend-Lease should supply arms to Russia as well as Great Britain. Churchill, desperate for American aid, believed a face-to-face meeting with FDR could bring America into the war.

The summer of 1941 also brought tragedy and an unexpected guest into the White House. Roosevelt was distracted and lethargic because of his blood disorder and anemia.[1] His closest advisors, including Hopkins, Ickes, and Morgenthau, were all disappointed at his lack of action on helping Churchill. In a conversation with Ickes, even the ever-loyal Missy LeHand declared that "we have a leader who won't lead."[2]

On June 4, 1941, President Roosevelt held a staff party in the Diplomatic Reception room. Mrs. Roosevelt was in Hyde Park, so Missy was the host. Staffers ate an informal dinner, then sat around the piano and sang songs. Still burdened by anemia, Roosevelt retired to his bedroom around 9:30 P.M. As the party was winding down, Missy began to wobble, called out in fear, and fainted, falling to the floor in a heap. She lay gasping for breath, her lips turning blue.[3] Dr. Ross McIntire gave mouth-to-mouth resuscitation and she was carried upstairs to her room. She told McIntire that her neck and chest hurt. Her heart was racing, and she was gasping for breath. So began a long painful decline caused by what was eventually diagnosed as a stroke. Private nurses provided round-the-clock care, paid for by Roosevelt, who visited her regularly. She never fully recovered.

The next day Franklin Roosevelt's private life entered a new phase as a ghost materialized. In 1914, when he was the Assistant Secretary of the Navy during World War I, Eleanor had hired a young woman, Lucy Mercer, to help her juggle her social responsibilities and the raising of five rambunctious children.[4] Franklin was attracted to the beautiful new addition to the household, leading to an affair. When Eleanor found out, she offered Franklin a divorce, but under pressure from his mother Sara, Franklin agreed never to see Lucy again. The Roosevelts' marriage survived, but with a radically changed dynamic. Their intimate life together was over, and their relationship evolved into a political partnership of extraordinary effectiveness. They never stopped loving and respecting each other, but they began to develop personal ties outside their marriage which provided the emotional connections both needed.

On June 5, 1941, Lucy Mercer Rutherfurd visited the White House for the first time that we know of. Franklin had honored the letter of his pledge, if not the spirit, and the two had kept up a secret correspondence for many years. Lucy was sent special invitations to FDR's inaugurations and attended all of them. She had married a wealthy socialite, Winthrop Rutherfurd, and lived a comfortable life. Her husband suffered a severe stroke in early 1941. In the aftermath Lucy reentered Franklin's life with her first recorded visit, under the pseudonym "Mrs. Paul Johnson." That name appears in the president's daily schedule twelve times between early June 1941 and April 1945.[5]

Franklin Roosevelt was also distracted during this time by the charming Princess Martha of Norway. Roosevelt had a special fondness for European royalty, especially if attractive, and much has been made of their friendship. There are reports of Roosevelt taking Martha for long rides in the country and before her stroke Missy feared she was losing her place of prominence among FDR's female friends. Roosevelt also took Lucy on rides in the country, and occasionally she would wait at a predetermined roadside location and he would insist his driver pick up the seeming damsel in distress.[6]

Certainly, on the surface it appeared that President Roosevelt was not devoting enough attention to a world in crisis. But FDR always operated on two levels: the outer-facing Franklin, always cheerful and merry, quick with a story or a joke, and the inner Franklin, with hidden compartments holding his most private thoughts. These he rarely shared with others, even his closest friends and advisors. And, while they feared he was not taking control of the situation with the war, in fact he was extremely focused on it.

The front page of the August 1, 1941, Washington *Evening Star* carried a large photo of Harry Hopkins being greeted by Soviet Premier Joseph Stalin in Moscow. Hopkins was now the head of the Lend-Lease program, and the president had sent him to Russia to size up Stalin and report back—as Hopkins had scrutinized and analyzed Winston Churchill back in January. With all the controversy surrounding the idea of extending Lend-Lease to the Soviet Union, Roosevelt needed to know exactly whom he was dealing with.[7]

It was hot and very humid that morning and at 11:00 A.M. a sweaty gaggle of reporters trudged into the Oval Office hoping for news. Roosevelt was feeling much better and in a very friendly mood.[8] "Mr. President, could you tell us if you have any word from Mr. Hopkins since he arrived in Moscow?"[9]

"Only a report of his arrival. That's all."

"Could you tell us whether there is any possibility of him coming back by way of China?"

"I don't know. I haven't the faintest idea."

"Would you care to comment sir on the Russian resistance up to the present time?"

The president paused. "I think only . . . that it is magnificent, and frankly, better than any military expert in Germany thought it would be!"

The reporters laughed. "Could we quote that, sir?" one asked.

"Yes."

"A direct quote?"

"Yes, if you want to."

"Does that include outstanding German military experts?"

"Now don't go and spoil it." More laughter from the reporters, and a change in subject.

"Mr. President, do you have any immediate travel plans?"

Roosevelt smiled and leaned back in his comfortable green swivel chair. "I really do hope I can get off early next week up the coast some-where, where at least the nights will be cool. And—er—I think I will take a week off."[10]

The president announced he would be cruising up the New England coast and visiting his family home on Campobello Island in New Bruns-wick, Canada, across the border from Maine. The remainder of his day was busy, including a lunch with Henry Morgenthau and a Cabinet meeting. He did not reveal that that evening he was dining with Lucy Mercer Rutherford, again using the name Mrs. Paul Johnson. She stayed until 11:00 P.M.[11] She returned again the next afternoon. Eleanor was in Eastport, Maine, meeting with an international student group.

President Roosevelt left muggy Washington, D.C., on August 3 aboard a train headed for New London, Connecticut. Riding with him were Dr. Ross McIntire and General "Pa" Watson. At New London the next evening at 8:30 he and his party boarded USS *Potomac*, the 165-foot white presidential yacht, waving to spectators and reporters on shore.[12] The following day *Potomac* docked at Nonquitt, Massachusetts, where the president went ashore to mingle with locals. He then spent the afternoon fishing in full sight of beachgoers. After sunset, *Potomac* headed north through Buzzards Bay toward the Cape Cod Canal.[13]

At 8:00 P.M., the yacht changed course, rendezvousing secretly with the U.S. Navy warship USS *Augusta* at the western tip of Martha's Vineyard. The president and guests transferred to the Northampton class cruiser, and at 6:30 A.M., *Augusta* and USS *Tuscaloosa*, escorted by five destroyers, headed north toward Placentia Bay in Newfound-land, where Roosevelt was to rendezvous clandestinely with Winston Churchill.

The president took special joy in tricking journalists, and to that end the crew and passengers of *Potomac* now spent several days cruising in the Cape Cod vicinity. Often the on-deck tableau featured a faux FDR, portrayed by a wheelchair-bound crewman or Secret Service agent, wearing a hat and sporting a cigarette holder while being waited on.[14] People on shore could clearly see the presidential flag flying from the topmast. Periodic bulletins declared that "all on board" were enjoying themselves. Roosevelt wrote to his cousin Margaret "Daisy" Suckley, one of his closest confidantes, "Even at my ripe old age I feel a thrill in making a get-away—especially from the American press."[15] Neither his Cabinet nor his wife knew his whereabouts.

PLACENTIA BAY, NEWFOUNDLAND

The prime minister had made an equally surreptitious departure aboard the pride of the Royal Navy, HMS *Prince of Wales*, from the Royal Navy's main base, Scapa Flow, at Scotland's northern tip.[16] Sailing west he was joined by Harry Hopkins, exhausted by his sojourn to Moscow to size up Joseph Stalin. When Hopkins flew into Scapa Flow, Royal Navy medicos had confined him to his berth, where he remained for the stormy and perilous crossing, laid low by the rigors of marathon diplomacy. Enforced rest restored his strength in time for the titans' meeting.[17]

Set against a beautiful mountainous backdrop, the town of Argentia on Placentia Bay was the site of what had been a Royal Navy base until the U.S. acquired the facility in the destroyer swap. The Americans had updated the base with an airstrip and U.S. Navy minesweepers and destroyers at anchor now dotted the bay. President Roosevelt arrived at 9:24 A.M. on Thursday, August 7. Exercising his authority as commander in chief, he had arranged for sons Elliott, an Army Air Corps pilot, and navy ensign Franklin Jr., to serve as his aides during the conference. Neither initially knew his destination. Elliott flew the British Minister of Supply, Lord Beaverbrook, to Placentia. Many years later Elliott wrote about his experience at this historic moment. Arriving aboard *Augusta* with instructions to go to the captain's cabin, he was shocked to find his brother and father about to have lunch. After a delighted reunion the table talk quickly centered on Lend-Lease and British concerns about Stalin.

"They'll be worried about how much of our production we're going to divert to the Russians," Franklin said, snapping his fingers.[18] "I know already how much faith the PM has in Russia's ability to stay in the war."

"I take it you have more faith than that?" Elliott asked.[19]

"I do."

The President had a good idea of what Churchill really wanted. "Watch and see if the PM doesn't start off by demanding that we immediately declare war against the Nazis," he told his sons.

There was a knock, and Elliott admitted a messenger delivering dispatches the president needed to review and sign. The younger Roosevelts were accustomed to serving their father as sounding boards when he was facing an important debate.

"The British Empire is at stake here," FDR said. "If in the past German and British economic interests have operated to exclude us from world trade, kept our merchant shipping down, closed us out of this or that market, and now Germany and Britain are at war, what should we do? America won't help England in this war simply so that she will be able to ride roughshod over colonial people."[20]

"I can see there will be a little fur flying here and there in the next few days," Elliott said, exchanging glances with his brother.

Roosevelt knew what Churchill wanted: a declaration of war and ever more Lend-Lease armaments. Roosevelt planned to give him words not weapons.

In settings like conferences, the president liked to have his sons with him, needing as he did people he knew intimately and trusted utterly to help with his personal care. The mundane but for him humbling and embarrassing details of getting into and out of bed, dressing, and using the bathroom all required significant physical assistance. In public his boys had long since mastered helping him pretend to walk, functioning as human crutches allowing him to balance and move assuredly in his heavy metal braces. Elliott's and Franklin's presence at Argentia would prove particularly important.

On the morning of August 9, the majestic *Prince of Wales*, escorted by two Royal Navy corvettes, glided out of a fog bank and into the still waters of Placentia Bay. The battleship, still scarred from its victory over *Bismarck*, anchored near *Augusta*. The dreadnoughts, bristling with cannon barrels and antiaircraft guns, had carried the most powerful men in the free world to their first meeting as the leaders of their countries.[21]

At 11:00 A.M., the prime minister climbed a gangway onto *Augusta* to the sound of shrill boatswains' pipes. A line of U.S. Navy officers turned their heads in unison and snapped a salute. Ranks of sailors stood on deck at attention. President Franklin Roosevelt, wearing a suit and hat, leaned against a railing. To stand on his own he was relying on painful steel braces concealed by his trousers. At his side, in their services' uniforms, were Elliott and Franklin Jr.[22] As the ship's band played "God Save the King," Churchill handed his letter of introduction from King George VI to Roosevelt, who accepted the document with formal dignity.[23] Both men were steeped in their nation's naval tradition, with its ritual pomp.

"At last," Roosevelt said with a smile. "We've gotten together."

"We have," Churchill replied.[24]

The Argentia conference's importance cannot be overstated. Each participant brought to the table contrasting, even conflicting agendas, and much was at stake. What might have happened if, as is all too common when powerful men first meet, Roosevelt and Churchill instantly took a disliking to one another? How would World War II have played out had the special relationship turned into a power struggle or, worse, a clash of egos? Tremendous tension already existed between the American and British military leaders standing nearby and deeply suspicious of each other.

The president invited the prime minister to his cabin for a private lunch, which he described to Daisy Suckley in a letter.

"Churchill stayed on board & lunched with me alone," he wrote. "He is a tremendously vital person . . . I like him & lunching alone broke the ice both ways."[25]

"Breaking" was the operative word, as their differences very quickly became apparent. The president's goal was to draft and issue a statement of guiding principles, a document both aspirational and inspirational. He wanted no formal strategy meetings of military leaders, no treaties requiring congressional approval, only discussions. Words were the weapons he wanted to use against Hitler. The prime minister's goal was to have Roosevelt provide something more metallic and pointed—in the best of all possible worlds, a declaration of war by the United States against Germany.[26]

But FDR was cautious, knowing his people still did not support the U.S. going to war. It had already taken so much to get Lend-Lease off the ground. In a clever gesture, Roosevelt urged Churchill to write the first draft of the declaration of principles he was after. Despite his disappointment, the prime minister accepted the assignment, which he turned over to Sir Alec Cadogan, the Undersecretary at the Foreign Office.[27] The Cadogan draft, which imagined the form a post-war peace would take, was a bitter pill for Churchill, who had hoped for so much more.

The president accepted Cadogan's draft the next day when the American entourage, plus three hundred American sailors, boarded *Prince of Wales* for a carefully scripted Sunday service and lunch.[28] Roosevelt demonstrated his remarkable capacity to adapt to any situation by mock-walking the entire length of the pitching quarter-deck holding onto Elliott's arm. The trek was one of his longest since becoming president. When FDR finally reached his chair he turned, and with a triumphant smile, installed himself on what instantly became his throne.

Churchill and Roosevelt sat together as the combined crews sang hymns the conferees had personally chosen, including "Onward, Christian Soldiers." Beneath the aft turret's massive fourteen-inch guns, all hands shared in a stirring and emotional experience that stood in sharp contrast to the destruction and death in besieged London, a moment of spiritual solidarity offering hope for a better future. Everyone present enjoyed a formal lunch hosted by the prime minister.[29]

Roosevelt brought together Harry Hopkins and his favorite diplomat, Undersecretary of State Sumner Welles, to rework the Cadogan draft. Knowing full well that Churchill wanted a declaration of war, Roosevelt wanted a declaration of peace, or at least a declaration of what would constitute peace after the war.[30]

It was paramount to avoid any hint of alliance or treaty that congressional isolationists could use to attack the document as unconstitutional. The resulting sequence of drafts illustrated the insurmountable differences in the leaders' philosophies. Roosevelt believed colonialism had to go. Churchill meant to preserve the British Empire. A related topic was a hot-button issue: Britain's favorable trade deals with countries belonging to its Commonwealth, a competitive edge FDR saw as unfair.

The final version of the Atlantic Charter—an opening statement and eight articles—was more press release than anything else. But the language carried immense weight and had unexpected consequences, especially for Churchill.

> The President of the United States of America and the Prime Minister, Mr. Churchill, representing His Majesty's Government in the United Kingdom, being met together, deem it right to make known certain common principles in the national policies of their respective countries on which they base their hopes for a better future for the world.
>
>   First, their countries seek no aggrandizement, territorial or other;

*Second, they desire to see no territorial changes that do not accord
with the freely expressed wishes of the peoples concerned;*

*Third, they respect the right of all peoples to choose the form of
government under which they will live; and they wish to see sovereign rights and self-government restored to those who have been
forcibly deprived of them;*

*Fourth, they will endeavor, with due respect for their existing
obligations, to further the enjoyment by all States, great or small,
victor or vanquished, of access, on equal terms, to the trade and to
the raw materials of the world which are needed for their economic
prosperity;*

*Fifth, they desire to bring about the fullest collaboration between
all nations in the economic field with the object of securing, for all,
improved labor standards, economic advancement, and social
security;*

*Sixth, after the final destruction of the Nazi tyranny, they hope
to see established a peace which will afford to all nations the means
of dwelling in safety within their own boundaries, and which will
afford assurance that all the men in all lands may live out their
lives in freedom from fear and want;*

*Seventh, such a peace should enable all men to traverse the high
seas and oceans without hindrance;*

*Eighth, they believe that all of the nations of the world, for
realistic as well as spiritual reasons, must come to the abandonment
of the use of force. Since no future peace can be maintained if land,
sea, or air armaments continue to be employed by nations which
threaten, or may threaten, aggression outside of their frontiers,
they believe, pending the establishment of a wider and permanent
system of general security, that the disarmament of such nations is
essential. They will likewise aid and encourage all other practicable
measures which will lighten for peace-loving peoples the crushing
burden of armaments.*

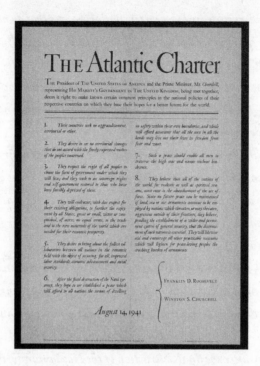

Though not at all to Churchill's liking, the Charter served Roosevelt's agenda well. Isolationists would have a tough time disputing its contents, sidestepping any need for congressional sign-off. Still, several elements raised red flags.

The third article respected people's right to choose their own form of government, and the restoration of rights and self-government to those who had lost them.

Churchill, ever the dedicated imperialist, read this stipulation as referring only to countries under the Axis boot. But discussion made clear that the Charter was endorsing global self-determination, as Roosevelt had intended.

The fourth Charter article, on trade and tariffs, also generated intense discomfort. Roosevelt wanted open trade. Churchill was desperate to maintain the privileges Britain had built into its ties to the countries of the Commonwealth.

The eighth article nettled Roosevelt. In an earlier iteration its central phrase had read "international organization for security." Recalling Americans' loathing for the failed League of Nations, FDR grasped that they would react identically to anything remotely similar. The final phrasing, "pending the establishment of a permanent system of general security," which suited him and went unnoticed by domestic isolationists, was the first reference to what became the United Nations. There was no signing ceremony, or even a signed copy. But the words to which they agreed would be the foundation for future change.

On Tuesday, August 12, Churchill bade farewell to Roosevelt, and *Prince of Wales* raised anchor. Aboard *Augusta*, Franklin Roosevelt held Elliott's arm as they stood on the foredeck and watched the pride of the Royal Navy sail out of Argentia Harbor, bound for Scapa Flow.[31] Four months later, just two days after Pearl Harbor, Japanese bombs and torpedoes sent the *Prince of Wales* and most of her crew to the bottom of the South China Sea off the coast of Malaya.[32]

In London the Prime Minister presented the conference as a great triumph. The Atlantic Charter buoyed both Parliament and public, implying as it did American involvement and a continuing flow of food, munitions, and support.[33] Shouldering aside his disappointment, Churchill put on a masterful display of enthusiasm and a sense of victory. Clinging to his goals, he had personally drafted a message for President Roosevelt to send Tokyo threatening reprisal if Japan continued its pattern of aggression against British holdings in the Western Pacific. The president declined to do so, but events soon rendered that matter moot.

Roosevelt did cut off shipments of American oil, pumping tensions in the Pacific to dangerous new levels. Both American and British naval chiefs believed that Japan was preparing to strike into Southeast Asia to seize that region's rich deposits of minerals and oil.

Isolationists in Congress flexed their strength the day Churchill departed Argentia, by nearly defeating a vote to extend the peacetime draft, which would have emasculated the reviving U.S. Army. Of that

203 to 202 tally, Senator Burton Wheeler bragged, "This vote clearly indicated that the administration could not get a resolution through the Congress for a declaration of war."[34]

Exactly one year before his return from the Atlantic Conference, Winston Churchill saluted Royal Air Force fighter pilots holding off the Luftwaffe in the Battle of Britain. Addressing the House of Commons, the prime minister made one of his most eloquent statements: "Never in the field of human conflict was so much owed by so many to so few."[35] He could have said the same for the Atlantic Charter. Churchill's words gave strength and comfort to a nation under tremendous stress. His unflinching bravery and commitment to victory were the foundation on which he earned the friendship and respect of the president of the United States.

In his Pulitzer Prize–winning book, *Roosevelt and Hopkins*, Robert Sherwood, one of FDR's speechwriters during this period, described the two leaders' relationship. "It would be an exaggeration to say that Roosevelt and Churchill became chums at this conference or at any subsequent time," Sherwood wrote. "They established an easy intimacy, a joking informality, and a moratorium on pomposity and cant—and also a degree of frankness in intercourse which, if not quite complete, was remarkably close to it."

But, as it had their prime minister, the Charter disappointed Britons. Sherwood noted: "In Britain, however, there had been the expectancy of tremendous action resulting from the meeting—of vast American armadas sweeping across the seas—and all that came out of it was a grouping of pious words."[36]

Reaction in America split along the increasingly fractious line dividing isolationists and internationalists. The anti-FDR *Chicago Tribune* screamed PACT PUSHES U.S. NEAR WAR. The *New York Times* was more measured: ROOSEVELT, CHURCHILL DRAFT 8 PEACE AIMS.

Franklin D. Roosevelt, September 11, 1941, at the White House in Washington, D.C., delivering a fireside chat. FDR wears a black arm band, mourning the recent death of his mother, Sara Delano Roosevelt.

18

LOSS AND LINDBERGH

MAINE—AUGUST 1941

A heavy summer mist on the Maine coast obscured the breakwater just off Rockland on August 16. Hundreds of people stood on Tilson's Wharf alongside stacks of lobster pots, straining to see. The town's police chief looked at his watch and shook his head; onlookers began to murmur. Suddenly at 2:55 P.M. a vague shape appeared, moving quickly toward shore. Another shape materialized right behind. In minutes, USS *Potomac*'s distinctive white silhouette hove into view. A small U.S. Navy escort vessel followed. The crowd cheered; police guided them off the dock so local dignitaries could greet the presidential yacht. A busload of reporters, photographers, and White House staff, arrived from the train station and pushed their way to the front.[1]

Potomac docked gracefully; crewmen secured lines and emplaced a gangplank. Members of the president's staff immediately boarded the yacht. After a few moments, the president's black Scottish Terrier Fala trotted down the gangplank, followed by several staffers. "Will the president still do his press conference?" a reporter yelled.

"Yes, he agreed to delay his departure for you," a staffer said. The reporters scrambled up the gangplank and into the *Potomac*'s wardroom to find the president seated. Wearing a tweed suit and a blue shirt, Roosevelt looked tanned and rested. Newsmen quickly filled the white-walled room. The afternoon sun streaming through the windows warmed reporters who had been waiting days for word of the president's whereabouts.

Waving a cigarette in his signature holder, Roosevelt was in an expansive mood.

"I'm glad to see you Mike," he said. "How are you?"[2]

"Very well, sir," replied Michael E. Hennessy of the *Boston Globe*, who had been covering Roosevelt for years.

"Sit down over here, Mike, and keep me straight," FDR said. "You've kept me straight for about fifty years."

"Fifty-two to be exact."

Roosevelt laughed.

"Can you tell us where this conference with Mr. Churchill was held?"

"I cannot, for obvious reasons."

First laying out strictures on the details of the meeting, location, times, and so on, the president described the moving Sunday service and the excellent relations between the American and British sailors and top military figures in attendance. Reporters flung a slew of queries.

"Put it this way. The conference was primarily an interchange of views relating to the present and the future," Roosevelt said. "A swapping of information, which was eminently successful."

Then came the question on every mind, as well as on the front page of the *Chicago Tribune*: "Are we any closer to entering the war, actually?"

"I should say no," FDR said.[3]

The president debarked to the train station for the trip to the White House. All along the rails people waited hours to wave and perhaps glimpse the president as his Pullman car passed.[4]

Newspapers journalists and radio pundits closely scrutinized and analyzed the text of the Atlantic Charter. Photos and newsreel footage were viewed by millions, and speculation was rampant about what it all meant. Truth be told, no one really did fully understand what had happened.

HYDE PARK

That summer Franklin Roosevelt had more on his mind than the war in Europe and the political situation at home. A second stroke disabled his devoted assistant Missy LeHand, Oval Office gatekeeper since he had moved into the White House and a fixture in his life for ten years before.[5] Insiders said she was the most powerful woman in Washington, and she certainly was closer to FDR than anyone else. Her convalescence was difficult and eventually she had to move out of the White House and live with her sister in Boston. Franklin personally paid her medical expenses.

An even graver blow than Missy's withdrawal into debility—she died in 1944—took his greatest advocate. Sara's death on September 7 at Hyde Park, with him by her side, deeply affected Franklin. These losses left voids that would never be filled.[6]

A few days after Sara's death, Franklin was in her room sorting through her things when Grace Tully brought him a box he had never seen.[7] Opening it, he discovered a trove from his childhood, including his first pair of shoes, his christening dress, and a lock of his baby hair. Tears flowed down his cheek as he began to sob. All the pent-up feelings he kept hidden deep inside came bursting out. Neither Grace nor anyone else in his inner circle had ever seen him show such emotion. Even Franklin Roosevelt's iron will and legendary good humor could not protect him from the crushing weight of the loss of his beloved mother. But events in the wider world demanded attention, and he had to set aside his grief and take up the mantle of command.

WASHINGTON

On September 11, 1941, in a fierce fireside chat, President Roosevelt addressed U-boat attacks on American destroyers and cargo ships flying the flags of neutral nations. He spent many hours on the text with Rosenman and Hopkins and shared the draft with the War, Navy, and State Departments. In addition to Churchill and Stalin, his own military advisors had been pressuring him to declare war. Grief-stricken but clearheaded, he delivered the most militant and aggressive speech possible, drawing a line in the waves of the Atlantic and authorizing his commanders to shoot first if necessary. When Secretary of State Cordell Hull saw the final draft, he insisted that it be toned down. The president refused.[8]

Seated before microphones in the Diplomatic Reception Room, empty save for a few family members, Harry Hopkins, and two staffers, Roosevelt channeled his anger and determination as he informed Americans that they were crossing into a new phase in the struggle.

"Normal practices of diplomacy—note writing—are of no possible use in dealing with international outlaws who sink our ships and kill our citizens," he said. "When you see a rattlesnake poised to strike, you do not wait until he has struck before you crush him. These Nazi submarines and raiders are the rattlesnakes of the Atlantic. They are a menace to the free pathways of the high seas. They are a challenge to our own sovereignty. They hammer at our most precious rights when they attack ships of the American flag—symbols of our independence, our freedom, our very life."[9]

Using imagery both provocative and proactive, Roosevelt painted a vivid picture of a snake coiling to attack. His deftness with visual metaphors was one of FDR's most effective rhetorical tools, in this case used brilliantly. He demonized the enemy while justifying a new "shoot first" dictate. He then made a pointed declaration that was akin to an act of war, except that it wasn't because he so precisely threaded the eye of the verbal needle.

"Our patrolling vessels and planes will protect all merchant ships—not only American ships but ships of any flag—engaged in commerce in our defensive waters," he said. "They will protect them from submarines; they will protect them from surface raiders. From now on, if German or Italian vessels of war enter the waters, the protection of which is necessary for American defense, they do so at their own peril."

Despite this provocation, Hitler refrained from declaring war on the United States. The Führer had his hands full with the invasion of the Soviet Union, the battle for North Africa, and his continued assault on Great Britain. He knew it was to his advantage to keep America out of the war as long as possible.

DES MOINES, IOWA

President Roosevelt's was not the only prominent voice on the air that night. Charles Lindbergh was in Des Moines to deliver a major address. A cartoon that day on the front page of the *Des Moines Register* showed Lindbergh at a podium, with Hitler and Mussolini clapping wildly. The caption read, "His Most Appreciative Audience."

A week earlier, Lindbergh had visited Henry Ford in Dearborn, Michigan, to discuss the war situation and the America First Committee.[10] "Every time I see Ford, I am impressed both by his eccentricity and his genius," he wrote in that night's diary entry. "I always come away refreshed and encouraged after a meeting with Ford. I only wish the country had more men like him."[11] Lindbergh did not comment on Ford's viciously antisemitic speeches and publications, and was probably there seeking a donation to America First.

The Des Moines Coliseum was filled with 8,000 people. A radio connection was set up so the audience could listen to FDR's speech, after which Lindbergh was to speak.[12]

The event started with a moment of silence marking Sara Roosevelt's death, followed by the national anthem. Owing to local technical difficulties, the President's broadcast came out distorted in Des Moines at the start, but the problem was quickly corrected.[13] The audience listened respectfully, occasionally cheering or applauding passages they agreed with.

When Roosevelt's speech ended, Charles Lindbergh walked out to sustained applause, with some unexpected boos. "It was the most unfriendly crowd of any meeting to date, by far," Lindbergh noted in his diary.[14] He had written his remarks with care, and despite Anne's pleas to soften his tone, he remained true to his beliefs. "Today, our country stands on the verge of war," he began, reiterating points he had made before. But he then went further than he ever had.[15]

"National polls showed that when England and France declared war on Germany less than 10 percent of our population favored a similar course for America," Lindbergh said. "But there were various groups of people, here and abroad, whose interests and beliefs necessitated the involvement of the U.S. in the war." Now, instead of making veiled hints, Lucky Lindy spoke his mind.

"The three most important groups who have been pressing this country toward war are the British, the Jewish, and the Roosevelt administration," Charles Lindbergh declared.[16]

A small section of the audience had audibly disapproved of several passages. This declaration drew a loud booing, which was immediately drowned out by cheers.[17] He resumed his prepared remarks.

"These war agitators comprise only a small minority of our people, but they control a tremendous influence," he said. "They have marshalled the power of their propaganda, their money, their patronage.

"It is not difficult to understand why Jewish people desire the overthrow of Nazi Germany. The persecution they suffered in Germany would be sufficient to make bitter enemies of any race. No person with a sense of the dignity of mankind can condone the persecution of the Jewish race in Germany . . . Instead of agitating for war, the Jewish groups in this country should be opposing it in every possible way for they will be amongst the first to feel its consequences."

Then as now, Lindbergh's defenders have claimed that in these sentences he was actually trying to honor the Jewish faith. But his words are his words.

"Their greatest danger to this country lies in their large ownership and influence in our motion pictures, our press, our radio, and our government," he said. "I am not attacking the Jewish or the British people. Both races, I admire. But I am saying that the leaders of both the British and the Jewish races, for reasons which are as understandable from their viewpoint as they are inadvisable from ours, for reasons which are not American, wish to involve us in the war."[18]

Now Lindbergh turned to the Roosevelt administration. "They have just used the war to justify the restriction of congressional power, and the assumption of dictatorial procedures on the part of the president and his appointees," he said. "The danger of the Roosevelt administration lies in its subterfuge. While its members have promised us peace, they have led us to war heedless of the platform upon which they were elected."

Louder boos were showering down from the coliseum's upper decks, but the majority of the audience was still cheering Lindbergh on.[19]

"We are on the verge of a war for which we are still unprepared, and for which no one has offered a feasible plan for victory," he told the audience. "We are on the verge of war, but it is not yet too late to stay out. The entire future rests upon our shoulders. If you oppose our intervention in the war, now is the time to make your voice heard."

America's most famous celebrity had directly attacked the president of the United States. The *Des Moines Register* front page the next day led with the headline U.S. NAVY TOLD TO SHOOT! subtitled "Roosevelt to the Axis: Enter Our Waters At Your Peril." The second-tier front page headline was LINDBERGH BLAMES BRITISH, ROOSEVELT AND JEWS.

Roosevelt's speech, broadcast as usual globally and in multiple languages, was very well received, and he began a delicate dance with Congress as he sought another modification to the Neutrality Act, this time to transform his "shoot on sight" rhetoric into legal language allowing specific military action.

Charles Lindbergh faced a backlash of outrage that took him by surprise and had the America First Committee near to foundering. He complained in his diary that *"New York Times* carries bitter attacks on my address from Jewish and other organizations and from the White House."[20] His unvarnished antisemitism drew fire from both Republicans and Democrats, and alienated once-vocal supporters. The Hearst newspapers declared that "The assertion that Jews are pressing this country into war is unwise, unpatriotic, and un-America," Hearst newspapers wrote, shocking many readers. "The voice is Lindbergh's, but the words are the words of Hitler." The *Des Moines Register* editorialized that "The speech was so intemperate, so unfair, so dangerous in its implications that it disqualifies Lindbergh from any pretensions of leadership."

Radio personality Walter Winchell portrayed the former aviator in painful terms, telling listeners, "Lindbergh's halo has become his noose."[21] Two weeks after his Des Moines appearance, at a rally in Fort Wayne, Indiana, Lindbergh suggested that President Roosevelt might try to suspend the 1942 midterm elections and impose a dictatorship in the

United States. A large number of America First members quit in protest, but a similar number of avowed American Fascists and Hitler supporters joined, further tarnishing the committee's image.[22] In the battle for public opinion, Roosevelt was winning. A Gallup poll released in late October asked what groups were most active "in trying to get us into a war." The Roosevelt administration came in first and Big Business came in second. Less than 7 percent named Jews as the culprits.

U.S. Navy destroyer USS Kearny *(DD-432) at Reykjavik, Iceland, on October 19, 1941, two days after she had been torpedoed by the German submarine U-568. A torpedo hole in* Kearny's *midships is visible. USS* Monssen *(DD-436) is alongside.*

19

RACE AGAINST TIME

WASHINGTON—SEPTEMBER 1941

Y ou know I am a juggler, and I never let my right hand know what my left hand does," Franklin Roosevelt famously and accurately said.[1] "I may have one policy for Europe and one diametrically opposite for North and South America. I may be entirely inconsistent, and furthermore I am perfectly willing to mislead and tell untruths if it will help win the war."

It is one of the most accurate self-assessments he ever made. In the late fall of 1941, surrounded by spinning plates of crisis—some domestic, some foreign—Roosevelt needed to be a master juggler to keep the whole balancing act from crashing down.

At home he had to prevent isolationists in Congress and on radio from scuttling Lend-Lease. Within the White House he needed to moderate between and among his advisors, some pushing him to declare war, others warning him to slow down. He faced serious labor fights with a coal miners' strike in the offing. On the Atlantic he had to push to protect ships carrying supplies to England from Nazi submarines and yet stay within the strict constraints of the Neutrality Act. In East Asia he had to pressure Japan with embargoes to slow its militant expansion without provoking an attack on American interests. And in the U.S.S.R., he needed to help Stalin counteract a relentless German advance that had impelled swastika-emblazoned tanks within thirty miles from Moscow even though most Americans opposed helping the Communists. This circus-worthy performance required extraordinary skill and exceptional leadership.

On October 9, the president formally requested that Congress again amend the Neutrality Law to permit the arming of American merchant ships, to free such vessels to visit ports in the war zones, and to allow U.S. Navy warships to escort convoys sailing under any nation's flag. On that amendment campaign Roosevelt had even less support on Capitol Hill than he had had for Lend-Lease, and a bitter debate broke out. After a German submarine fired torpedoes at the USS *Kearny*, killing eleven American sailors, President Roosevelt again took to the airwaves.

Navy Day, designated in 1922, was October 27, a date chosen because it was Theodore Roosevelt's birthday—a perfect occasion for another president named Roosevelt to speak his mind. The U.S. Navy had always held a special place in FDR's heart, and like his cousin Teddy he had served as the Assistant Secretary of the Navy. He intended that evening's speech to be historic, and out of longstanding habit huddled with Hopkins, Rosenman, and Sherwood.[2] White House logs show they worked on October 26 from dinner until after midnight and again during dinner on October 27 before leaving for the event at 9:30 P.M.[3]

Roosevelt, Eleanor, his speechwriters, and his press secretary were driven a few blocks north to the luxurious Mayflower Hotel on

Connecticut Avenue NW. The ornate Grand Ballroom, with its painted columns, balustraded balconies, and heroic stage, had hosted hundreds of prestigious occasions. That night it was filled with tuxedo-clad military leaders, their wives in glittering gowns, and a dozen radio technicians. The attack on the *Kearny* and the Senate's agreement to take up FDR's proposed Neutrality Act changes gave the evening an atmosphere of significance. Onstage, VIPs clustered around the president; two long tables of large bouquets flanked the podium. Hundreds of the most influential people in Washington sat at round tables with an air of expectation.[4]

"General Donovan, ladies and gentlemen . . ." the president began, referring to his friend and guest, General William Donovan of the U.S. Army. FDR then paused so those onstage could get to their seats. Flashbulbs popped. Reporters scribbled. From the railings of the balcony behind the stage hung two white life preservers separated by a U.S. Navy flag. The crowd settled; Roosevelt continued.

"Five months ago tonight, I proclaimed to the American people the existence of a state of unlimited emergency," he said, summarizing the drama of recent months, the attacks on merchant shipping and naval vessels, and the deaths under fire of American sailors.

"We have wished to avoid shooting, but the shooting has started," FDR said. "And history has recorded who fired the first shot. In the long run, however, all that will matter is who fired the last shot."[5]

Describing Hitler's ambition to rule the seas, he revealed the existence of a secret Nazi map along with the dictator's intention to conquer Central and South America and remake those regions into five new countries under German domination. He accused Hitler of plotting to abolish every religion and replace them with a Nazi theology.

"These grim truths will of course be hotly denied tonight and tomorrow in the controlled press of the Axis powers," he said. "And some Americans—not many—will continue to insist that Hitler's plans need not worry us. The motives of such Americans are not the point at issue. All of us Americans are faced with the choice between the kind of world we want to live in and the kind of world which Hitler and his hordes would impose upon us." It was later discovered that the map was a covert operation by British Intelligence.

The audience applauded as he pivoted to his quest to help his countrymen find their true better angels and retrieve the soul of America. To that end, he explained, he had asked Congress to protect merchant ships and access to British ports. He enumerated the perils awaiting on the seas sailed by America's navy. "It can never be doubted that the goods will be delivered by this nation, whose Navy believes in the tradition of 'Damn the torpedoes; full speed ahead!'" he declared.

The audience erupted in wild cheers at Admiral David Farragut's words, barked under fire during the Battle of Mobile Bay in 1864. Roosevelt made an impassioned case for providing arms to Russia and described the horror of Hitlerism. His ending summoned the essence of America's naval identity and rallied citizens to his cause: "Today in the face of this newest and greatest challenge of them all, we Americans have cleared our decks and taken our battle stations. We stand ready in the defense of our nation and the faith of our fathers to do what God has given us the power to see as our full duty."

The next day's Washington *Evening Star* trumpeted ROOSEVELT'S ADDRESS CALLS FOR HOLY WAR AGAINST HITLER REGIME. McCormick's *Chicago Tribune* was terse—ROOSEVELT: SHOOTING BEGUN. Stories inside explained how a coal strike would disrupt war production and throw the economy into chaos. The juggler went on juggling.

On November 7, the Senate voted 50 to 37 to amend the Neutrality Act, mirroring the House's earlier passage 212 to 194.[6] On November 12, Charles Lindbergh met with Henry Ford[7] and enlisted the auto maker's support to keep the American First Committee going. Public perceptions of Lindbergh as an antisemite, while attractive to Ford, had plunged the Committee into a financial crisis. In Washington, German chargé d'affaires Hans Thomsen wired the Foreign Ministry in Berlin that the

Reich's most effective partner, the America First Committee, was in trouble, and that Lindbergh might take over.[8]

The Wehrmacht had savaged their way across Russia, getting within miles of the capital, and starting a siege that induced terror in the hearts of Muscovites. Reports had reached London that in Nazi-controlled areas death squads were slaughtering tens of thousands of Jews. With Lend-Lease now incorporating the U.S.S.R., envoys and convoys began heading to the Russian port of Arkhangelsk. On November 17 Congress repealed the Neutrality Act, something FDR had been pushing for years.

The British Empire was teetering. In North Africa, General Erwin Rommel's Panzer Group Afrika had the British Army on the defensive, and the Royal Navy's fleet in the Mediterranean had been devastated by aerial and submarine attacks.[9] Despite American efforts in the North Atlantic, cargo ships were being sunk faster than manufacturers could replace them. The Allies were tracking a massive Japanese fleet posing a threat to British colonies in Asia.

Based at Pearl Harbor, Hawaii, for a year, the U.S. Navy's Pacific Fleet was staying in trim with exercises at sea but returning to base weekends so crews could be with their families. An American embargo on oil was pushing Japanese militarists to develop plans for attacking Pearl Harbor. The fate of democracy, freedom, even organized religion, was hanging in the balance. Players in this multinational drama were hitting their marks on the global stage; all that remained was for the curtain to rise on the next act.

A navy photographer snapped this photograph of the Japanese attack on Pearl Harbor in Hawaii on December 7, 1941, just as the USS Shaw *exploded.*

20

INFAMY

The headline for the lead story on the morning of December 7, 1941, of the *New York Times* declared, ROOSEVELT APPEALS TO HIROHITO AFTER NEW THREATS TO INDO-CHINA.

The president had released the contents of a very personal letter he had conveyed to the Japanese emperor seeking to ease the escalating hostility between the two nations. His optimism may have been misplaced, but his words were sincere. "I address myself to Your Majesty at this moment in the fervent hope that Your Majesty may, as I am doing, give thought in this definite emergency to ways of dispelling the dark clouds," FDR wrote. "I am confident that both of us, for the sake of the peoples not only

of our own great countries but for the sake of humanity in neighboring
territories, have a sacred duty to restore traditional amity and prevent
further death and destruction in the world."[1]

Roosevelt's message never reached Hirohito. At the White House that
Sunday morning optimism was in short supply. American intelligence
had intercepted a top-secret diplomatic cable from Tokyo instructing
Japan's ambassador in Washington to deliver final demands to the
Americans and, for security's sake, to begin burning documents.[2] This
sure sign that war was coming was validated by British reports of a large
Japanese fleet steaming south toward Singapore; the Allies expected the
attack to occur in Indochina, Malaya, or the Philippines.

That afternoon, skipping a luncheon Eleanor had arranged, Franklin
Roosevelt was with Harry Hopkins in his private study on the second
floor of the White House. He was working on his stamp collection at
1:47 P.M. when the phone rang.

His caller was Frank Knox. "Mr. President, we just picked up a radio
call from Pearl Harbor advising all our stations that an air raid attack
was on and that it was no drill," the Secretary of the Navy said.

"*No!*" FDR exclaimed, so startling Hopkins that he jumped to his feet.
"The Japs have attacked Pearl!" Roosevelt told Hopkins.[3]

"I don't believe that, it must be a mistake," Hopkins said. "Japan would
never attack Honolulu."

Stunned, Roosevelt hung up the heavy black handset. "I had hoped
to finish my term without getting into war, but if the reports are true,
it takes the matter out of my hands," he said. "The Japs have made the
decision for me."

For months he and his advisors had been pondering where Japan
might strike, and how to respond if its forces struck a British or Dutch
colony. Churchill had repeatedly demanded to know American policy
regarding an attack on Britain's Asian bases. Just as often Roosevelt had
no response. Among his military advisors, consensus was elusive, except
on certainty that the American people would never support going to war

with Japan over Bangkok or Singapore. Much later, Robert Sherwood summed up the sole factor that would have crystallized domestic support for martial action.

"There was just one thing that they could do to get Roosevelt completely off the horns of the dilemma, and that is precisely what they did, at one stroke, in a manner so challenging, so insulting and enraging, that the divided and confused American people were instantly rendered unanimous and certain."[4]

Shortly after 2:00 P.M. Roosevelt called Hull, who was about to meet with the Japanese Ambassador Nomura Kichisaburo and Saburo Kurusu, an envoy from the emperor. Briefing his secretary of state, FDR told Hull to keep mum about Pearl Harbor.

Admiral Harold Stark, Chief of Naval Operations called twenty minutes later confirming FDR's worst fears—the surprise attack had inflicted massive damage, killed nearly 2,500 people and ravaged the Pacific fleet.[5] Roosevelt ordered Stark to issue battle orders committing American forces to war in the Pacific, then dictated a statement for the press to Steve Early and convened his top military advisors. Updates from Hawaii detailed the extent of the death and destruction and the treachery the Japanese had concealed with their false diplomacy.

It was the worst day of his presidency, the worst day of his life—and the worst military defeat in American history. President Franklin Roosevelt's beloved Navy lay in smoking ruins in Pearl Harbor as the Japanese Empire launched well-coordinated attacks across a 4,000-mile front. Disaster and defeat enshrouded the White House.

But as the smoke cleared from the mangled wreckage, it revealed a genuinely great commander in chief. Franklin Roosevelt rose to the occasion, providing a staggered nation vision and confidence. He took the weight of the free world on his paralyzed legs and carried America into the future—away from its isolationist past and into the age of the global superpower. After he had devoted years of effort to persuade the American people that isolationism betrayed the spirit and the soul of this country's commitment to freedom, Japanese warlords had made the case in hours.

Franklin was at his desk when Grace Tully came into the room. Winston Churchill was on the phone, she said.

"Mr. President, what's this about Japan?" the prime minister asked.

"It's quite true. They have attacked us at Pearl Harbor. We are all in the same boat now."

"This certainly simplifies things; God be with you."[6]

Secretly, the British leader was pleased. He had feared Japan would attack only British colonies and that a hamstrung Roosevelt would not be able to intervene. "But now at this very moment I knew the United States was in the war, up to the neck and into the death," Churchill wrote in his memoir. "So, we had won after all! I went to bed and slept the sleep of the saved and thankful."[7]

In the Oval Office, Roosevelt was now face to face with Army Chief of Staff George Marshall, Secretary of War Henry Stimson, Secretary of the Navy Frank Knox, Secretary of State Cordell Hull, Chief of Naval Operations Admiral Harold Stark, and Harry Hopkins. Once the commander in chief had described events half a world away, he and his lieutenants began making plans for what to do about it. By telephone from Honolulu, Hawaiian Governor Joseph Poindexter confirmed the reports, adding details as he was learning them.

"My God!" Roosevelt exclaimed, looking around at his companions. "There's another wave of Jap planes over Hawaii right this minute!"[8]

"What is the situation with our troops, and where are our planes?" Roosevelt asked Marshall.

"I've ordered General MacArthur to execute all the necessary movement required in event of an outbreak of hostilities with Japan," the army chief of staff replied.

"I want the Japanese Embassy and all their consulates protected, and all Japanese citizens picked up," Roosevelt said. "We need to know what they are up to."

"Nomura and Kurusu were in my waiting room when you called to tell me what happened," Hull told the president, his voice shaking with anger.

Hull suggested the Department of Justice take the lead. To Knox and Stimson, the president said, "We need guards placed not only on our own arsenals but on all private munitions factories and all bridges."

"The Army will guard the War Department from now on," Marshall said, meaning the executive building next door.

"That's fine but I don't want military guards around the White House."

The conversation turned to Capitol Hill.

"I am going to give a short, powerful statement tomorrow to Congress and ask for a declaration of war," the president said. His statement would be brief and firm, he said.

Secretary Hull insisted that any remarks at the Capitol include a detailed history of Japanese duplicity. He and Roosevelt argued, with FDR giving no ground in his refusal to go for the interminable tick-tock Hull was prescribing. The debate reverberated on and off through the day.[9]

The meeting broke up around 4:15 P.M. Word went out to Cabinet members to convene at the White House at 8:30 P.M., with congressional leaders to follow at 9:00. Dispatches from Pearl continued to arrive, each driving the dagger in his heart deeper: eight battleships sunk or damaged; thousands injured and killed; the U.S. Pacific Fleet crippled.

After the advisors left, the president called Grace Tully into the oval study. She found him sitting behind the desk smoking.

"Sit down, Grace," he said. "I am going before Congress tomorrow. I would like to dictate my message. It will be short."

Tully sat and took out her notebook. The president took a drag on his cigarette, looked at the ceiling, and in a clear, slow voice dictated his speech start to finish, uninterrupted. He articulated each word, taking care to note every punctuation mark and paragraph break.[10]

"Yesterday, comma, December 7, comma, a date which will live in world history, comma, the United States was simultaneously and deliberately attacked by naval and air forces of the Empire of Japan, period. The United States was at the moment at peace with that nation and was continuing in conversations with its government and its Emperor looking toward the maintenance of peace in the Pacific, period."[11]

His off-the-cuff composition illustrates both leadership and literacy. Beyond the pro forma requirement to obtain a declaration of war from Congress, FDR needed to engage the entire world with a battle cry on behalf of freedom, a righteous call to arms. On the worst day of his presidency, bombarded with calls and questions, Franklin Roosevelt dictated the first draft of one of the greatest speeches of the twentieth century, arguably one of the greatest speeches in American history. "He began in the same calm tone in which he dictated his mail," Tully wrote in her autobiography. "Only his diction was a little different as he spoke each word incisively and slowly. The entire message ran under five hundred words, a cold-blooded indictment of Japanese treachery and aggression, delivered to me without hesitation, interruption, or second thoughts."

Amid chaos, shouldering the weight of an embattled free world, Franklin Roosevelt calmly and precisely composed this clear and decisive statement in his head. Tully typed what he had dictated and gave it to FDR to review.

He made a series of edits, including the most famous to grace any presidential speech—changing "world history" to "infamy" and adding dashes to indicate pauses.

At 8:40 P.M., Vice President Wallace and Cabinet members arrived. They sat in a semicircle facing the president, seated at his desk in the Oval Study. The mood was somber.

"This is the most important Cabinet meeting since 1861, when Lincoln called his advisors about the start of the Civil War," FDR said. Despite their differences they all shared a deep commitment to defending democracy, and on this night, they were a band of brothers, united in their determination to avenge their country's honor.[12]

Outwardly he seemed calm; inside, he was raging with a cold fury. He described the massive loss of life and destruction of his cherished battleships. He read aloud the text he had drafted. Hull and Stimson, who had brought a seventeen-page blow by blow chronicling Japan's decade of mendacity, objected. The earlier debate resumed until FDR agreed to review their text. That typescript, archived at the Franklin D. Roosevelt Presidential Library, shows no handwritten notes; it is unlikely that the president even read it.

At 9:45 P.M., the president undertook the day's most challenging task. The Cabinet members stood up to make room for a contingent of congressional leaders to sit down. Now Roosevelt was face to face with a bipartisan audience that included bitter enemies.[13] The only Republican leader excluded had been Hamilton Fish. The politicians had a basic grasp of events at Pearl but, thanks to censorship, they knew few details. As the president was filling them in, they gasped, asking why the navy and army had been caught off guard. Even as he was confessing that he had no satisfactory answer, FDR showed no fear, no hesitation about what needed to be done. He read them the text of his speech and asked for their support. House Republican Leader Joseph Martin (R-Massachusetts), of "Martin, Barton, and Fish" fame, told the president, "Where the integrity and honor of the nation is involved, there is only one party."[14] Agreeing that the next day at 12:30 P.M. the president would address both houses of Congress and the world, the informal caucus dispersed.

But Franklin was not to be the first Roosevelt to address the nation about Pearl Harbor. At 6:45 P.M., Mrs. Roosevelt began her regular Sunday night NBC broadcast. Neither her husband or anyone else at the White House had previewed what she had written.

"Good evening, ladies, and gentlemen. I am speaking to you tonight at a very serious moment in our history," she began. "The Cabinet is convening and the leaders in Congress are meeting with the President. The State Department and Army and Navy officials have been with the President all afternoon. For months now the knowledge that something of this kind might happen has been hanging over our heads and yet it seemed impossible to believe, impossible to drop the everyday things of life and feel that there was only one thing which was important—preparation to meet an enemy no matter where he struck. That is all over now, and there is no more uncertainty. We know what we have to face, and we know that we are ready to face it."[15]

"I should like to say just a word to the women in the country tonight. I have a boy at sea on a destroyer, for all I know he may be on his way to the Pacific," she said, referring to Franklin Jr. "Two of my children are in coast cities on the Pacific. Many of you all over the country have boys in the services who will now be called upon to go into action. You have friends and families in what has suddenly become a danger zone. You cannot escape anxiety. You cannot escape a clutch of fear at your heart and yet I hope that the certainty of what we have to meet will make you rise above these fears. We are the free and unconquerable people of the United States of America."

This was one of Eleanor Roosevelt's finest moments, for which she rarely received the credit she earned. Her voice, filled with sorrow, was nonetheless steadfast and comforting. She was direct, honest, and vulnerable, connecting with listeners on a deeply personal level.

All four Roosevelt sons served during the war, including in ferocious battles in the Pacific, Africa, and Europe. In saying, "I should like to say just a word to the women in the country tonight . . ." Eleanor created a maternal bond with half the country, even women who disliked her policies. Amid nationwide shock and fear, with rumors rampant about an attack on the West Coast looming, her reassuring voice, even speaking hard truths, steadied an America knocked back on its heels.

The Roosevelts had invited CBS newsman Edward R. Murrow and his wife to dinner that evening. Given the circumstances, Janet Murrow called to confirm. "We still want you to come," Eleanor said. "We still have to eat."

The Murrows arrived around 8:00. Eleanor, fresh from her broadcast, presided over a small group dinner of scrambled eggs and pudding. Franklin was absent. Eleanor herself served. hiding her concern behind the silver serving trays. Around 10:30, as the Murrows were preparing to leave, Eleanor told Ed the president had asked that he stay if he could. Janet left by herself.

Edward R. Murrow, among the most famous of American journalists, now sat on a bench outside the president's study, watching the most powerful men in the free world enter and depart the inner sanctum of Franklin Roosevelt's private study.[16]

Not until after midnight, was Murrow summoned to the president's side. Roosevelt, comfortable in a shapeless "sack jacket" looked sallow and exhausted.[17] Sitting beside World War I hero General William J. Donovan, a longtime FDR friend and political ally who lately had been working informally to gather intelligence for the president, FDR was eating a sandwich that he washed down with gulps from a bottle of beer on the table in front of him.

"Never have I seen one so calm and so steady," Murrow wrote later. In chat mode, the president asked Murrow about people they both knew in London, and how Britons were holding up. Then his talk turned darker. He raged against his military's failings. He listed the losses of ships and the human toll, and when he decried the destruction of planes, he banged his fist on the table. "They were on the ground, by God," he shouted. "On the ground!" He did not yet know that the Japanese had also bombed Clark Field near Manilla, destroying American fighters and bombers left exposed on the runway.

Murrow left the White House with the scoop of the century, an incredible first-person account of President Roosevelt's reaction to the attack. Putting patriotism above professional glory, Murrow never reported what he learned that night.

What Roosevelt learned that night was that his efforts to prepare the country for war might not have been enough. The attack on Pearl Harbor revealed exactly how complacent the American armed services were, even in the face of Fascist victories across the globe. In truth, the president's campaign to force a reluctant Congress to fund his rearmament program, despite intense opposition, may have been his greatest accomplishment. According to historian and author Michael Beschloss, "If Roosevelt had not persuaded the nation to rearm before Pearl Harbor, the Allies might conceivably have lost the war. After the Japanese assault, his conspicuous personal self-confidence, through the public hysteria and beyond, was a powerful weapon of war."[18]

THE U.S. CAPITOL

President Roosevelt arrived at the Capitol a little after noon on December 8. As he entered the House, the audience stood and cheered for several minutes. He made the long walk out into the grand chamber holding onto James and balancing himself with his cane. Once in position, he took a deep breath and began.[19]

"Yesterday, December 7th, 1941—a date which will live in infamy—the United States of America was suddenly and deliberately attacked by naval and air forces of the Empire of Japan."

"A date which will live in infamy." Not only does FDR's phrase mark the date Japan attacked the United States, but the date on which America embarked on its journey from isolationist nation to superpower.

"The United States was at peace with that Nation and, at the solicitation of Japan, was still in conversation with its Government and its Emperor looking toward the maintenance of peace in the Pacific," he continued. "Indeed, one hour after Japanese air squadrons had commenced bombing in the American Island of Oahu, the Japanese Ambassador to the United States and his colleague delivered to our Secretary of State a formal reply to a recent American message. And while this reply stated that it seemed useless to continue the existing diplomatic negotiations, it contained no threat or hint of war or of armed attack."

The political elite on the House floor and onlookers cramming the galleries above listened in silence. The president's tone was grave, with a razor-sharp edge.

"The attack yesterday on the Hawaiian Islands has caused severe damage to American naval and military forces," he said. "I regret to tell you that very many American lives have been lost. In addition, American ships have been reported torpedoed on the high seas between San Francisco and Honolulu. Yesterday the Japanese Government also launched an attack against Malaya.

"Last night Japanese forces attacked Hong Kong. Last night Japanese forces attacked Guam. Last night Japanese forces attacked the Philippine Islands. Last night the Japanese attacked Wake Island. And this morning, the Japanese attacked Midway Island."

We know FDR wrote this without his usual team of speechwriters. He did incorporate one suggestion by Vice President Henry Wallace, a line that summed up the president's own feelings and generated the loudest round of applause: "No matter how long it may take us to overcome this premeditated invasion, the American people will in their righteous might win through to absolute victory."[20]

He wasted no words, his language honed and pointed like a bayonet, leaving no doubt that he meant to wage war: "With confidence in our armed forces—with the unbounding determination of our people—we will gain the inevitable triumph—so help us God. I ask that the Congress declare that since the unprovoked and dastardly attack by Japan on Sunday, December 7th, 1941, a state of war has existed between the United States and the Japanese Empire."

Here was a clarion call, a profound statement of national values, and a fierce show of determination to obtain justice. In its brevity—seven minutes, for the record—FDR's text expressed his outrage, his sense of betrayal, and his complete confidence that, in the end, the United States would avenge this treachery. Just twenty-five sentences, about twice the length of Lincoln's Gettysburg Address, it is extraordinary in its clarity of purpose and call to action.

Four hours later, he signed the declaration of war that Congress had passed. Franklin Roosevelt's words that day launched the greatest armada, largest air force, and most mechanized infantry in history. The racing industrialization that enabled the arsenal of democracy became turbocharged with patriotic fervor and lust for revenge. Within two years, Roosevelt would be the undisputed leader of the free world, commander in chief of the mightiest international military force ever assembled, and the last great hope of conquered people everywhere.

On December 9, 1941, Roosevelt wrote in a dispatch to Churchill, "The Senate passed the all-out declaration of war eighty-two to nothing and the House has passed it three hundred eighty-eight to one. Today all of us are in the same boat with you and the people of the Empire and it is a ship which will not and cannot be sunk."[21]

Churchill immediately began planning to use that metaphorical vessel and in a literal ship sail across the Atlantic bound ultimately for 1600 Pennsylvania Avenue NW.

On December 11, Hitler's foreign minister Joachim von Ribbentrop summoned American chargé d'affaires Leland B. Morris to his office and at 2:18 P.M. informed him that "Germany, as from today, considers herself as being in a state of war with the United States of America." Ribbentrop then screamed at Morris "Your president wanted this war, and now he has it!" and stormed out of the room.

NEW YORK

On December 8, Charles Lindbergh, speaking for the America First Committee, issued a statement of his own: "We have been stepping closer to war for many months. Now it has come, and we must meet it as united Americans regardless of our attitude in the past toward the policy our government has followed. Whether or not that policy has been wise, our country has been attacked by force of arms and by force of arms we must retaliate, our own defenses and our own military positions have already been neglected too long. We must now turn every effort to building the greatest and most efficient army, navy, and air force in the world. When American soldiers go to war, it must be with the best equipment that modern skill can design, and that modern industry can build."[22]

The isolationist movement had been sunk by the Japanese bombs that landed on Pearl Harbor. Within days of the attack the FBI, with particular attention to Charles Lindbergh and the America First Committee, began investigating leaks to Germany of secret military plans, portions of which McCormick's *Chicago Tribune* had published. At an America First Committee party in Greenwich Village ten days after Pearl Harbor, Charles Lindbergh and several dozen other guests bemoaned their movement's undoing. Urged to speak, Lindbergh reluctantly agreed. He did not know that there were two undercover informants for the FBI and Military Intelligence standing right in front of him.

"There is only one danger in the world," he said. "That is the yellow danger. China and Japan are really bound together against the white race. There could have only been one efficient weapon against this alliance. Underneath the surface, Germany itself could have been this weapon. The ideal setup would have been to have Germany take over Poland and Russia, in collaboration with the British, as a bloc against the yellow people and Bolshevism. But instead, the British and the fools in Washington had to interfere. The British envied the Germans and wanted to rule the world forever. Britain is the real cause of all the trouble in the world today."[23]

Lindbergh went on to say that America First needed to lay low until Americans wearied of war, giving the committee an opportunity to reemerge as a political power.

The world-famous pilot believed himself a patriot, and with the country now at war he wanted to serve. Realizing it would be an arduous task, he set out to rejoin the military. On December 20, 1941, he wrote a personal letter to General Hap Arnold, offering to serve in the Army Air Corps. An acquaintance of many years' standing, Arnold had profound respect for Lindbergh, but when the aviator's offer hit the papers the

public howled disapproval, and a meeting with army secretary Henry
Stimson went badly.[24] Lindbergh later learned that at a meeting with
senators, President Roosevelt bragged, "I will clip that young man's
wings."[25] Rejected, albeit politely everywhere he went, Lindbergh was
offered a job in late March 1942 by auto tycoon Henry Ford, who took
delight in annoying Franklin Roosevelt.

Ford, who had just completed the massive mile-long Willow Run
factory, designed to produce a B-24 Liberator heavy bomber every hour,
wanted Lindbergh to improve the design, increase efficiency, and test
aircraft. The pilot jumped at the chance and performed admirably. He
unquestionably helped make the B-24 a better bomber, and over time
he earned grudging respect from critics, a painful journey whose initial
trajectory was summed up by a sister-in-law of his: "In 15 years he has
gone from Jesus to Judas."[26]

Late in the war, Lindbergh traveled to the Pacific as a civilian technical consultant to improve Marine warplanes' performance. He ended up
flying fifty combat missions, earning high praise from General Douglas
MacArthur and fellow pilots.

In the years following the attack on Pearl Harbor books, articles,
movies, and multiple congressional and Pentagon investigations have
explored what happened and why. The Army and Navy commanders
on Pearl Harbor were criticized and forced to retire in disgrace, though
many feel they were unfairly scapegoated. The investigations led to cries
of coverup, and a multitude of conspiracy theories. There are still unanswered questions. Should FDR and Marshall have been more aggressive
in alerting their field commanders of the danger? Should they have shared
the top secret intelligence that came from the broken codes of the Japanese? Why were the military bases so unprepared? There are no definitive
answers. Robert Sherwood posits that their concern that "undue alarm
might be caused" helps explain why Roosevelt and Marshall were so
hesitant to raise a more urgent alarm.

"Marshall and Roosevelt were far more afraid of the isolationists at home—the "portions of our public that doubted our integrity"—than they were of the enemies abroad. They were afraid of being called "alarmists" a word which was then interchangeable with "warmongers."[27] Therefore, neither one of them, nor Admiral Stark, ever reached out to push the button which rang the General Alarm, for that precautionary measure might have been construed as the overt act."

Franklin Roosevelt at microphones, Winston Churchill to his right watching the lighting of the White House Christmas Tree, December 24, 1941.

21

CHRISTMAS AT THE
WHITE HOUSE

THE COAST OF SCOTLAND—DECEMBER 1941

The great ship rumbled as her engines engaged. Moving slowly up the river Clyde she left Glasgow headed west. HMS *Duke of York*, commissioned six weeks earlier, was the newest addition to the Royal Navy. At 740 feet and displacing more than 37,000 tons, she had a maximum speed of 32 mph, making her one of the world's fastest warships. *York* was a King George V class battleship like HMS *Prince of Wales*, which in August had brought Churchill to the Atlantic Conference. Japanese bombers had sunk *Wales* off the coast of Malaya two days before *York* left port.

The *Duke of York* was setting forth less than a week after Pearl Harbor, carrying Prime Minister Winston Churchill and fifty of his top military advisors, assistants, and his traveling map room.[1] The Britons were on a secret pilgrimage to the United States, seeking audience with their savior, Franklin Roosevelt.

The North Atlantic welcomed the voyagers with the worst weather imaginable. Massive swells broke across the dreadnought's bow. *York*'s complement of destroyers and other smaller ships struggled against headwinds. Fearful that slowing his pace to keep the flotilla together would draw German submarines, the captain sheared off onto a solo course westward.[2]

The ship was fully battened down, with passengers confined below decks. The ten-day trip wore on even the most seaworthy among them but also allowed Churchill and his inner circle to draft three briefing papers on battle strategy to share with their American counterparts.

WASHINGTON

HMS *Duke of York* arrived at Norfolk Navy Yard, Virginia, on December 22, 1941. Churchill immediately flew north to Washington. At Anacostia Naval Air Station, President Roosevelt was waiting for him in the back seat of his car. They shook hands and greeted each other as old friends.[3] At the White House, Churchill got a room right across the hall from Harry Hopkins, who since the men met in England a year earlier had become the prime minister's strongest advocate. The president and the prime minister sat up until after midnight, drinking and smoking and talking about the war and the world they now faced. Churchill's aides set up his traveling map room, which fascinated Roosevelt. He soon ordered one for himself. The two champions of freedom, normally separated by 3,500 miles of ocean, now slept just yards from one another. For several wondrous weeks they wandered in and out of each other's rooms whenever they had a yen to talk. Both had much to say.

The following day Churchill joined the president for a rowdy press conference. The visitor's presence had drawn twice the typical number of journalists, everyone jostling for a better look at the prime minister. Secret Service agents vetted all seeking entry, and it was minutes before the ritual session-starting call of "All In!"[4]

"I am sorry to have taken so long for all of you to get in, but apparently—I was telling the Prime Minister the object was to prevent a wolf from coming in here in sheep's clothing," Roosevelt told his audience. The president then described the British press as lambs compared to the American wolves posing as journalists.

The reporters laughed, and those in the back leaned forward to hear better. Roosevelt explained the purpose of the meetings and listed other countries as participants in the coalition now engaged in defeating the Axis powers. The room was so crowded that the diminutive prime minister was obscured.

"I wish you would just stand up for one minute and let them see you," FDR said. "They can't see you."

Winston Churchill stood to applause and calls of "We can't see you!" from the back. The rotund, sixty-seven-year-old prime minister of Great Britain climbed onto the seat of his chair and waved, eliciting wild cheering and more applause. Smiling, he took questions, and then described his perspective on how the new military alliance might work.

"The key to the whole situation is the resolute manner in which the British and American democracies are going to throw themselves into the conflict. As a geographical and strategic point, it obviously is of very high importance." Asked whether Germany might collapse under the weight of the new international coalition he replied, "I have always been feeling that one of these days we might get a windfall coming from that quarter. And then, as we did in the last war, we may wake up and find we ran short of Huns."

The reporters laughed and continued to fling questions at him. Always happy to be the center of attention, Churchill charmed his inquisitors, answering with directness and humor.

"I can't describe the feelings of relief with which I find Russia victorious, the United States and Great Britain standing side by side," he said "It is incredible to anyone who has lived through the lonely months of 1940. It is incredible. Thank God."

"How long do you think it will take to lick these boys?"

"If we manage it well, it will only take half as long as if we manage it badly," he said to a chorus of laughter.

The final questioner spoke for millions worldwide.

"Mr. Minister, do you have any doubt about the ultimate victory?"

Churchill straightened. Leaning forward, and in a deep, powerful voice, he answered, "I have no doubt whatever."[5]

Churchill's arrival and comments rated headlines even in the *Chicago Tribune*. President Roosevelt had achieved his key victory of the war, and for America, it had only just begun. Finally, America had awoken from its naive isolationist slumber and donned the uniform of liberation. Churchill stayed at the White House for five weeks while British and American military leaders plotted strategy. He delivered a remarkable address to a special session of congress in which he ended by declaring, "I avow my hope and faith, sure and inviolate, that in the days to come the British and American peoples will, for their own safety and for the good of all, walk together in majesty, in justice, and in peace."

At twilight on Christmas Eve, Churchill joined the president to watch the lighting of the national Christmas tree on the South Lawn of the White House. As the two men looked out from the mansion's south portico at the towering East Oriental spruce draped with lights, they formed a solemn tableau of friendship and uplift. Britons' last two Christmases had been subdued, darkened by its blackout rules. In many a home, empty chairs around the holiday table invoked memoires of those far away or gone forever. In remarks broadcast internationally, both spoke from the heart.

"The year 1941 has brought upon our Nation a war of aggression by powers dominated by arrogant rulers whose selfish purpose is to destroy free institutions. They would thereby take from the freedom-loving peoples of the earth the hard-won liberties gained over many centuries. We have joined with many other nations and peoples in a very great cause. Millions of them have been engaged in the task of defending good with their lifeblood for months and for years."

"One of their great leaders stands beside me. He and his people in many parts of the world are having their Christmas trees with their little children around them, just as we do here. He and his people have pointed the way in courage and in sacrifice for the sake of little children everywhere. And so, I am asking my associate, my old and good friend, to say a word to the people of America, old and young."[6]

When Churchill began speaking, his voice was heavy with emotion.

"I spend this anniversary and festival far from my country, far from my family, yet I cannot truthfully say that I feel far from home. This is a strange Christmas Eve. Almost the whole world is locked in deadly struggle, armed with the most terrible weapons which science can devise, the nations advance upon each other. . . . We may cast aside for this night at least the cares and dangers which beset us and make for the children an evening of happiness in a world of storm.

"Here, then, for one night only, each home throughout the English-speaking world should be a brightly lighted island of happiness and peace. Let the children have their night of fun and laughter. Let the gifts of Father Christmas delight their play. Let us grown-ups share to the full in their unstinted pleasures before we turn again to the stern task and the formidable years that lie before us, resolved that, by our sacrifice and daring, these same children shall not be robbed of their inheritance or denied their right to live in a free and decent world."

Their words brought hope to people from Malaya to Moscow, from Palestine to Poland, from Paris to Pearl Harbor, at a time of deepening darkness. Their comments reflected absolute faith in their victory and the value of manifesting the spirit of Christmas for children facing an uncertain future. Lit by the nation's Christmas tree they stood in unity, the embodiment of democratic ideals, giving voice to expressions of freedom that touched the soul of America and inspired its citizens with a righteous cause.

Franklin, Eleanor, and Winston attended a simple church service at the Foundry United Methodist Church on Christmas morning. The rector had placed lilies on the altar in memory of Sara Roosevelt. They prayed for "those who are dying on land and sea this Christmas morning." There was much singing, but one carol was unfamiliar to Churchill, "O Little Town of Bethlehem." He noted in his memoir that its lyrics left a lasting impression.[7]

Yet in thy dark streets shineth
The everlasting light.
The hopes and fears
Of all the years
Are met in thee tonight.

President Franklin Roosevelt and delegates from twenty-six countries sign
the Statement of United Nations at the White House, January 1, 1942.

22

THE STATE OF THE UNION

WASHINGTON—JANUARY 1942

The limousine stopped beside a small red brick structure layered in ivy behind an iron gate. President Roosevelt, his wife, and Prime Minister Churchill exited the car and in a few steps were at the tomb of George and Martha Washington. Standing under an umbrella, Roosevelt and Churchill removed their hats. The prime minister lifted a large wreath of iris and camellias and carried the floral arrangement to its intended location. He gently placed the wreath on Washington's white marble sarcophagus and bowed his head in silent meditation. Walking from the tomb Churchill turned to Mrs. Roosevelt. "What a wet day," he said.[1]

President Roosevelt had declared January 1, 1942, a National Day of Prayer. The prime minister had returned to Washington that morning from Canada. Before paying their respects at Mount Vernon the two men attended a service at Christ Church in Alexandria, Virginia, sitting in a pew that once belonged to America's first president.

"We are to pray for three gifts from God," the Reverend Edward Welles declared from the pulpit. "Pardon, power, and peace. Pardon for past shortcomings, power for the present task of achieving victory and peace—enduring peace—by God's help in the days to come."

Those days proved historic. The convergence of Great Britain's and America's highest military officials and political leaders was given the code name "Arcadia." FDR's highest priority was creation of a grand coalition allying countries willing to fight fascism. The two sovereign teams worked on a declaration of intent to be signed by participating nations—a consortium initially referred to as "the Associated Powers," a label not to Roosevelt's liking.

Upon returning from Mount Vernon, Roosevelt hosted a working lunch in the White House dining room. He wanted the formal declaration signed that day, but certain issues remained unresolved. Prime Minister Churchill, Soviet Ambassador Maxim Litvinov, Chinese Minister Dr. T. V. Soong, Harry Hopkins, and Roosevelt debated those points. The president pushed to include freedom of religion. Litvinov refused.

"The Kremlin might possibly agree to include freedom of conscience," the ambassador said.

"The phrase 'religious freedom' means the same thing," Roosevelt insisted. "I want to use the word 'religion' because it is part of the Four Freedoms. The original Jeffersonian principle of religious freedom was so broadly democratic that it included the right to have no religions at all—it gave the individual the right to worship any God he chose, or no god."[2]

Litvinov also wanted to clarify that signatories were agreeing to oppose "those members of the Tripartite pact and its adherents with which such government is at war." Russia was not at war with Japan and did not want to commit to opening a second front. In the end Roosevelt got religious freedom and Litvinov absolved the Soviet Union from having to fight Japan.

After lunch the president, now upstairs in the White House quarters, had an inspiration to christen this new international coalition the United Nations. Excited, he wheeled himself into Churchill's room just as Colonel Ian Jacob was helping the prime minister get out of the bath.[3] Roosevelt apologized and started to withdraw. But Winston Churchill proudly stood half-naked and squared his shoulders. "The Prime Minister of Great Britain has nothing to hide from the President of the United States," he declared.

And thus, the phrases "United Nations" and "special relationship" were born.

The final edit to the declaration was the insertion of the term "United Nations," and a copy was printed for ceremonial purposes. At 10:00 P.M. that evening Roosevelt, Churchill, Litvinov, and Soong signed the "Declaration by United Nations." The following day representatives of another twenty-two countries signed. The declaration announced that the United Nations "are now engaged in a common struggle against savage and brutal forces seeking to subjugate the world." Roosevelt released the text to the press at 3:00 P.M. on January 2.

The Arcadia Conference shifted into a flurry of strategic planning, technical discussions, weapons production, and arguments and agreements regarding command structure. During a two-week period of this critical summit Churchill, Roosevelt, and their most senior advisors toiled in formal session eight times, augmented by countless informal talks. Military teams met on their own an additional twelve times.

Roosevelt insisted on establishing a Combined Chiefs of Staff, based in Washington, to coordinate all military activity and to ensure clear lines of command between the two sovereign states' armed forces.[4] The chiefs worked out complicated logistical issues and deployments. The most important decision was assigning defeat of Hitler's Germany top priority. The Allies' success in World War II was a product of the United Nations and its unprecedented collaboration. The alliance established in the White House at Christmas 1941 has lasted more than eighty years.

The White House

Roosevelt needed time to work on his State of the Union message, set to be delivered January 6. Fierce pressure to keep the Arcadia Conference on track and Churchill's unusual schedule of mid-afternoon naps and late-night drinking was pushing the president to the edge of exhaustion. He squeezed in meetings with his writing team of Robert Sherwood, Sam Rosenman, and Harry Hopkins at odd times: early morning, over lunch, late in the evening. He read a draft aloud to Churchill, afterward telling the writers the prime minister "had loved the speech."[5] FDR and his wordsmiths were driving themselves without relent, fearing FDR's message to Congress and the nation would be judged, perhaps unfavorably, against Churchill's rousing December 26 oration to a special session of Congress.

On Monday, January 5, the writers and Grace Tully were huddling in the Cabinet Room. Usually a paragon of order, their improvised workspace reflected the urgency of the task before them—papers cascading across a long mahogany table, research materials balanced haphazardly on chairs, everywhere stacks or folders bulging with notes and clippings. At 1:00 P.M. Roosevelt rolled in for another working lunch. He was in a good mood, and excited about their progress on the text. Attorney General Francis Biddle was to meet with them at 2:00 P.M. and Roosevelt, a dedicated practical joker, had an idea.

"You know Francis is terribly worried about civil liberties—especially now," he told his cowriters. "He has been on my neck asking me to say that the war will not curtail them too much. Now don't laugh and give it away, but I'm going to hand him a little line."[6]

"Ask Francis to come right in here," the president told General Pa Watson.

The attorney general entered and took a seat at the table.

"Francis, I'm glad you came," a stony-faced Roosevelt said in stern tones. "All of us have just been discussing here the question of civil liberties in the war, and I have finally come to a decision to issue a proclamation—which I am going to ask you to draft—abrogating so far as possible all freedom of discussion and information during the war, it's a tough thing to do, but I'm convinced that it's absolutely necessary, and I want to announce it in this speech we are working on now."

The group sat in funereal silence as Biddle, obviously distressed, looked from face to face. He launched into a passionate defense of civil liberties, arguing with vehement eloquence against curtailing those liberties. He stood and began pacing back and forth, gesticulating as he railed. After several minutes FDR and the writers could hold back no longer, and laughter erupted. A stunned Biddle, realizing he had yet again been a victim of the court jester in chief, smiled sheepishly.

Tensions eased, and Biddle joined in finalizing the speech, providing input from the Department of Justice. The team worked until 2:00 A.M. The final version was delivered to FDR when he woke the next morning. Of the president he served, Sam Rosenman wrote, "He never allowed the seriousness of the job in hand to become depressing. He enjoyed laughter, he enjoyed a good story, he enjoyed telling humorous incidents and anecdotes. He made these serious sessions pleasant, light, and enjoyable experiences."

But Biddle's concern about civil liberties was prescient. Six weeks later President Roosevelt signed Executive Order 9066, creating a special military exclusion zone along the West Coast. His order allowed the military to remove and relocate any persons who might pose a threat to the United States. This resulted in the unconstitutional incarceration of approximately 120,000 people of Japanese descent, 80,000 of whom were American citizens, and many of whom had sons actively serving in the American military. The episode stands as one of the most shameful engineered by the Roosevelt administration, and reflects fear and racism unleashed by the attack on Pearl Harbor. Biddle was one of only a few members of the administration to oppose Executive Order 9066.

THE U.S. CAPITOL

An arctic wind was sweeping Pennsylvania Avenue on January 6 as President Roosevelt and his entourage headed toward the Capitol. The temperature was 12°, the coldest day of the new year. Even so, the president, with Princess Martha and Prince Olav of Norway, rode in an open car.[7] At the Capitol a bipartisan escort of lawmakers accompanied him into the House chamber. On General Watson's arm, the president slowly made his way to the podium in front of the rostrum, where Vice President Wallace and Speaker Sam Rayburn were sitting. The assembly rose and applauded as he reached the lectern. His voice calm and firm, Roosevelt delivered his first wartime address to Congress.

"In fulfilling my duty to report upon the State of the Union, I am proud to say to you that the spirit of the American people was never higher than it is today—the Union was never more closely knit together—this country was never more deeply determined to face the solemn tasks before it,"[8] he said. The chamber echoed with applause in the first of more than thirty ovations to greet FDR's message.

"The response of the American people has been instantaneous, and it will be sustained until our security is assured. The act of Japan at Pearl Harbor was intended to stun us—to terrify us to such an extent that we would divert our industrial and military strength to the Pacific area, or even to our own continental defense. The plan has failed in its purpose. We have not been stunned. We have not been terrified or confused. This very reassembling of the Seventy-seventh Congress today is proof of that; for the mood of quiet, grim resolution which here prevails bodes ill for those who conspired and collaborated to murder world peace. That mood is stronger than any mere desire for revenge. It expresses the will of the American people to make very certain that the world will never so suffer again."

Roosevelt paused, letting the applause play out. His stare was unblinking, his jaw firm, his countenance severe.

"The militarists of Berlin and Tokyo started this war. But the massed, angered forces of common humanity will finish it. They know that victory for us means victory for freedom. They know that victory for us means victory for the institution of democracy—the ideal of the family, the simple principles of common decency and humanity. They know that victory for us means victory for religion. And they could not tolerate that. The world is too small to provide adequate 'living room' for both Hitler and God. In proof of that, the Nazis have now announced their plan for enforcing their new German, pagan religion all over the world—a plan by which the Holy Bible and the Cross of Mercy would be displaced by *Mein Kampf* and the swastika and the naked sword."

President Roosevelt enumerated goals for weapons and equipment manufacture—ambitious estimates far exceeding those from his own advisors.

"First, to increase our production rate of airplanes so rapidly that in this year, 1942, we shall produce 60,000 planes, 10,000 more than the goal that we set a year and a half ago. The rate of increase will be maintained and continued so that next year, 1943, we shall produce 125,000 airplanes, including 100,000 combat planes." Roosevelt stunned lawmakers, and any arms makers listening, as he promised to deliver 45,000 tanks in 1942 and 75,000 tanks in 1943, 20,000 antiaircraft guns then 35,000 the following year, 6,000,000 tons of shipping rising to 10,000,000 tons of shipping. The total cost would be $68 billion.

"We know that we may have to pay a heavy price for freedom. We will pay this price with a will. Whatever the price, it is a thousand times worth it. No matter what our enemies, in their desperation, may attempt to do to us—we will say, as the people of London have said, 'We can take it.' And what's more we can give it back and we will give it back—with compound interest." As the audience clapped, Franklin Roosevelt smiled and nodded.

"But we of the United Nations are not making all this sacrifice of human effort and human lives to return to the kind of world we had after the last world war. We are fighting today for security, for progress, and for peace, not only for ourselves but for all men, not only for one generation but for all generations. We are fighting to cleanse the world of ancient evils, ancient ills. We are fighting, as our fathers have fought, to uphold the doctrine that all men are equal in the sight of God. Those on the other side are striving to destroy this deep belief and to create a world in their own image—a world of tyranny and cruelty and serfdom. That is the conflict that day and night now pervades our lives. No compromise can end that conflict. There never has been—there never can be—successful compromise between good and evil. Only total victory can reward the champions of tolerance, and decency, and freedom, and faith."

Republicans and Democrats on the floor and spectators in the gallery jumped to their feet in approval as Roosevelt turned from the microphones to thank Vice President Wallace and Speaker Rayburn.[9]

Response to Roosevelt's address was wildly positive. In a Gallop poll that week 84 percent of respondents approved of Roosevelt's job performance. Senate Majority Leader Alben Barkley (D-Kentucky) said, "It was a fighting address—the American people will respond with fighting determination." Across the aisle Senator Warren Austin (R-Vermont) hailed "the speech of a military leader who uttered a great battle cry pitched to the heavens." Speaker Rayburn, who had turned sixty that day, declared, "Of all his great speeches this is the greatest." And House Majority Leader John McCormack (D-Massachusetts) said, "One of the greatest speeches of all time. Without regard to our religious convictions, we can all thank God that in this crisis he gave us as our leader Franklin D. Roosevelt."[10]

Even FDR's most strident critics offered faint praise. Isolationist bigwig Senator Burton Wheeler (D-Montana) said he approved of FDR's plans to build more planes and tanks. Senate Minority Leader Charles L. McNary (R-Oregon) was quoted as saying, "A scrappy speech, but this is going to cost mountains of money and each item of the expense must be carefully scrutinized." The ultra-isolationist Roosevelt-hater Hamilton Fish III (R-New York) sarcastically congratulated the president on "a good pep talk."

Roosevelt's closing for his tenth State of the Union—"Only total victory can reward the champions of tolerance, and decency, and freedom, and faith"—marked a turning point in FDR's battle to awaken the spirit of America. He no longer needed to cajole and convince the people into rejecting isolationism and embracing their destiny as warriors against tyranny. Americans nationwide had united in a commitment to defend freedom and democracy everywhere in the world.

Doris Kearns Goodwin explained how FDR was able to rally the country to recognize itself as the "Arsenal of Democracy."

"Roosevelt's success in mobilizing the nation to this extraordinary level of collective performance rested on his uncanny sensitivity to his followers, his ability to appraise public feelings, and to lead the people one step at a time."[11]

And lead people he did, through the global cataclysm that was World War II. Having triumphed in his war of words, Roosevelt now had to wage a real war, leading the combined military might of the United Nations to defeat Hitler and the Axis powers, forcing them to surrender unconditionally. On June 6, 1944 he delivered his D-Day Prayer, which reveals in eloquent prose his true beliefs about the soul of America.

> *Almighty God: Our sons, pride of our Nation, this day have set upon*
> *a mighty endeavor, a struggle to preserve our Republic, our religion,*
> *and our civilization, and to set free a suffering humanity. Lead them*

straight and true; give strength to their arms, stoutness to their hearts, steadfastness in their faith.

With Thy blessing, we shall prevail over the unholy forces of our enemy. Help us to conquer the apostles of greed and racial arrogancies. Lead us to the saving of our country, and with our sister Nations into a world unity that will spell a sure peace, a peace invulnerable to the scheming of unworthy men. And a peace that will let all men live in freedom, reaping the just rewards of their honest toil.

*This is the last photograph of FDR, taken on April 11, 1945,
at the Little White House in Warm Springs, Georgia.*

EPILOGUE

Winston Churchill departed Washington on January 14, 1942 and headed home to face his critics in the House of Commons, who questioned his leadership in the face of bitter defeats across the globe. Harry Hopkins sent presents for Mrs. Churchill, his host while he was in London. He included a note which says much about his relationship with the Churchills. "You would have been quite proud of your husband on this trip," Hopkins wrote. "First because he was ever so good natured. I didn't see him take anybody's head off, and he eats and drinks with his customary vigor, and still dislikes the same people."[1]

The Roosevelt-Churchill-Hopkins alliance remains one of the most consequential elements in the creation of today's world. Despite personal flaws and idiosyncrasies, those figures' wisdom, actions, and words inspired freedom-loving people to risk everything in the battle between good and evil. Between democracy and fascism. This trio's adventures from 1942 to 1945 have been well documented. Battles and summits, shocking setbacks and glorious victories have solidified into a wartime mythology of inevitable triumph. But in the early dark days, defeat and disaster were constant companions. The strain of leadership during these years took a terrible toll on all three men. Churchill suffered at least one heart attack and other serious ailments. Hopkins endured almost constant pain from his stomach problems and after the Yalta summit was taken directly to the Mayo Clinic where he almost died, for a second time. Franklin Roosevelt literally worked himself to death in the cause of liberty and did not live to see the end of that terrible war. His final days were bittersweet. Sweet with the knowledge that Nazi Germany's demise was near and that the United Nations, meant to protect the peace achieved by the war, would soon convene for its inaugural meeting. Bitter due to Roosevelt's dismal health. Cardiac and circulatory failure rendered his countenance grey and drawn, bags under his eyes purple and swollen. When longtime friends saw him, they gasped at his frailty.

As he had so many times before, Roosevelt visited Warm Springs, Georgia in early spring 1945, seeking rejuvenation after the exhausting journey to Yalta to meet with Stalin and Churchill. The United Nations meeting was on his mind, and he was determined to give the founding delegates an inspirational welcome. But his most immediate concern was the annual Jefferson Day speech on April 13. He penned most of the text himself.

He never delivered that speech. On April 12, 1945 a massive cerebral hemorrhage struck him down. His death shocked a world at war. For hundreds of millions his passing ended an era of unrelenting crisis answered by his unselfish leadership.

On the day after he died, the *New York Times* predicted, "Men will thank God on their knees a hundred years from now that Franklin D. Roosevelt was in the White House . . . in that dark hour."

Addressing Parliament, Prime Minister Winston Churchill saluted his comrade in arms:

> For us, it remains only to say that in Franklin Roosevelt there died the greatest American friend we have ever known and the greatest champion of freedom who has ever brought help and comfort from the new world to the old. Of Roosevelt . . . it must be said that had he not acted when he did, in the way he did, had he not resolved to give aid to Britain and to Europe in the supreme crisis through which we have passed, a hideous fate might well have overwhelmed mankind and made its whole future for centuries sink into shame and ruin.

Under different circumstances Churchill once noted, "Meeting Franklin Roosevelt was like opening your first bottle of champagne; knowing him was like drinking it."

In his biography of Lindbergh, A. Scott Berg wrote "The passing of Franklin Roosevelt did not affect Washington's official attitude toward Lindbergh overnight. It took a week."[2] As the war in Europe neared its end, Lindbergh was summoned back to the States and was asked to join a Naval Technical Mission to Germany to study Nazi aircraft technology. In the 1950s, President Eisenhower recognized Lindbergh's contributions and, after reinstating the reserve commission Lindbergh resigned in the 1930s, promoted him to brigadier general in the U.S. Air Force.

Charles Lindbergh died in 1974, having spent the final years of his life living mostly in Hawaii, a passionate advocate for environmental causes. In 2003 there was a shocking revelation that Lindbergh had multiple secret families in Germany, beginning in 1957. Three of his secret children revealed he had fathered seven children with three different women.[3] DNA tests and more than one hundred love letters to their mother confirmed their story. The children had been sworn to secrecy regarding their father, but finally went public with their stories.

★

FDR's undelivered Jefferson Day speech articulates his vision of the future, his faith in America, and his firm belief in Jefferson's ideals.

> Today, this Nation which Jefferson helped so greatly to build is playing a tremendous part in the battle for the rights of man all over the world. Today we are part of the vast Allied force—a force composed of flesh and blood and steel and spirit—which is today destroying the makers of war, the breeders of hatred, in Europe and in Asia. We, as Americans, do not choose to deny our responsibility. Nor do we intend to abandon our determination that, within the lives of our children and our children's children, there will not be a third world war . . . I ask you to keep up your faith. And to you, and to all Americans who dedicate themselves with us to the making of an abiding peace, I say: The only limit to our realization of tomorrow will be our doubts of today. Let us move forward with strong and active faith.

As final words go, they have survived the test of time.

Like so many of Franklin Roosevelt's words, these resonate now—as doubts undermine our commitment to democracy, to social justice, to human progress. Our faith in our neighbors has been shaken. Again "breeders of hatred" both foreign and domestic threaten our democracy, in much the same way Charles Lindbergh and the America First Committee did. To actualize America's true potential, we must move forward with a strong and active faith in ourselves, our fellow citizens, and our fragile democracy.

Franklin Delano Roosevelt was not a perfect man, nor a perfect president. Critics rightfully point to his responses to the Jewish refugee crisis and the Holocaust, the unconstitutional incarceration of Americans of Japanese descent, his consolidation of power in the Oval Office, and his expansion of the federal government's role in the everyday life of Americans.

Balancing those debts are his accomplishments: societal safety nets; the forty-hour work week; worker's compensation; rural electrification and the TVA; millions of acres of National Parks and protected lands; the Four Freedoms; the GI Bill; the defeat of Nazi Germany, Fascist Italy, and Imperial Japan; the United Nations. And so much more. FDR was neither a perfect man nor a perfect president. There is no such thing as complete human perfection. But he sought to evolve and grow his outlook as the face of America also changed. Perhaps because of his multitudes, Franklin Delano Roosevelt was the perfect man to be president at that moment in history.

ACKNOWLEDGMENTS

There are so many people who have helped me along during the unusual career path that led me to write this book. A music major in college performing avant-garde electronic music, sound recordist, film and video editor, TV producer, museum executive and curator, director of a presidential library. The one person who helped me the most is my wife, Meris, who has supported me, advised me, and read every one of the many versions of this book.

Old friends who reviewed the manuscript and provided critical feedback include Doug Kroll, former journalists and authors Michael Zuckerman and Phil Lerman. Harvey Kaye, the great history professor and author of several books on Roosevelt's speeches, gave me positive feedback at a critical moment, and carries the torch for FDR's most progressive policies. Ron Collins, noted First Amendment scholar and author, provided me with a better understanding of what a book proposal really is, and gave generous support and encouragement along the way. And Michael Dolan, who did the first editorial review and provided wise and helpful guidance.

When I arrived at the FDR Presidential Library and Museum, I was welcomed into a multifaceted community of family members, National Archives staff, Trustees, and historians. Nancy Roosevelt Ireland, the chair of the Trustees, proved to be a wonderful friend and ally, helping and inspiring me with her calm advice. Anne Roosevelt, the chair of the Roosevelt Institute helped me understand the complex relationship between the private foundation that supports the library and the National Archives. They also provided insight and perspective on their grandfather and "grand mere." All of the Roosevelt extended family that I met were gracious, intelligent, and committed to educating the public about their family legacy. Although not a family member, the late Ambassador William vanden Heuvel was perhaps Franklin and Eleanor Roosevelt's greatest champion. He was the leader of the Roosevelt Institute for many years, and a mentor to me. His generosity flowed to every major Roosevelt project, the FDR Memorial in Washington, D.C., the Roosevelt House at Hunter College, Four Freedoms Park on Roosevelt Island, the annual Four Freedoms Awards, and of course the FDR Library.

I owe a special thanks to David Ferriero, former archivist of the United States, and Susan Donius, director of the Office of Presidential Libraries, for selecting me to oversee the remarkable archive, museum, and cultural institution that is the FDR Library. The staff of the library, especially Supervising Archivist Kirsten Carter, Supervising Curator Herman Eberhardt, and Public Programs and Communications Manager Cliff Laube, all showed great patience and good humor in teaching me about how the National Archives works, and the things I should and should *not* do. And to Mary Jikhars and Joanne Morse who are the best administrative team I have ever worked with. I am fortunate to have had an experienced deputy director, William Harris, who is now the director and doing a terrific job. There are too many to mention, but all of the staff at the library helped me in their own way, and I am grateful to them all. One secret to my successful tenure at the library was the amazing friendships I made with the former director, Lynn Bassanese, and the twelve other presidential library directors, who all share a passion and commitment to the task of protecting and providing access to our nation's most precious presidential documents and artifacts.

Franklin Roosevelt established the Trustees of the Library back in 1938 to raise private funds to build the beautiful Dutch Colonial building. Today they continue to provide financial support and advice to the director. Fredrica Goodman and her husband Jack were friends of Franklin Roosevelt Jr. and served the library for almost four decades. They welcomed me into the community and provided valuable advice and enlightening stories about the Roosevelts. Through the Trustees I met many brilliant experts including Allida Black, Douglas Brinkley, Steven Lomazow, Geoffrey Ward, and the historian's historian, William E. Leuchtenburg, and I learned much from them.

I also want to thank the many scholars and writers I met through programs and conferences. Michael Beschloss, Richard Breitman, Jared Cohen, Blanche Weisen Cook, Susan Dunn, Rebecca Erbelding, David Kennedy, Eric Rauchway, and David Woolner. They all showed me different aspects of the Roosevelts; the complexity, the humanity, the humor and the tragedy that mark their legacy. The historian who influenced me the most was Doris Kearns Goodwin. I first read her book *No Ordinary Time* long before I arrived at the library and it motivated me to delve deeply into the stories of those chosen to lead this country. She also invited me to work with her on the History Channel miniseries *FDR* that has reached millions of viewers. Doris continues to inspire people the world over.

Then there are those who are no longer with us but whose work influenced my perspective and are referenced throughout the book, including Sam Rosenman, Robert Sherwood, Joe Lash, William Manchester, and Eleanor, Elliott, and James Roosevelt.

Finally, I need to acknowledge my agent Leah Spiro whom I have known since we were children growing up on Long Island. She guided me through the publishing labyrinth, always confident even after a series of rejections. Her diligence brought me to Jessica Case, my editor at Pegasus who believed in me, a first-time author, and raised the quality of the book several levels.

There are so many more who helped me along the way, and I am thankful to them all.

ILLUSTRATION CREDITS

p. 152   Charles Lindbergh delivering a radio address on CBS, 1940. *Library of Congress, Harris & Ewing Collection.*

p. 157   Franklin Roosevelt and press secretary Stephen Early in the White House, January, 1941. *FDR Library 7836(39).*

p. 160   Senator Burton Wheeler and Charles Lindbergh raising their hands at a rally at Madison Square Garden, May 23, 1941. *Copyright Getty Images.*

p. 167   Winston Churchill is cheered by workers during a visit to bomb damaged Plymouth on May 2, 1941. The Prime Minister was accompanied by Lady Nancy Astor on this visit, who can be seen behind Churchill. *War Office Second World War Official Collection, photographer, Capt. Horton, @IWM.*

p. 178   German troops at the Soviet state border marker, photographed by Johannes Hahle, June 22, 1941. *Wikimedia Commons, public domain.*

p. 189   Prime Minister Winston Churchill and President Franklin D. Roosevelt standing aboard HMS *Prince of Wales.* Supporting Franklin Roosevelt on his left side is his son, Captain Elliott Roosevelt USAAF. A presidential aide stands nearby. *August 10, 1941. @IWM, public domain.*

p. 200   *From the National Archives and Records Administration, photo 44-PA-426.*

p. 203   Franklin D. Roosevelt, September 11, 1941 at the White House in Washington, D.C., delivering a fireside chat. FDR wears a black arm band, mourning the death of his mother, Sara Delano Roosevelt. 1941. *FDR Library, public domain.*

p. 212   U.S. Navy destroyer USS *Kearny* (DD-432) at Reykjavik, Iceland, on October 19, 1941, two days after she had been torpedoed by the German submarine U-568. A torpedo hole in *Kearny*'s midships is visible. USS *Monssen* (DD-436) is alongside. U.S. Navy photo 80-G-28788, *public domain.*

p. 217   A navy photographer snapped this photograph of the Japanese attack on Pearl Harbor in Hawaii on December 7, 1941, just as the USS *Shaw* exploded. *U.S. National Archives and Records Administration, public domain.*

p. 232   Franklin Roosevelt at microphones, Winston Churchill to his right watching the lighting of the White House Christmas Tree, December 24, 1941. *FDR Library, public domain.*

p. 238   President Franklin Roosevelt and delegates from twenty-six countries sign the Statement of United Nations at the White House, January 1, 1942. *FDR Library, public domain.*

p. 249   This is the last photograph of FDR, taken on April 11, 1945 at the Little White House in Warm Springs, Georgia. Photograph by Nicholas Robbin, courtesy Elizabeth Shoumatoff *FDR Library, public domain.*

BIBLIOGRAPHY

Asbell, Bernard. *Mother and Daughter* (New York: Fromme International, 1988).

Anderson, Jervis. *A. Philip Randolph: A Biographical Portrait* (Berkeley: University of California Press, 1986).

Askey, Nigel. *Operation Barbarossa* (Self-published, 2018).

Baynes, Norman, H. ed., *The Speeches of Adolf Hitler*, vol. 1 (London: Oxford University Press, 1942), 731–32.

Berg, A. Scott. *Lindbergh* (New York: G. P. Putnam's Sons, 1998).

Berle, Adolf. *Navigating the Rapids* (New York: Harcourt Brace Jovanovich, 1973).

Beschloss, Michael. *Presidents of War* (New York: Crown, 2018).

Black, Conrad. *Franklin Delano Roosevelt* (New York: Public Affairs, 2003).

Brands, H. W. *Traitor to his Class* (New York: Anchor Books, 2008).

Breitman, Richard. *FDR and the Jews* (Cambridge: The Belknap Press, 2013).

Breitman, Richard. *Berlin Mission* (New York: Public Affairs, 2019) 10.

Bullitt, Orville. *For the President: Personal and Secret* (New York: Houghton Mifflin, 1972).

Churchill, Winston. *Memoirs of the Second World War, Abridged* (Boston: Houghton Mifflin Co., 1959).

Cook, Blanche Wiesen. *Eleanor Roosevelt*, vol. 3 (New York: Viking, 2016).

Doyle, William. *Inside the Oval Office: From FDR to Clinton* (New York: Kodansha 1999).

Duffy, James P. *Lindbergh vs. Roosevelt* (Washington, D.C.: Regnery Publishing, 2010).

Dunn, Susan. *A Blueprint for War* (New Haven: Yale University Press, 2018).

Dunn, Susan. *1940* (New Haven, Yale University Press, 2013).

Erbelding, Rebecca. *Rescue Board* (New York: Doubleday, 2018).

Foner, Eric. *Give Me Liberty!: An American History,* 3 ed. (New York: W. W. Norton & Company 2012).

Goodwin, Doris Kearns. *No Ordinary Time* (New York, Simon & Schuster, 1994).

Hamilton, Nigel. *The Mantle of Command* (New York: Houghton Mifflin Harcourt, 2014).

Hart, Bradley W. *Hitler's American Friends* (New York: St. Martin's Press, 2018).

Holzer, Harold. *The Presidents vs. the Press* (New York: Dutton, 2020).

Ickes, Harold L. *The Secret Diary of Harold Ickes VIII The Lowering Clouds* (New York: Simon & Schuster, 1955).

Ickes, Harold L. *The Autobiography of a Crumudgeon* (New York: Reynal and Hitchcock, 1943).

Katznelson, Ira. *Fear Itself* (New York: Liveright Publishing, 2013).

Kaye, Harvey J. *The Fight for Four Freedoms: What Made FDR and the Greatest Generation Truly Great* (New York: Simon & Schuster, 2015).

Kaye, Harvey J. *FDR on Democracy: The Greatest Speeches and Writings of Franklin D. Roosevelt* (New York: Skyhorse, 2020).

Kennedy, David. *Freedom from Fear* (Oxford: Oxford University Press, 1999).

Larson, Eric. *The Splendid and the Vile* (New York: Crown, 2020).

Lash, Joseph P. *Eleanor and Franklin* (New York: W. W. Norton and Company, 1971).

Lindbergh, Anne Morrow. *Bring Me a Unicorn: Diaries and Letters of Anne Lindbergh* (New York: Harcourt Brace, 1972).

Lindbergh, Charles. *The Wartime Journals of Charles A. Lindbergh* (New York: Harcourt Brace Jovanovich, 1970).

Lomazow, Steven and Eric Fettmann. *FDR'S Deadly Secret* (New York: Public Affairs, 2009).

Manchester, William. *The Last Lion: Alone* (New York: Little, Brown and Company, 1988).

Manchester, William and Paul Reid. *The Last Lion: Defender of the Realm* (New York: Bantam Books, 2013).

Meacham, Jon. *Franklin and Winston* (New York: Random House, 2003).

Michaelis, David. *Eleanor* (New York: Simon & Schuster, 2020).

Olson, Lynne. *Citizens of London* (New York Random House, 2010).

Persico, Joseph E. *Edward R. Murrow: An American Original* (New York: McGraw-Hill, 1988).

Persico, Joseph E. *Franklin and Lucy* (New York: Random House, 2008).

Pfeffer, Paula F. *A. Philip Randolph, Pioneer of the Civil Rights Movement* (Baton Rouge: Louisiana State University Press, 1990).

Prange, Gordon W. *At Dawn We Slept* (New York: McGraw-Hill, 1981).

Ray, John. *The Battle of Britain* (London: Cassell, New Edition, 2001).

Reilly, Michael and William Slocum. *Reilly of the White House* (New York: Simon & Schuster, 1947).

Roden, Robert N. *Saving the Jews* (New York: Thunder's Mouth Press, 2006).

Roosevelt, Eleanor. *This I Remember* (New York: Harper and Brothers, 1949).

Roosevelt, Elliott and James Brough. *A Rendezvous With Destiny* (New York: G.P. Putnam's Sons, 1975).

Roosevelt, Elliott (Editor). *The Roosevelt Letters*, vol. 3 (London: George G. Harrap and Company, 1952).

Roosevelt, Elliott and James Brough. *Mother R.* (New York: G. P. Putnam's Sons, 1977).

Roosevelt, James. *My Parents: A Differing View* (Chicago: Playboy Press, 1976).

Rosenman, Samuel I. *Working with Roosevelt* (New York: Harper Brothers, 1952).

Sherwood, Robert. *Roosevelt and Hopkins* (New York: Harper Brothers, 1948).

Shirer, William L. *The Rise and Fall of the Third Reich* (New York: Simon & Schuster, 1959).

Smith, Jean Edward. *FDR* (New York: Random House, 2008).

Smith, Kathryn. *The Gatekeeper* (New York: Touchstone, 2016).

Tully, Grace. *F.D.R. My Boss* (Chicago: Peoples Book Club, 1949).

Wallace, Max. *The American Axis* (New York: St. Martin's Press, 2003).

Ward, Geoffrey C. *Closest Companion* (New York, Houghton Mifflin, 1995).

Watts, Jill. *The Black Cabinet: The Untold Story of African Americans and Politics in the Age of Roosevelt* (New York: Grove Press, 2020).

Wyman, David S. *The Abandonment of the Jews* (New York: Pantheon Books, 1984).

Online Resources

British Pathe Newsreel, *Atlantic Conference with Churchill and Roosevelt, August 1941*, https://www.youtube.com/watch?v=s_Gae3AUs4U.

Citino, Robert "Operation Barbarossa: The Biggest of All Time," The National WWII Museum (June 18, 2021).

Franklin D. Roosevelt Presidential Library and Museum website, https://www.fdrlibrary.org/.

FDR Library Henry Morgenthau Jr. Diaries, http://www.fdrlibrary.marist.edu/archives/collections/franklin/index.php?p=collections/findingaid&id=535.

FDR Library Map Room Papers, http://www.fdrlibrary.marist.edu/archives/collections/franklin/?p=collections/findingaid&id=51.

FDR Library Master Speech Files, http://www.fdrlibrary.marist.edu/archives/collections/franklin/index.php?p=collections/findingaid&id=582.

FDR Library Presidential Press Conferences, http://www.fdrlibrary.marist.edu/archives/collections/franklin/?p=collections/findingaid&id=50.

FDR Library Selected Documents on the Holocaust and Refugees, http://www.fdrlibrary.marist.edu/archives/collections/franklin/index.php?p=collections/findingaid&id=505.

George Washington University, Eleanor Roosevelt (ER) Papers, *My Day*, https://erpapers.columbian.gwu.edu/my-day.

George Washington University, Eleanor Roosevelt (ER) Papers, Speeches, https://erpapers.columbian.gwu.edu/miscellaneous-documents.

Ibiblio, *"Hitler's New Year's Order of the Day to the German Armed Forces"* Dec. 31, 1940, http://www.ibiblio.org/pha/policy/1940/1940-12-31b.html.

Library of Congress—Franklin D. Roosevelt Resource Guide, https://guides.loc.gov/franklin-d-roosevelt.

National Archives—Google Arts and Culture: Vincent Astor, https://artsandculture.google.com/story/vincent-astor-u-s-national-archives/EgVxQyhXXB8A8A?hl=en.

Thompson, W. H. "I Guarded Winston Churchill" (*Maclean's* magazine, Oct. 15, 1951), https://archive.macleans.ca/article/1951/10/15/i-guarded-winston-churchill .

USHMM "Americans and the Holocaust" exhibit, https://exhibitions.ushmm.org/americans-and-the-holocaust/how-many-refugees-came-to-the-united-states-from-1933-1945

NOTES

Chapter 1

1 Grace Tully, *F.D.R. My Boss* (Chicago: Peoples Book Club, 1949), 235.

2 Kathryn Smith, *The Gatekeeper* (New York: Touchstone, 2016), 213.

3 Franklin D. Roosevelt Presidential Library, PPF 3737.

4 William L. Shirer, *The Rise and Fall of the Third Reich* (New York: Simon and Schuster, 1959), 599.

5 Ibid.

6 George Washington University, ER Papers, *My Day*, September 2, 1939.

7 Shirer, *The Rise and Fall of the Third Reich*, 598.

8 Ibid.

9 Franklin D. Roosevelt Presidential Library, *Day by Day*, September 1, 1939.

10 Harold Holzer, *The Presidents vs. the Press* (New York: Dutton, 2020), 154.

11 Franklin D. Roosevelt Presidential Library, Master Speech File, Press Conferences, September 1, 1939.

12 Ibid.

13 William Manchester, *The Last Lion: Alone* (New York: Little, Brown and Company, 1988), 519.

14 Manchester, *The Last Lion: Alone*, 520.

15 Winston Churchill, *Memoirs of the Second World War, Abridged* (Boston: Houghton Mifflin Co., 1959), 167.

16 Adolf Berle, *Navigating the Rapids* (New York: Harcourt Brace Jovanovich, 1973), 251.

17 FDR Library, Master Speech File, September 1, 1939.

18 Samuel I. Rosenman, *Working with Roosevelt* (New York: Harper Brothers, 1952), 189.

19 Charles Lindbergh, *The Wartime Journals of Charles A. Lindbergh* (New York: Harcourt Jovanovich, 1970), 249.

20 A. Scott Berg, *Lindbergh* (New York: G. P. Putnam's Sons, 1998), 394.

21 Charles Lindbergh, *The Wartime Journals of Charles A. Lindbergh* (New York: Harcourt Jovanovich, 1970), 250.

22 Ibid., 251.

23 Max Wallace, *The American Axis* (New York: St. Martin's Press, 2003), 203.

24 Lindbergh, *The Wartime Journals of Charles A. Lindbergh*, 245.

25   FDR Library, Map Room Papers, FDR to WC.
26   William Manchester, *The Last Lion: Alone* (New York: Little, Brown and Company, 1988), 549.

Chapter 2
1   Max Wallace, *The American Axis* (New York: St. Martin's Press, 2003), 204.
2   A. Scott Berg, *Lindbergh* (New York: G. P. Putnam's Sons, 1998), 397.
3   Washington *Evening Star*, September 16, 1939, 7.
4   Ibid, *New York Times*, September 16, 1939, 1.
5   Charles Lindbergh, *The Wartime Journals of Charles A. Lindbergh* (New York: Harcourt Brace Jovanovich, 1970), 345.
6   Max Wallace, *The American Axis* (New York: St. Martin's Press, 2003), 207.
7   Max Wallace, *The American Axis* (New York: St. Martin's Press, 2003), 208.
8   Samuel I. Rosenman, *Working with Roosevelt* (New York: Harper Brothers, 1952), 189.
9   Adolf Berle, *Navigating the Rapids* (New York: Harcourt Brace Jovanovich, 1973), 186.
10   Washington *Evening Star*, September 21, 1939, 1.
11   FDR Library, Master Speech File, September 21, 1939.
12   *New York Times*, September 21, 1939, 1.
13   Berg, *Lindbergh,* 398.
14   Washington *Evening Star*, October 14, 1939.
15   *New York Times*, October 14, 1939, 1.
16   *New York Herald Tribune,* October 14, 1939, Berg, 392.

Chapter 3
1   German newsreel footage.
2   Norman H. Baynes, ed., *The Speeches of Adolf Hitler*, I, (London: Oxford University Press, 1942), 731-732.
3   David S. Wyman, *The Abandonment of the Jews* (New York: Pantheon Books, 1984), 1.
4   FDR Library, PSF. Correspondence. FDR to Gov. Herbert Lehman.
5   Richard Breitman, *Berlin Mission* (New York, Public Affairs, 2019), 10.
6   *New York Times*, March 13, 1938, 1.
7   FDR Library, HM Jr. Diary. Vol. 115, 380–1.
8   FDR Library, Press Conferences, March 25, 1938.
9   USHMM "Americans and the Holocaust" exhibit.
10   Berg, *Lindbergh,* 379.
11   Ibid., 381.
12   Washington *Evening Star*, October 17, 1939, 1.
13   FDR Library, Master Speech File, October 17, 1939.
14   Ibid.

Chapter 4
1   GWU ER Papers, *My Day*, March 19, 1940.

2   Washington *Evening Star*, March 16, 1940, 1.

3   Ibid.

4   *New York Times*, March 17, 1940, 37.

5   Washington *Evening Star*, March 17, 1940, 1.

6   FDR Library, Master Speech File, March 16, 1940.

7   *The Atlantic, March, 1940.*

8   FDR Library, Master Speech File, March 16, 1940 .

9   *Poughkeepsie Journal,* April 7, 1940, 1.

10   FDR Library, *Day by Day*, April 7, 1940.

11   Ibid.

12   FDR Library Press Conferences, April 10, 1940.

13   Ibid.

14   Adolf Berle, *Navigating the Rapids* (New York: Harcourt Brace Jovanovich, 1973), 304.

15   FDR Library, Henry Morgenthau Jr. Diaries, phone transcript, April 10, 1940.

16   Ibid.

17   William Manchester, *The Last Lion: Alone* (New York: Little, Brown and Company, 1988), 637.

18   Ibid., 640.

Chapter 5

1   Kathryn Smith, *The Gatekeeper* (New York: Touchstone, 2016), 222.

2   FDR Library, HMJ Diaries, May 10, 1940.

3   FDR Library, Press Conference, May 10, 1940.

4   FDR Library, *Day by Day,* May 13, 1940.

5   Robert Sherwood, *Roosevelt and Hopkins* (New York: Harper Brothers, 1948).

6   Manchester, *The Last Lion: Alone,* 679.

7   Ibid., 680.

8   Winston Churchill, *Memoirs of the Second World War, Abridged* (Boston: Houghton Mifflin, 1959), 231.

9   Manchester, *The Last Lion: Alon,* 682.

10   FDR Library, Map Room Papers, WC to FDR, May 15, 1940.

11   FDR Library, Map Room Papers, FDR to WC, May 16, 1940.

12   Washington *Evening Star*, May 16, 1940, 1.

13   Ibid.

14   FDR Library, Master Speech File, May 16, 1940.

15   Ibid.

16   A. Scott Berg, *Lindbergh* (New York: G. P. Putnam's Sons, 1998), 401.

17   *New York Times*, May 19, 1940, 8.

18   Ibid.

19   Charles Lindbergh, *The Wartime Journals of Charles A. Lindbergh* (New York: Harcourt Brace Jovanovich, 1970), 350.

20   Berg, *Lindbergh,* 402.

21   Max Wallace, *The American Axis* (New York: St. Martin's Press, 2003), 213.

22   FDR Library, HMJ Diaries, May 20, 1940, 563.

23   Manchester, *The Last Lion: Alone*, 684.
24   Ibid.
25   Washington *Evening Star*, June 11, 1940, 5.
26   FDR Library, Master Speech File, May 10, 1940.
27   Sherwood, *Roosevelt and Hopkins*, 143.
28   Ibid., 150.
29   William Manchester and Paul Reid, *The Last Lion: Defender of the Realm* (New York: Bantam Books, 2013), 114.
30   FDR Library Map Room Papers, WC to FDR, July 31, 1940.

Chapter 6
1   Blanche Wiesen Cook, *Eleanor Roosevelt, vol. 3* (New York: Viking, 2016), 299.
2   *Chicago Tribune*, 07/19/1940, 1.
3   George Washington Univ., ER Papers, Speeches, July 18, 1940.
4   Doris Kearns Goodwin, *No Ordinary Time* (New York, Simon & Schuster, 1994) 133.
5   Cook, *Eleanor Roosevelt, vol. 3*, 300.
6   *Chicago Tribune*, July 19, 1940, 1.
7   FDR Library, Master Speech File, July 19, 1940.
8   *Chicago Tribune*, July 20, 1940, 1.
9   Lindbergh, *The Wartime Journals*, 374.
10   *Chicago Tribune*, August 5, 1940, b, 4.
11   Ibid.
12   FDR Library, Photograph id# 51115139.
13   FDR Library, PSF Box 3, Joseph Kennedy correspondence.
14   FDR Library Map Room Papers WC to FDR, August 15, 1940.
15   FDR Library HMJ Presidential Diaries, August 13, 1940.
16   FDR Library Map Room Papers WC to FDR.
17   Jean Edward Smith, *FDR* (New York: Random House, 2008), 475.
18   Washington *Evening Star*, September 3, 1940, 1.
19   FDR Library Master Speech File, September 2, 1940.
20   Bradley W. Hart, *Hitler's American Friends* (New York: St. Martin's Press, 2018), 109
21   Washington *Evening Star*, September 1, 1940, 1
22   Hart, *Hitler's American Friends*, 104. Rachel Maddow podcast "Ultra."
23   Hart, *Hitler's American Friends*, 100.
24   Ibid., 102.
25   Ibid., 108.
26   Ibid., 109.
27   National Archives—Google Arts and Culture: Vincent Astor.
28   Ibid.
29   Ibid., 8.
30   Eric Foner, *Give Me Liberty!: An American History*, 3rd ed. (New York: W. W. Norton & Company 2012), 697.
31   Robert C. Weaver, "With the Negroes Help," *The Atlantic*, June 1942.

32   Joseph P. Lash, *Eleanor and Franklin* (New York: W. W. Norton and Company, 1971), 534.

33   FDR Library, *Day By Day*, September 27, 1940.

34   William Doyle, *Inside the Oval Office: From FDR to Clinton* (New York: Kodansha, 1999).

35   Lash, *Eleanor and Franklin*, 530.

36   Doyle, *Inside the Oval Office.*

37   Lash, *Eleanor and Franklin*, 530.

38   David Kennedy, *Freedom from Fear* (Oxford: Oxford University Press, 1999), 766.

Chapter 7

1   Berg, *Lindbergh*, 173; *New York Times*, December 14, 1927, 1.

2   *New York Times*, December 15, 1927, 2.

3   Washington *Evening Star*, December 15, 1927, 4.

4   Berg, *Lindbergh*, 173.

5   Anne Morrow Lindbergh, *Bring Me a Unicorn: Diaries and Letters of Anne Lindbergh* (New York: Harcourt Brace, 1972), 142.

6   Ibid.

7   Berg, *Lindbergh*, 406.

8   Ibid., 407.

9   Lindbergh, *The Wartime Journals*, 404.

10   *New York Times*, October 15, 1940, 1; Washington *Evening Star*, October 15, 1940, 5.

11   Lindbergh, *The Wartime Journals*, 409.

12   Sherwood, *Roosevelt and Hopkins*, 183.

13   Rosenman, *Working with Roosevelt*, 229.

14   Sherwood, *Roosevelt and Hopkins*, 184.

15   Rosenman, *Working with Roosevelt*, 233.

16   FDR Library, *Day By Day*, October 23, 1940.

17   *Philadelphia Inquirer*, October 24, 1940, 2.

18   Ibid.

19   FDR Library, Master Speech File, October 23, 1040.

20   Rosenman, *Working with Roosevelt*, 238.

21   FDR Library, Master Speech File, October 23, 1940.

22   Rosenman, *Working with Roosevelt*, 240.

23   Sherwood, *Roosevelt and Hopkins*, 189.

24   FDR Library, HMJ Presidential Diaries, October 28, 1940.

25   FDR Library, Master Speech File, October 29, 1940.

26   FDR Library, HMJ Presidential Diaries, October 29, 1940.

27   Ibid.

28   Rosenman, *Working with Roosevelt*, 243.

29   *Boston Globe*, October 31, 1940, 1.

30   Ibid.

31   Ibid.

32   James Roosevelt, *My Parents: A Differing View* (Chicago: Playboy Press, 1976), 160.

Chapter 8

1   *New York Times*, November 6, 1940, 2.
2   FDR Library Master Speech File, November 5, 1940.
3   Lash, *Eleanor and Franklin*, 631.
4   *New York Times*, November 6, 1940, 1.
5   Washington *Evening Star*, November 7, 1940, 1.
6   FDR Library Press Conferences, November 8, 1940.
7   Ibid.
8   Manchester and Reid, *The Last Lion: Defender of the Realm*, 210.
9   W. H. Thompson, "I Guarded Winston Churchill," *Maclean's*, October 15, 1951.
10   Ibid.
11   Eric Larson, *The Splendid and the Vile* (New York: Crown, 2020), 298.
12   Ibid., 303.
13   *New York Times*, November 24, 1940, 1.
14   FDR Library, Day by Day, November 25, 1940.
15   FDR Library HMJ Presidential Diaries, November 24, 1940.
16   Washington *Evening Star*, November 25, 1940, 1, 5.
17   *New York Times*, November 26, 1940, 1.
18   Ibid.
19   FDR Library Press Conferences, November 27, 1940.

Chapter 9

1   *Miami Herald*, December 4, 1940, 1.
2   *Miami Herald*, December 4, 1940, 1.
3   Ibid.
4   FDR Library, YouTube, FDR's December 1940 Caribbean Cruise, Part 1.
5   FDR Library, Caribbean Cruise Travel Log, December, 1940.
6   Sherwood, *Roosevelt and Hopkins*, 222.
7   FDR Library, Caribbean Travel Log.
8   Churchill, *Memoirs of the Second World War*, Abridged, 384.
9   FDR Library, Caribbean Travel Log.
10   FDR Library, YouTube, FDR's December 1940 Caribbean Cruise, Part 2.
11   FDR Library Map Room Papers, WC to FDR, December 7, 1940, 123.
12   Sherwood, *Roosevelt and Hopkins*, 223.
13   FDR Library Caribbean Travel Log.
14   Ibid.
15   Ibid.
16   FDR Library Press Conferences, December 14, 1940.
17   Ibid.
18   Sherwood, *Roosevelt and Hopkins*, 224.

Chapter 10

1   Sherwood, *Roosevelt and Hopkins*, 225.

2   FDR Library Press Conferences, December 17, 1940.

3   FDR Library *Day By Day*, December 29, 1940.

4   *Hollywood Citizens News*, December 30, 1940, 1.

5   FDR Library, Master Speech File, December 29, 1940.

6   Joseph E. Persico, *Edward R. Murrow: An American Original* (New York: McGraw-Hill, 1988), 182.

7   FDR Library Master Speech File, December 29, 1940.

8   Rosenman, *Working with Roosevelt*, 261.

9   Conrad Black, *Franklin Delano Roosevelt* (New York: Public Affairs, 2003), 607.

10   *New York Times*, December 30, 1940, 1.

11   Eisenhower Presidential Library, Master Speech File, Farewell Address.

12   Churchill, *Memoirs of the Second World War*, Abridged, 401.

13   FDR Library, Press Conferences, January 3, 1941.

14   Rosenman, *Working with Roosevelt*, 261.

15   FDR Library, *Day By Day*, January 6, 1941.

16   Ibiblio, *Hitler's New Year's Order of the Day to the German Armed Forces*, December 31, 1940.

17   FDR Library, Master Speech File, January 6, 1941.

18   Ibid.

19   Rosenman, *Working with Roosevelt*, 263.

20   Ibid., 265.

Chapter 11

1   Thompson, "I Guarded Winston Churchill."

2   Manchester and Reid, *The Last Lion: Defender of the Realm*, 280.

3   Churchill, *Memoirs of the Second World War*, Abridged, 402.

4   Larson, *The Splendid and the Vile*, 346.

5   Ibid., 347.

6   Sherwood, *Roosevelt and Hopkins*, 238.

7   Churchill, *Memoirs of the Second World War*, Abridged, 402.

8   Larson, *The Splendid and the Vile*, 347.

9   Sherwood, *Roosevelt and Hopkins*, 236.

10   Ibid., 229.

11   Washington *Evening Star*, January 20, 1941, 3.

12   Ibid., 1.

13   FDR Library Master Speech File, January 20, 1941.

14   Rosenman, *Working with Roosevelt*, 268.

15   FDR Library Master Speech File, January 20, 1941.

16   Washington *Evening Star*, January 20, 1941, 3.

Chapter 12

1   Washington *Evening Star*, January 23, 1941, 1.

2   Berg, *Lindbergh*, 414.

3   *New York Times*, January 24, 1941, 1.

4   Berg, *Lindbergh*, 414.

5   *New York Times*, January 24, 1941, 6.
6   Black, *Franklin Delano Roosevelt*, 615.
7   Sherwood, *Roosevelt and Hopkins*, 261.
8   International Churchill Society, Speeches/1941–1945—War Leader: "Give us the Tools" https://winstonchurchill.org/resources/speeches/1941-1945-war-leader/give-us-the-tools/.
9   Ibid.
10 National Archives, Exhibits, *Treasures of Congress—HR 1776*, https://www.archives.gov/exhibits/treasures_of_congress/Images/page_20/65c.html.

Chapter 13

1   Washington *Evening Star*, March 16, 1941, 1.
2   FDR Library Master Speech File, March 15, 1941.
3   Washington *Evening Star*, March 16, 1941, 43.

Chapter 14

1   *Chicago Tribune*, April 18, 1941, 1.
2   Berg, *Lindbergh*, 417.
3   Ibid.
4   John Ray, *The Battle of Britain* (London: Cassell, New Edition, 2001), 215.
5   Hart, *Hitler's American Friends*, 162.
6   Ibid., 161.
7   Berg, *Lindbergh*, 417.
8   FDR Library Press Conferences, April 25, 1941.
9   Ibid.
10 Wallace, *The American Axis*, 277.
11 *New York Times*, April 29, 1941, 10.
12 Ibid.
13 Wallace, *The American Axis*, 284.
14 Ibid.

Chapter 15

1   British Pathe Newsreel—Churchill Visits Plymouth, 1941 YouTube, https://www.youtube.com/watch?v=I5Tr-iPL01U.
2   Larson, *The Splendid and the Vile*, 441.
3   *Plymouth Herald*, December 3, 2017, https://www.plymouthherald.co.uk/news/history/remembering-winston-churchill-came-plymouth-869912.
4   FDR Library, Map Room Papers, WC to FDR May 3, 1941, 47.
5   Ibid.
6   Larson, *The Splendid and the Vile*, 450.
7   Ibid., 452.
8   Steven Lomazow and Eric Fettmann, *FDR'S Deadly Secret* (New York: Public Affairs, 2009), 83.
9   Washington *Evening Star*, May 28, 1941, 2.

10   Sherwood, *Roosevelt and Hopkins*, 297.

11   FDR Library Master Speech File, May 27, 1941.

12   Sherwood, *Roosevelt and Hopkins*, 298.

13   FDR Library Master Speech File, May 27, 1941.

14   Washington *Evening Star*, May 28, 1941, 3.

15   Ibid.

16   Lash, *Eleanor and Franklin*, 534.

17   Paula F. Pfeffer, *A. Philip Randolph, Pioneer of the Civil Rights Movement* (Baton Rouge: Louisiana State University Press, 1990), 58.

18   Jervis Anderson, *A. Philip Randolph: A Biographical Portrait* (Berkeley: University of California Press, 1986), 247.

19   Ibid.

20   Kennedy, *Freedom from Fear*, 767.

21   Ibid.

22   Lash, *Eleanor and Franklin*, 534.

23   Anderson, *A. Philip Randolph*, 257.

24   Kennedy, *Freedom from Fear*, 768.

25   *Pittsburg Courier*, June 28,1941, 1.

26   Kennedy, *Freedom from Fear*, 768.

Chapter 16

1   *Los Angeles Times*, June 21,1941, 1, 9.

2   Robert Citino "Operation Barbarossa: The Biggest of All Time," The National WWII Museum, (June 18, 2021).

3   Nigel Askey, *Operation Barbarossa* (Self-published, 2018), 105.

4   John Graham Royde-Smith, "Operation Barbarossa," Britannica online, June 15, 2011.

5   Manchester and Reid, *The Last Lion: Defender of the Realm*, 378.

6   International Churchill Society, Speeches/1941–1945—War Leader: Alliance with Russia, https://winstonchurchill.org/resources /speeches/1941-1945-war-leader/alliance-with-russia/.

7   *Poughkeepsie Journal*, July 1, 1941, 1.

8   *New York Times*, July 1, 1941, 1.

9   FDR Library, Master Speech File, June 30, 1941.

10   Lindbergh, *The Wartime Journals*, 506.

11   Berg, *Lindbergh*, 422.

12   *San Francisco Examiner*, July 2, 1941, 1.

13   Wallace, *The American Axis*, 284.

14   *New York Times*, July 15, 1941, 1.

15   Lindbergh, *The Wartime Journals*, 518.

16   Harold L. Ickes, *The Secret Diary of Harold Ickes, The Lowering Clouds* (New York: Simon & Schuster, 1955), 581.

17   Ibid., 582.

Chapter 17

1   Lomazow and Fettmann, *FDR'S Deadly Secret*, 84.

2   Smith, *The Gatekeeper*, 242.

3   Ibid.

4   Joseph E. Persico, *Franklin and Lucy* (New York: Random House, 2008), 87

5   FDR Library, *Day By Day*, June 5, 1941 and various dates, Ushers' log.

6   Persico, *Franklin and Lucy*, 262.

7   Sherwood, *Roosevelt and Hopkins*, 321.

8   FDR Library, HMJ Presidential Diaries, September 5, 1941, 65.

9   FDR Library Press Conferences, September 1, 1941.

10   Ibid.

11   Persico, *Franklin and Lucy*, 256

12   *New York Times*, August 4, 1941, 1

13   FDR Library Travel Log, Atlantic Conference, August 1941.

14   Nigel Hamilton, *The Mantle of Command* (New York: Houghton Mifflin Harcourt, 2014), 6.

15   Geoffrey C. Ward, *Closest Companion* (New York, Houghton Mifflin, 1995), 205.

16   Churchill, *Memoirs of the Second World War*, Abridged, 489.

17   Sherwood, *Roosevelt and Hopkins*, 347.

18   Elliot Roosevelt and James Brough, *A Rendezvous With Destiny* (New York: G.P. Putnam's Sons, 1975), 291.

19   Hamilton, *The Mantle of Command*, 18.

20   Roosevelt and Brough, *A Rendezvous With Destiny*, 292.

21   FDR Library, Travel Log, August, 1941, Newfoundland.

22   Roosevelt and Brough, *A Rendezvous With Destiny*, 293.

23   British Pathe Newsreel, *Atlantic Conference with Churchill and Roosevelt*, August, 1941.

24   Jon Meacham, *Franklin and Winston* (New York: Random House, 2003), 108.

25   Ward, *Closest Companion*, 222.

26   Manchester and Reid, *The Last Lion: Defender of the Realm*, 393.

27   Hamilton, *The Mantle of Command*, 30.

28   Manchester and Reid, *The Last Lion: Defender of the Realm*, 394.

29   Ibid., 395.

30   Sherwood, *Roosevelt and Hopkins*, 359.

31   Roosevelt and Brough, *A Rendezvous With Destiny*, 298.

32   Manchester and Reid, *The Last Lion*, 433.

33   Churchill, *Memoirs of the Second World War*, Abridged, 492.

34   *New York Times*, August 13, 1941, 1.

35   Churchill, *Memoirs of the Second World War*, Abridged, 366.

36   Sherwood, *Roosevelt and Hopkins*, 362.

Chapter 18

1   *Portland Press Herald*, August 24, 1941, 1.

2   FDR Library, Press Conferences, August 16, 1941.

3   Ibid.

4   *New York Times*, August 17, 1941, 1.

5   Smith, *The Gatekeeper*, 245.

6   Kearns Goodwin, *No Ordinary Time*, 271.
7   Tully, *F.D.R. My Boss*, 105.
8   Rosenman, *Working with Roosevelt*, 292.
9   FDR Library, Master Speech File, September 11, 1941.
10   Wallace, *The American Axis*, 288.
11   Lindbergh, *The Wartime Journals*, 534
12   *Des Moines Register*, September 11, 1941, 1, 4.
13   Berg, *Lindbergh*, 426.
14   Lindbergh, *The Wartime Journals*, 537.
15   *New York Times*, September 12, 1941, 1.
16   Berg, *Lindbergh*, 427.
17   Wallace, *The American Axis*, 290; *Des Moines Register*, September 12, 1941, 1.
18   CharlesLindbergh.com, "Des Moines Speech," September 11, 1941, http://www.charleslindbergh.com/americanfirst/speech.asp.
19   *Des Moines Register*, "Des Moines Speech," 1941, 1.
20   Lindbergh, *The Wartime Journals*, 538.
21   Wallace, *The American Axis*, 292.
22   Ibid., 296.

Chapter 19
1   FDR Library, HMJ Presidential Diaries, May 15, 1942, 35.
2   Sherwood, *Roosevelt and Hopkins*, 382.
3   FDR Library *Day By Day*, October 27, 1941.
4   British Pathe, YouTube, "President Roosevelt's Navy Day Speech," 1941.
5   FDR Library, Master Speech File, October 27, 1941.
6   Sherwood, *Roosevelt and Hopkins*, 382.
7   Wallace, *The American Axis*, 297.
8   Ibid., 298.
9   Churchill, *Memoirs of the Second World War*, Abridged, 504.

Chapter 20
1   *New York Times*, December 7, 1941, 1.
2   Hamilton, *The Mantle of Command*, 47.
3   Sherwood, *Roosevelt and Hopkins*, 429.
4   Ibid., 430.
5   Hamilton, *The Mantle of Command*, 45, 46.
6   Churchill, *Memoirs of the Second World War*, Abridged, 506.
7   Ibid.
8   Tully, *F.D.R. My Boss*, 255.
9   Sherwood, *Roosevelt and Hopkins*, 432.
10   Tully, *F.D.R. My Boss*, 256.
11   FDR Library, Master Speech File, December 7, 1941.
12   FDR Library, HMJ Presidential Diaries, December 7, 1941, 55.
13   FDR Library, *Day By Day*, December 7, 1941.
14   Gordon W. Prange, *At Dawn We Slept* (New York: McGraw-Hill, 1981), 559.

15 George Washington University, ER Papers, radio addresses, Ep. 11, December 7, 1941, Pan-American Coffee Bureau Series.
16 Persico, *Edward R. Murrow*, 193.
17 Ibid., 194.
18 Michael Beschloss, *Presidents of War* (New York: Crown, 2018), 433.
19 Washington *Evening Star*, December 7, 1941, 1.
20 Sherwood, *Roosevelt and Hopkins*, 436.
21 FDR Library, Map Room Papers, FDR to Winston Churchill, December 9, 1941, 80.
22 *New York Times*, December 9, 1941, 1.
23 Wallace, *The American Axis*, 301.
24 Ibid., 305.
25 Berg, *Lindbergh*, 437.
26 Ibid., 433.
27 Sherwood, *Roosevelt and Hopkins*, 434.

Chapter 21
1 Churchill, *Memoirs of the Second World War*, Abridged, 512.
2 Manchester and Reid, *The Last Lion: Defender of the Realm*, 441.
3 Churchill, *Memoirs of the Second World War*, Abridged, 518.
4 FDR Library, Press Conferences, December 23, 1941.
5 Ibid.
6 FDR Library, Master Speech File, December 24, 1941.
7 Churchill, *Memoirs of the Second World War*, Abridged, 519.

Chapter 22
1 Washington *Evening Star*, December 25, 1941, 1.
2 Sherwood, *Roosevelt and Hopkins*, 449.
3 Hamilton, *The Mantle of Command*, 139.
4 Ibid., 140.
5 Rosenman, *Working with Roosevelt*, 321.
6 Ibid.
7 FDR Library, *Day By Day*, January 6, 1941.
8 FDR Library, Master Speech File, January 6, 1942.
9 Washington *Evening Star*, January 6, 1942, 1.
10 *New York Times*, January 7, 1942, 4.
11 Kearns Goodwin, *No Ordinary Time*, 608.

Epilogue
1 Sherwood, *Roosevelt and Hopkins*, 478.
2 Berg, *Lindbergh*, 463.
3 Charles Lindbergh House and Museum, https://www.mnhs.org /lindbergh/learn/family/double-life.

INDEX